Warwick Unive

Paradise Overseas

The Dutch Caribbean: Colonialism and its Transatlantic Legacies

Gert Oostindie

MACMILLAN
CARIBBEAN

Macmillan Education
Between Towns Road, Oxford OX4 3PP
A division of Macmillan Publishers Limited
Companies and representatives throughout the world

www.macmillan-caribbean.com

ISBN 1-4050-5713-0

Text © Gert Oostindie 2005
Design © Macmillan Publishers Limited 2005
Map © KITLV, Leiden, The Netherlands

First published 2005

Typeset by EXPO Holdings Sdn Bhd
Cover design by Gary Fielder, AC Design
Cover image: Attentive public at a judicial court, Paramaribo, Suriname.
Watercolour, Arnold Barret, 1881. Collection KITLV, Leiden, The Netherlands.

For Ingrid, with love

2009   2008   2007   2006   2005
10 9   8   7   6   5   4   3   2   1

Warwick University Caribbean Studies

The Centre for Caribbean Studies at the University of Warwick was founded in 1984 in order to stimulate interest and research in a region which is now receiving academic recognition in its own right.

In conjunction with the University of Warwick, Macmillan Caribbean has published a comprehensive list of titles which study the complexity and variety of a remarkable region and reflect the pan-Caribbean, inter-disciplinary approach of the Warwick University Centre for Caribbean Studies.

The Series features new titles in the fields of history, sociology, economics and development, literature, anthropology and politics as well as the re-issue of major works. Some are contributed by individual authors while others are collected papers from symposia held at the University of Warwick or elsewhere.

Warwick University Caribbean Studies

Series Editors: Alistair Hennessy and Gad Heuman

Contents

Preface

The Dutch were in the Caribbean for four centuries. They arrived there with high expectations which were more often dashed than they were fulfilled. By the time they wanted to leave the West Indies, it was no longer possible to do so; reluctantly, perhaps, they are still a significant presence in the region today. In the intervening period, new societies were created out of more or less nothing: Suriname on the Wild Coast of the South American continent and six islands in the Caribbean Sea. Only in more recent times did these acquisitions lose – from a Dutch perspective – their 'foreignness' and in their own way become increasingly Dutch. This development was regarded with mixed emotions by the 'mother country'.

Paradise Overseas presents a tour around the main themes of a history that continues to link the former colonies with the Netherlands. This is a book about the often-appalling self-interest, negligence and naivety of the Dutch; it is also a book about occasional, desperate attempts to redeem the situation. It is about the Surinamese, Antilleans and Arubans, their experiences under colonial rule and their laborious forging of unique identities. It is about the nebulous nature of what is so deceptively called the 'Dutch Caribbean', a collection of regions which have never been culturally uniform and whose inhabitants have been difficult to define even in terms of geography since the start of the mass exodus to the Netherlands in the 1970s.[1]

This book does not offer a comprehensive history of the Dutch Caribbean. The rare attempts that have been made to write such a book have above all illustrated the inadequacy of this label in the face of a multifarious reality. Neither does it attempt to address in equal measure all parts of the Netherlands' modest empire in the West Indies or all periods of this history. I will only in passing mention themes and episodes which, although important, are not of immediate relevance to the frame of reference of this book, which is to analyze the growth of this collection of societies over the centuries towards its contemporary dualistic character – apparently at least Caribbean and Dutch at the same time.

The chapters of this book may all be read as individual texts, each departing from a different angle, jumping in both time and space. The first chapters are the most historical, while the subsequent chapters become increasingly explicit in their examination of the present. The emphasis moves from the Caribbean colonies, to the mother country, to the interaction within the asymmetrical triangle that connects the Caribbean islands, Suriname and the Netherlands.

The title, *Paradise Overseas*, is a variation on the title of the novel *Het paradijs van Oranje* (The Paradise of Orange, 1973) by the Surinamese author Bea Vianen which addresses Surinamese migration to the Netherlands. My title, *Paradise Overseas*, reaches somewhat further back in history, referring to the high expectations harboured on both sides of the Atlantic. Expectations which centuries ago led the Dutch to embark on a voyage towards the Caribbean, expectations which were fostered by the descendants of those Dutch settlers and, above all, the descendants of the slaves and contract workers imported by the Dutch, when they made the same journey in the opposite direction. That paradise was rarely found might well be sad, but it is hardly surprising. Nonetheless, I respect the dreams, the old as well as the new; there may be a touch of irony in my chosen title, but I have tried to give the dreamers the respect they deserve.

Paradise Overseas has its roots in a book I published in Dutch in 1997 under the title *Het paradijs overzee*.[2] Although the book was well received in the Dutch-speaking world and is now in its third edition, I thought long and hard before deciding on an English version. Despite being convinced of the need for an authoritative study of the 'Dutch' Caribbean, that illegible and – in part, consequently – forgotten corner of the Atlantic world, I doubted whether a simple translation of *Het paradijs overzee* would be able to fulfil this demanding role. That this book is being published is partly attributable to the encouragement I received from many 'overseas' colleagues, and partly because it gradually became clearer to me what elements I would have to change for an English-language audience, which is likely to be familiar with the main features of Atlantic history and which would therefore mainly be interested in how Dutch-Caribbean history 'fits' into the stories of the surrounding countries.

Paradise Overseas is therefore a heavily abridged and revised version of the Dutch original. Whereas *Het paradijs overzee* was divided into ten essays in four sections, here I present seven consecutive chapters. I have omitted the introductions to each of the four sections as well as the penultimate chapter, because these sketch a broader Caribbean context for the Dutch reader which I judged unnecessary for an English-language audience. I have also left out two chapters which deal in detail with affairs from the Dutch orbit.[3]

In contrast to this ruthless cutting there was a critical re-reading and in many places revision and updating of the other essays, which in particular led to the augmentation of the first and closing chapters. I have also included references to and, where applicable, discussion of crucial recent publications by other authors as well as of my own recent work.[4] As a result, the present book is up-to-date both in its rendering of the subject matter of this book and as a guide to the most significant literature. I have been particularly careful to include relevant literature in English. Three chapters were previously published in English and have been revised for this book.[5] I wrote parts of the present book in English, while others parts were translated for me from the Dutch original by Annabel Howland and Peter Mason. I thank the Netherlands Organization for Scientific Research (NWO) for the translations grant that made this possible.

During the writing of *Het paradijs overzee* and later of *Paradise Overseas,* I received critical responses from many sources, sometimes in relation to a single chapter, sometimes on many different parts of the manuscript; I have considered all of these comments and in many cases have worked them into the text. I would especially like to thank Michiel Baud, Allison Blakely, Frank Bovenkerk, Aart G. Broek, Seymour Drescher, Pieter C. Emmer, Ruben Gowricharn, Gad Heuman, Rosemarijn Hoefte, Michiel van Kempen, Inge Klinkers, Franklin W. Knight, Boeli van Leeuwen, Emy Maduro, Sidney W. Mintz, Richard and Sally Price, Alex van Stipriaan, Michel-Rolph Trouillot and Peter Verton.

I am particularly indebted to Harry Hoetink and Ingrid Koulen who read large parts of early versions of *Het paradijs overzee* and provided me with their invaluable criticism. My gratitude goes out to both of them who, each in their own way, have had such a profound influence on me over so many years. Like the Dutch original, this book is dedicated to Ingrid, my companion for over two decades.

– GJO, September 2003

Notes

1   Nonetheless, to avoid a laborious use of quotation marks I shall use the collective term Dutch Caribbean, without the intellectually and perhaps politically more satisfying quotation marks – a nod to legibility. A second gesture towards simplicity is the use of the term 'Antillean' to include Aruba, even though this country has had an autonomous status in the Kingdom of the Netherlands since 1986 and is separate from the five islands that have made up the Dutch Antilles since that date.

2   Oostindie 1997, 1998, and reprinted again by KITLV Press in 2001.
3   The third chapter in *Het paradijs overzee* ('Voltaire, Stedman, en de Surinaamse slavernij') was published in English in *Slavery & Abolition* 14/2, 1993:1–34), under the title 'Voltaire, Stedman and Suriname Slavery'. In this essay I examine the historiographic clichés of the allegedly exceptional cruelty of Surinamese slavery. This chapter was misunderstood by many as an *apologia* for Dutch colonialism. That it obviously gave grounds for this reading was one reason for not reprinting it here. A second, somewhat more pragmatic reason was that it is already available in English and would not have contributed significantly to the context of *Paradise Overseas*.

Due to the nature of the material, the seventh chapter in the original book, 'Het voorspel tot exodus' ('Prelude to the Exodus'), offers an unavoidably anecdotal account of the early history of Antillean and Surinamese immigrants in the Netherlands. However precious these stories are to me, they are merely footnotes to the history of the recent exodus to the Netherlands from the Caribbean, as I argue in the later chapter published here under the title 'The Delusive Continuities of the Diaspora'. See also Oostindie 1990.

Stripped of ceremony and largely also of its footnotes, Chapter 9, 'Caraïbische dilemma's' ('Caribbean Dilemmas'), formed the text of the inaugural lecture I gave on assuming my chair as Professor of Caribbean Studies at Utrecht University on 18 January 1994 (Leiden: KITLV Uitgeverij 1994). The body of this oration presented a brief outline of Caribbean and contemporary research themes against the background of which I placed the Dutch Caribbean. In this English edition the former description is unnecessary, while I have striven explicitly and, in my view, sufficiently to deal with the latter in the other essays, particularly in Chapter 5.
4   Especially Oostindie 1999a and b, 2001; Oostindie & Verton 1998; Oostindie & Klinkers 2001 and 2003.
5   Chapter 2 is reprinted with minor revisions in the footnoting from 'Same Old Song? Perspectives on Slavery and Slaves in Suriname and Curaçao', in Gert Oostindie (ed.), *Fifty Years Later; Antislavery, Capitalism and Modernity in the Dutch Orbit*, pp. 143–78 (Leiden: KITLV Press 1995, Pittsburgh: University of Pittsburgh Press 1996). Chapter 5 is a thoroughly revised and updated version of 'Ethnicity, Nationalism, and the Exodus: The Dutch Caribbean Predicament', in Gert Oostindie (ed.), *Ethnicity in the Caribbean; Essays in Honor of Harry Hoetink*, pp. 206–231 (London: Macmillan 1996). Chapter 6 is a modified version of 'The Delusive Continuities of the Dutch Caribbean Diaspora', in Mary Chamberlain (ed.), *Caribbean Migration; Globalised Identities*, pp. 127–47 (London: Routledge 1998).

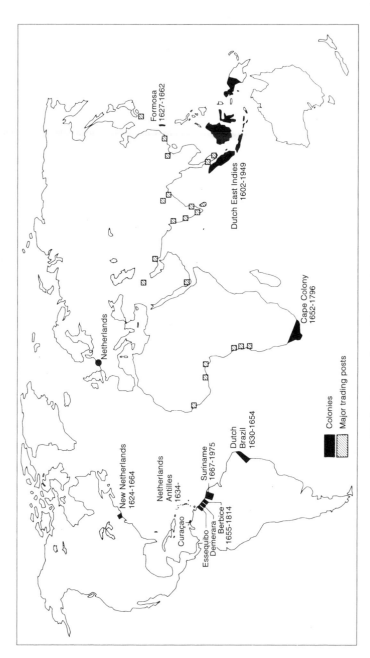

Main Areas of the 'Dutch Empire'

Formosa 1627-1662

Dutch East Indies 1602-1949

Cape Colony 1652-1796

Netherlands

New Netherlands 1624-1664

Netherlands Antilles 1634-

Curaçao

Suriname 1667-1975

Essequibo

Demerara

Berbice 1655-1814

Dutch Brazil 1630-1654

Colonies

Major trading posts

1 | Worlds apart

At first glance the history of the Dutch in the Caribbean appears, in one way or another, to be literally out of place. Holland in the tropics it was not, but what then was it? Though the topography suggests otherwise, the Dutch colonies on the South American mainland had little to do with their Latin environment, as was true of most of the Antilles. However far back in time we go, the role of the Dutch in Latin American history has generally been marginal. Only in the Caribbean did the Dutch play a part of any significance and they are still a presence there today. Yet even in that small part of the New World, the Netherlands' role remained a modest one.

The apparent dullness of this history can also make it appear 'out of place'. Latin-American culture, which Europeans have readily received one-sidedly as if it were a single culture, evokes associations with what the Cuban writer, Alejo Carpentier once called *lo real maravilloso*: a fascinating mixture of bizarre realities and impossible dream worlds which we are unable to grasp. Dutch history in this part of the world pales in comparison. It is a world of sugar plantations and merciless slavery, but above all it is a prosaic story of the West Indian interests of the Dutch trading houses, an insignificant episode in the grand narrative of history.

Yet closer examination reveals an extraordinary history, rather than a dull one. Dutch colonialism in these parts was not heroic and was often cruel. Built on unfounded expectations it was, remarkably, only to a limited extent the work of the Dutch themselves. The result was a few barely viable countries, which more as exception than rule were liabilities rather than assets to the Netherlands. Above all, a re-reading of this history engenders amazement at so much incongruity and naturally raises the question as to why a line was not drawn under this chapter much earlier.[1]

From Brazil to the Caribbean

The Dutch America story began as a consequence of the Low Countries' revolt against the Spanish, which in turn led to the Eighty Years' War

1

(1568–1648) and the foundation of the Dutch Republic. The Caribbean became a new battlefront where the rebels shattered the Spanish monopoly and, moreover, assured a supply of Caribbean salt for the herring industry – a mainstay of the Republic's economy. The distinction between war and piracy at that time was a vague one. The Dutch West India Company, which was founded on the model of the successful Dutch East India Company, was initially no more than an instrument of war and privateering. Hence, Piet Heyn's interception of a treasure fleet in the Cuban bay of Matanzas in 1628 was regarded as an 'heroic deed'; it is still sung about today by Dutch soccer fans today who haven't the faintest idea of its historical background.[2] Ships and islands were seized and lost; were captured, lost, re-captured and re-lost.

The Dutch also tried to gain a foothold in Brazil, a colony of Portugal which at that time had been temporarily brought under Spanish rule. The Dutch West India Company was in control of north-eastern Brazil between 1624 and 1654. It was there that the Netherlands became embroiled in the Atlantic system of slave trading and plantation production, that knot of economic illusions, modern technologies and marketing, moral indifference and plain cruelty. The need to supply the Brazilian plantations with slaves took the Dutch to the African coast where they retained their trading posts until well into the nineteenth century. The importance of the slave trade rapidly increased. During the Brazilian period, the provinces of Holland and Zeeland were probably among the largest transatlantic slave traders. However, this 'heyday' – moral objections were barely raised at the time – was brief. From the late seventeenth century on, the Dutch were forced to limit themselves to supplying their own colonies. The Dutch share of the entire transatlantic slave trade is now estimated to have been about five per cent; trading houses in Holland and Zeeland registered around half a million slaves who travelled the horrifying 'middle passage'.[3]

With the loss of Brazil, the centre of Dutch America shifted permanently to the Caribbean – New Amsterdam (now New York), the Netherlands' settlement in North America, was also lost at this time. By the end of the seventeenth century the first round of wars and redistribution in the archipelago had been completed. In the end, Spain held on to the Greater Antilles, and Britain and France seized a series of islands from Spain, which had been weakened by the Dutch. What remained as the Netherlands' consolation prize were six islands in the Caribbean and a few colonies on the northern, 'Wild Coast' of South America, the most important of which was Suriname.

One legacy in particular bound Dutch Brazil with the Caribbean. During their escapades in Brazil, Dutch entrepreneurs – largely of Iberian origins – helped to export plantation sugar production to the

Caribbean. Using Dutch credit, they delivered the technology and the first contingents of slaves to the British island of Barbados. While the Spanish Caribbean plantations, which dated from the beginning of the sixteenth century, had led a languid existence, the sugar plantation of Barbados became the model which was to leave its mark on the non-Spanish Caribbean within the space of a few generations. The Dutch Republic developed its own colonies on the Wild Coast according to this model. The Netherlands and its new, formerly Iberian citizens have the dubious honour of having begun this 'plantation revolution' in the Caribbean. The loss of Brazil added an important impulse to this process because the many Sephardic colonists who had settled there chose not to await the return of the Catholic Portuguese, but to move to the Netherlands or her colonies. The Sephardic transatlantic networks were to play a decisive role in the further development of the Dutch Caribbean.

To a certain degree this outlines the early history of the Dutch Caribbean. Within a few decades the new colony of Suriname was transformed into a thriving, or at least rapidly growing plantation colony. Curaçao, unsuitable for plantation agriculture, proved suitable as a trade (smuggling) centre and a slave depot. The remaining islands were, with the exception of a few episodes, of little significance. The three small colonies on the Wild Coast – Berbice, Demerara and Essequibo – never escaped the shadow of neighbouring Suriname. It was not until after 1800 that these regions were really developed by the United Kingdom as British Guiana. The colonial history of the Dutch Caribbean up to the twentieth century is, therefore, primarily the story of Suriname and Curaçao.

After Eldorado

So what motivated the first colonists? The founders of the 'Dutch West Indies' cannot be accused of excessive missionary zeal. The many pamphlets produced by Willem Usselinx, the *auctor intellectualis* of the Dutch West India Company, teem with economic and geopolitical arguments for the foundation of an empire in the New World. Any trace of religious fervour tends to rail against the Spanish; Usselinx was writing around 1600, at the time of the Dutch uprising against the Spanish, and religion clearly played an important part in that war. However, barely any effort was made to tie in the colonization of the New World – which was primarily an expansion of the theatre of war into the tropics – with a religious offensive. As Usselinx remarked, 'the holy Gospel should also be spread and God's church propagated among the blind heathens. This is the main task to be carried out there and we must not let the opportunity slip.'[4]

Yet this cursory encouragement is dwarfed by the bulk of his writings, in which he spurs his compatriots on to colonize the West. Colonization and trade, power and gold were Usselinx's real concerns, and he presented an example which most of his successors were to take to heart. Those who made the journey to the Dutch West Indies generally did so in the hope of finding a tangible Eldorado rather than a spiritual Walhalla or purification through self-sacrifice.

And so it would remain until well into the nineteenth century. The Dutch came to the New World in the hope of making their fortunes and to establish themselves as a prominent nation. Ideological and religious considerations were utterly subordinate to these aims. It is often claimed that Dutch foreign policy is marked by a continuous swing between the poles of 'merchant' and 'preacher'. Not only is such an assertion debatable in a general sense, and impossible to verify because so vague, it in no way applies to early Dutch colonialism in the Caribbean. Whatever brought the Dutch to these regions, missionary zeal was the least of their motives.

Neither were the first Dutch colonists naive fortune hunters, blinded by the myth of Eldorado, an imaginary land of fabulous wealth. This dream was initially one of the few things shared by the European countries who, ever since Columbus, had tried to take a piece of the New World for themselves. In the Caribbean, and in particular in present-day Peru and Mexico, the Spanish had already confiscated large quantities of gold when, in around 1535, a story began to circulate about El Dorado, the gilded man. This story implied new and even more wonderful prospects. Somewhere in the Americas, probably in what today is Colombia or Venezuela, there was said to be a kingdom of such unimaginable wealth that the king was dressed daily in a layer of gold dust. He would make offerings to the gods and then wash away his precious decoration in a lake. In the search for El Dorado, one of the possible locations was shifted further and further eastwards to the Guyanas on the 'Wild' North coast of South America. In the interior of the Guyanas was to be found Lake Parima where El Dorado was said washed the dusty riches off his body every day. After the Spanish, it was primarily the British who sent expeditions into the interior in the late seventeenth century. Time and again, the craving for gold and fame led such men as Walter Raleigh to journey along the wide rivers into the inhospitable interior, navigating by the compass of the vaguest of ideas. Time and again, desire crumbled into despair, and all too often ended in a miserable death.

By the time the Netherlands became lord and master over the Guyanas in the second half of the seventeenth century, gold fever had subsided, although various expeditions to find Lake Parima and the kingdom of Eldorado continued into the eighteenth century. Yet Dutch expansion in the New World was never dominated by gold fever – probably not because the Dutch were so level-headed but because they arrived too late to be able to seize the parts of the Americas that *were* rich in gold and silver. In Aruba and Suriname, the Dutch mined a certain amount of precious metals, but it never was a major industry. It soon became apparent that profit for the Dutch colonies lay primarily in other ventures. The Guyanas thus developed into an enormous accumulation of plantations and the Antilles became the crossroads of international trade, including smuggling. Great things could be achieved in the West as long as there was investment – as an old Dutch saying has it, *de kost gaat voor de baat uit*, 'expenditure precedes profits'.

It was in this spirit that enterprising characters such as Usselinx published their pamphlets explaining how the Dutch entrepreneurial spirit could turn the West Indies into a kind of Eldorado. Many were to concur, particularly in relation to the agricultural potential of Suriname. The frequently exaggerated talk about the incomparable fertility of the region and the accompanying belief in the profits to be made there would never subside. The present-day Surinamese fiction of inexhaustible natural wealth ('stick a walking stick in the ground and a week later you'll have a fruit tree') echoes early colonial notions which confused the exotic environment with infinite growth. The first books on Suriname exude boundless optimism. In 1718, J.D. Herlein compared the colony, with 'her wealth of blessedly fertile assets, exceptionally elegant, enticing and lustrous', with paradise. Even in the region Suriname's fertility achieved proverbial status; planters from Barbados apparently hatched the fantastic plan to ship soil from Suriname to replace their own, exhausted top soil. In 1822 the influential civil servant A.F. Lammens declared that one may 'expect anything of a country where the fertility of the soil has triumphed for more than century over man's most extravagant attempts to destroy it.'[5]

Far less was written during the colonial period about the six islands – the Leeward Islands of Aruba, Bonaire and Curaçao, and the Windward Islands of Saba, St Eustatius and St Martin. And what was written was far less laudatory. It was not without reason that the Spanish had spurned the Antilles as *islas inútiles*, useless islands. The landscape of the islands was not as majestic as that of Suriname, the agriculture was unproductive and their importance for trade, however significant for the Caribbean as a whole, was modest in Dutch eyes. As J.H. Hering, one of the first authors to write on Curaçao, put it:

> One cannot describe the island of Curaçao as a treasure trove
> of the most valuable products of nature: its entrails are not

pregnant with gold, silver or gems, and its fertile plains, between rocks and stony ground, produce little that is exceptional; all that grows and waxes is usually for personal use or to feed the Negro slaves. This island can therefore be regarded as a warehouse, or supply shed, for products that are shipped from the mainland or the Netherlands, or any land out of whose lap Europe enjoys notable benefits.[6]

A history of migration

The history of the Caribbean is made by migrants. With the arrival of Columbus, history not only took a new turn, it more or less began anew. In a short time the Amerindian populations on the islands were wiped out, while in the Guyanas they were relegated to the margins of colonial society. Immigration provided steady repopulation. The current population is descended from these newcomers: European colonists, African slaves, Asian contract workers and small minorities from elsewhere. The flora and fauna were also to a large extent imported. Coffee, cotton, even sugar – the product considered to have given the region its identity – were all foreign crops. Beef cattle, horses, pigs, even the *kabrieten* (goats) so typical of the Leeward Islands were all brought from the Old World to the New. It is hard to find another part of the world that has been so utterly 'remade' as the Caribbean following the arrival of Columbus.

The Caribbean colonies differed considerably from one another. The history of migration was an essential element in this. Slavery was introduced everywhere, but not at all to the same degree. In the Spanish-speaking Caribbean there were proportionally far fewer Africans and their descendants than in the colonies of the North-West Europeans, including the Dutch. The abolition of slavery was followed by a period of Asian contract labour which was to drastically alter the face of several countries, including Suriname. And then there was the enormous range of colonists; the Spanish, British, French and Dutch all left their mark on their colonies. As a consequence a rich variety of languages, religions, educational systems and political orientations still exist in the region today. Even when the United States began to eclipse European influence in the twentieth century, many of the diverse legacies of a colonial past held their ground.

The ties between the Netherlands and her colonies were remarkably loose, at least until the twentieth century. Britain and France cherished their Caribbean colonies. And just as France had fought for Haiti around 1800, so in the late-nineteenth century the Spanish battled in vain to retain Cuba, *la perla de las Antillas*. Conversely, from the Netherlands' perspective, the Dutch West Indies rarely emerged from the shadow of the Dutch East Indies.

In many respects, colonial Suriname, the jewel of the modest West Indian domain, was an average Caribbean plantation colony. When Suriname became Dutch in 1667, in an exchange of colonies which included the transfer of Manhattan from Dutch to English rule, it had less than 10,000 inhabitants. The small Native American population was soon driven into the interior and the coastal region transformed into plantations where African slaves laboured on the cultivation of sugar, coffee and cotton. What recognizably linked this colony to Holland was the polder system which the planters had introduced to transform the swampy coastal area into one suitable for plantation agriculture. Within a few decades this water management on the sugar plantations had developed into an ingenious system of separate water circuits which provided drainage, irrigation, transportation through the expansive cane fields, and a source of energy for the sugar mills where the cane sap was extracted. While the working conditions for the slaves were extremely harsh, the level of productivity for the planters was spectacular. In 1774 Abbé Raynal wrote with amazement that 'the Dutch have earned the honour of having tamed the ocean in the New World as they did in the Old.'[7] Sugar and coffee were the mainstay of the plantation economy, with cotton and cocoa as minor competitors. Around 1770 the average number of slaves on a Surinamese sugar plantation was 150, compared with 125 on an average coffee plantation. A good half century later the average number of slaves on a sugar plantation had risen to 170, while the numbers on the coffee plantations had dropped to ninety-five. About 125 slaves lived and worked on cotton plantations.[8]

Apart from the polders, Suriname had little that could be described as typically Dutch. The origins of the few white inhabitants lay mainly outside the Netherlands. The largest group of white colonists were Sephardic Jews, joined later by Ashkenazi Jews. There were also French Huguenots, British, Germans, and so on. The most successful Dutch planters were captivated by what the eighteenth-century governor Mauricius denounced as the *animus revertendi*, the desire to return as quickly as possible – and rich – to the patria. The local elite had strong economic ties with the mother country, but little in the way of cultural ties. New governors and other Dutch who passed through the colony were constantly confronted with how little they had in common with their expatriate 'compatriots'.

The large majority of the Surinamese was made up of African slaves and their descendants. The success of the plantations entailed an increasing dependence on slavery – not only were millions of guilders sunk into the fertile ground of Suriname, so too were the bodies of innumerable slaves and their descendants. The demographic development was frightful: until deep into the eighteenth century the negative growth ratios were generally in the order of five per cent; only after Emancipation did the Afro-Surinamese population begin to reproduce itself. That the population of Suriname increased at all was due entirely to a constant supply of new slaves, which did not dry up until the late eighteenth century. A total of 215,000 Africans were taken to Suriname. This large-scale slave trade caused the population of Suriname to reach a pinnacle in the 1770s with more than 70,000; slaves formed almost ninety-five per cent of that population. The number of white colonists and free citizens of (partly) African origin was extremely small. At the time of Emancipation in 1863 the colony still had around 63,000 inhabitants, about sixty per cent of which were slaves.[9] Relations between planters and slaves were initially strictly limited to the routines of work and discipline. Not until the nineteenth century did the Christianization of the slaves begin, by which time the slaves had long since created their own religious and cultural worlds, which would far outlive the empire of the planters.

The contrast between Suriname and the Antilles is striking. These islands were colonized slightly earlier than Suriname: Curaçao, the main island, in 1634, and the others around the same time. The differences between the history of Suriname and the Antilles is considerable and even the differences between the islands are more obvious than their similarities. These six islands, which were once described as 'Curaçao and dependencies', fall into two geographical groups: the three Leeward Islands and the three Windward Islands. The distance between Paramaribo and Curaçao measures more than 1500 km, the distance between this island and the Windward Islands further north is another 750 km. While Suriname is four times the size of the Netherlands – though most of it is uninhabited and, indeed, for all but Amerindians and Maroons practically uninhabitable tropical rain forest – the Antillean islands are all very small.

Almost from the beginning of the colonization, the Antilles formed an exception to the general pattern of European expansion in the Caribbean. This was due simply to their geographical and ecological features. Where sugar, coffee and slavery dominated elsewhere, this was no option on these islands. The Leeward Islands were simply too dry for the large-scale cultivation of tropical export crops; crop production and goat breeding never really developed beyond local supply. In terms of climate, the Windward Islands of the Antilles were more suitable for plantation agriculture, yet their small surface area and, in the case of St Martin and Saba, mountainous terrain largely offset this 'advantage'.

Although there were sugar plantations on St Martin and St Eustatius, they were never significant. Food production for local consumption was more important. As on the Leeward Islands, slaves were put to work in the salt pans. The real significance of the Antilles, however, lay in their commercial capacity; Curaçao and St Eustatius were to play a crucial part in trade between Europe and the New World in different periods, and they were especially important to trade within the Caribbean and between the Caribbean and the mainland. This trade was mainly smuggling, as hazardous as it was potentially profitable for merchants and the opportunistic colonial power.

The limited size and the modest economic significance of these islands implied small populations. In 1817, the first year for which figures are available for all islands, Curaçao had a population of 12,000, the islands of Aruba and Bonaire a little over 1,700 and 1,100 respectively, and the Windward Islands almost 7,300. At the time of the abolition of slavery in 1863, the total population of the Antilles was recorded as 33,000, of whom 19,000 lived on Curaçao. The number of slaves was far smaller than in Suriname and, moreover, steadily declined. On Curaçao in 1789, two thirds of the population were slaves; by 1814 the figure had dropped to less than half and by 1863 to only a third. During slavery the Antillean population had mixed racially far more than in Suriname, with the consequence that the 'free coloured' population was considerably larger. A striking testimony to the intensity of the interracial relations was the gradual adoption of the language of Papiamentu by the entire island's population. Today it is the only Creole language in the Caribbean which does not bear the stigma of inferiority and which is spoken by all local social and ethnic groups on the Leeward Islands.

The white elite of the islands were more inclined to permanent residence than their counterparts in Suriname, where only the Jewish colonists remained from the early days of colonization through to the twentieth century. Both Protestants and Sephardic Jews established themselves on the Leeward Islands, joined in the twentieth century only by Ashkenazi Jews; through their successful mercantile activities in the region at large, both groups became more Latinized over the centuries, and have held their ground to the present day.

The composition of the white population on the Windward Islands reflects other whims of fate. These three islands were originally British possessions. With Dutch consent, the resident white population remained on these islands after the handover of power to the Netherlands in the mid-seventeenth century. The Dutch arrived too late in the day and with too few colonists and too little interest to have a significant cultural impact. The lingua franca was English and the islands were mainly oriented towards their immediate surroundings; of the entire Dutch Caribbean, the Windward Islands continue to have the weakest links with their distant mother country.

Thus the contrasts in natural resources determined not only the way the colonists exploited their new possessions, but also the diverging ways each of these colonial societies and their populations developed as a consequence. The resultant distinctions in ethnicity and cultural orientation still underlie the profound differences between territories which only from the outside might appear to form a single, uniform cultural sphere.[10]

Plantations and profit

The whole system of African slave markets, American plantations and European commercial centres was a paradoxical one. On the one hand it was a remarkably advanced system, a structure of multinationals centuries before the term was invented. The logistics of intercontinental trade and related financial regulations; the extensive organization and standardization of production processes on the plantations; products which had previously been exclusively aimed at European elites now became available in ever increasing quantities and at ever lower prices for the diets of greater numbers of Europeans – all these points attest to a remarkable modernity. But the crux of this devil's triangle was slavery, a form of labour which gradually became stigmatized in Western Europe; if not perceived as economically obsolete, it was increasingly deemed morally reprehensible.[11]

Two of the most intriguing issues in the historiography of the Americas prior to the late eighteenth century are the widespread lack of politically relevant scruples regarding the Atlantic slave trade and New World slavery, and that moves to abolish slavery and the slave trade were not followed through. For the moment suffice it to say that in the Netherlands the question of a moral justification of slavery in the colonies barely arose. Dutch involvement in the slave trade dates from the late-sixteenth century; it was not until three hundred years later that slavery in the Dutch Caribbean was brought to an end. The length of this episode is all the more remarkable when we consider that the Netherlands was one of the first powers in the world to abolish this form of bondage for its own citizens at home. In this respect too there was a gaping divide between the mother country and her colonies in the Caribbean.[12]

Unfortunately for the colonists, Dutch colonialism in the Caribbean deviated from the regional norm in terms of metropolitan protection. While other European powers wholeheartedly supported the trade of

their slave colonies – naturally with a view to reaping the benefits there-
of – the Netherlands largely refused to provide this support. For the
Antilles this was no disaster, because their trading economy was only to
a limited degree aimed at the Netherlands. However, this policy did hurt
the Dutch colonies in the Guyanas. In the mercantile tradition, Suriname
was only permitted to trade exclusively with the Netherlands. Dutch
traders brought slaves from Africa to Suriname, Dutch ships transported
the tropical products to Dutch markets, and Dutch capital financed the
Surinamese plantation system. The Netherlands was vital to Suriname,
but the relationship was in no way mutual. Sugar and coffee from
Suriname made up only a small share of the Dutch staple market. The
colony was forced to compete with foreign competitors without any
domestic support. This step-motherly behaviour, which contrasted starkly with the protectionism practised by other European powers, would
turn out to be fatal.

Suriname did not live up to the expectations of the paradise that
Herlein had described, and even less so of the colony Usselinx and
numerous other investors after him had dreamed of. The productivity of
Suriname's sugar plantations contrasted favourably with the results
obtained elsewhere and hence became the source of sweet illusions. The
coffee sector entered a deep crisis in the late eighteenth century, but prior
to this it had experienced a period of excellent harvests. However, following a boom period, which already came to an end in the last quarter
of the eighteenth century, the balance sheet was extremely disappointing.
As a consequence of the half-hearted Dutch mercantilism, to remain
profitable Suriname was forced to achieve standards of productivity and
cost efficiency considerably above those of its competitors. This turned
out to be too demanding in the long term, leading to an increased and
ultimately unsustainable dependence on credit from the Netherlands.
These loans were often extended with unrealistic expectations. Inevitably
more and more plantations went bankrupt at the expense of their lenders.
Consequently the flow of credit to Suriname had dried up by the end of
the last quarter of the eighteenth century. It was a long time before the
'collapsed credit' was restored and Suriname would never again fulfil the
high expectations metropolitan investors, rulers and colonial planters
and merchants had once had of her.[13]

However prosaic it might be, there is something absurd about this
entire history of capital finance. The lending of capital to Suriname and
the running of the plantations became increasingly the domain of representatives who were paid a salary or commissions without having to
share the financial risks associated with owning the capital involved. In
exchange for all kinds of attractive rewards, they organized transportation around the transatlantic triangle and managed the plantations. In

due course, however, this management role became an end in itself. Instead of becoming profitable businesses, the plantations increasingly became bottomless pits in which investment rarely generated the desired results. Descendants of planters who generations earlier had 'repatriated' to the Netherlands discovered how their overseas possessions continuously deteriorated under external management. In the end they often ended up subsidizing the plantations rather than the other way round. Small savers in the Netherlands who had bought a few shares in these Surinamese companies also got a rude awakening. While the plantation overseers and their commercial agents in Suriname were sitting pretty, Dutch trading houses were forced to take ever greater risks; this game of economics, which had blinded many with the delusion of easy profit, eventually led to the collapse of several large firms. The colony became a graveyard of unrealistic expectations of easy gains.

The bitter irony is that the colony truly was a graveyard. Year after year more slaves died on the plantations than were born there. Only by constantly importing new slaves from Africa were the planters able to maintain the slave labour force and thereby production. However, the considerable investment that this entailed contributed to a significant extent to the disappointing financial results. Thence arose the absurd and cruel phenomenon of the plantation that devoured both the lives of slaves and the owner's capital.

In a typical Caribbean colony such as Suriname, a majority of the slaves worked on the plantations under a strictly regulated, industrial labour regime. Slavery on the Antilles followed a very different model. The small size of the Windward Islands hampered their development into true plantation colonies; the ecological features of the Leeward Islands had the same effect. Deforestation, begun by the Spanish and enthusiastically completed by the Dutch, had made the islands unsuitable for the farming of tropical export crops. Although there was sufficient rain, the ground was unable to retain water, as is still the case today. Hence the apparent aridity of the islands, which forced the colonists to limit themselves to modest-sized companies geared only towards production for local consumption.

These differences translated into a broad range of economic profiles and thence into a different and less intensive use of slave labour. Curaçaoan 'plantations' were in fact small, mixed farms. Maize and some green vegetables were grown, some cattle, pigs, goats and poultry were kept and bred. The number of slaves on these plantations could usually be counted by the dozen, whereas a typical Caribbean sugar plantation commonly had at least a hundred slaves – and at later stages many more. Similarly, on the Antilles slaves were used in many non-agricultural activities. They worked in the salt pans of Bonaire and St Martin, in shipbuilding, as dockers, sailors and fishermen on and around Curaçao and St Eustatius, as gardeners and domestic servants on all the islands. Far more than in Suriname they were used to working alongside whites and free coloureds and their masters frequently only owned a few slaves.

The significance for the Antillean economies of a separate class of slaves gradually declined. While in the mid-nineteenth century planters in Suriname were still making fierce attempts to delay the abolition of slavery and were bent on finding ways to bind freed slaves to the plantations, the slave owners of Curaçao were more concerned about the impending idleness of the slaves once they had gained their freedom. They reasoned that there was not enough work on the islands. This is why they had released so many slaves in the preceding decades, even expecting and hoping that after Emancipation many of them would migrate to nearby Venezuela. Curaçao was as crowded as Suriname was empty, even then.

Unlike Suriname, the demographic development of the islands, including the slaves, was favourable. The milder labour regime for the slaves may have been significant in this, although it is probable that the more favourable climate and a less pernicious servitude were more important factors. Whatever the case, the life of the slaves on the islands was physically less merciless. This was also of benefit to their owners; they did not have to constantly buy new slaves to maintain labour levels. This was no longer a priority for them. The slave trade dried up here faster then anywhere else in the non-Spanish Caribbean and the proportion of slaves in Antillean society declined as that of free labour of (partially) African origins increased. Slavery was of marginal importance in the Antilles long before it was abolished in the Dutch Caribbean. In this respect the islands differed fundamentally from Suriname, which followed the typical Caribbean model.

Intermezzo: East and West

At one point the Dutch colonial empire stretched across many parts of Asia, Africa and the Americas. However, many of the colonies were lost before or around 1800. The colonial domain that had stabilized by the first half of the nineteenth century comprised what are today Indonesia, Suriname, the islands of the Antilles and a few settlements on the West coast of Africa. By this time Berbice, Demerara and Essequibo had already been handed over to Britain, as had the Cape Colony (the heart of today's South Africa) and, 150 years earlier, New Amsterdam (now

New York). In fact, New Amsterdam and the Cape Colony – not co-incidentally territories outside the tropics – were the only two colonial enterprises which expanded into settler colonies, becoming extensions abroad of the colonial mother metropolis in a region where European colonists would come to form a significant proportion of the population. However, in both instances these developments only materialized after the departure of the Dutch.

The remaining colonies, the core of the colonial empire, lay in the tropics and offered a dubious 'home' to colonists forming only a small minority of the population. The differences between these colonies were enormous. Firstly, in terms of scale: whereas the population of the Dutch East Indies was counted in millions, in the Caribbean it remained in the tens of thousands; the trading settlements in West Africa, which were handed over to the British in 1870, had negligible populations. In all cases the colonists were minority populations: their numbers were negligible in the 'Indies' (Indonesia) – which were not colonized in the traditional sense until the twentieth century; they made up only a small percentage of the population in Suriname; and less than a quarter of the Antillean population.

The backgrounds of the rest of the colonies' populations varied substantially from one colony to another. In Asia the populations were almost entirely 'native' with roots going back millennia. Only Suriname and Aruba had small Native American populations. In the West Indies, and only there, the Dutch ruled over a large majority of colonized peoples whom they themselves had transported there. Whereas in Africa and Asia they had been intruders, who in retrospect may be said to have left no more than scratches on the rocks, in the Caribbean they created their own colonial subjects. In the Caribbean a majority of these subjects were African slaves and their offspring, while in the East Indies slaves formed only a small section of the population and were predominantly recruited locally or in the region. This too was a fundamental difference between the East and West.

That this gulf between the Dutch East Indies and West Indies remained deep is hardly surprising. Indonesia was and is in all respects – geographically, economically, politically – of a completely different scale and significance compared with Suriname, the Netherlands Antilles and Aruba. The Dutch miracle of its seventeenth, 'Golden' century and the prosperity which was maintained thereafter was primarily based on domestic economic growth and intra-European trade. The colonial contribution had long paled in comparison. Yet, particularly from the nineteenth century on, Indonesia and not the West Indies made a significant contribution to Dutch economic growth. By the early twentieth century, Indonesia alone was thought by some to be the 'cork that buoyed up the Dutch economy', the colonial prosthetic that lent the Netherlands the air of an international player.

This was to be clearly expressed in the post-war process of decolonization. Only after outright warfare in Asia and bitter political conflict at home did the Netherlands resign itself to Indonesian independence. It became apparent in the mid-nineties when Queen Beatrix visited Indonesia that the old wounds on the Dutch side had not healed. The debate in Dutch politics and media was dominated by the question of whether and how the monarch should express regret for the colonialism of the past and particularly of the post-War colonial warfare, regardless of whether Jakarta was actually awaiting such an apology. No straightforward apology has been voiced by the Dutch state to date.

Dutch policy in the Caribbean, on the other hand, evoked an image of a – in effect failed – process of 'upside-down decolonization'. In around 1970, The Hague tried to erase the postcolonial ties laid out in the Charter of 1954, whereby the Caribbean countries became internally autonomous countries within the Kingdom of the Netherlands but could still count on substantial support from The Hague in many spheres. There was limited but politically just enough support for a move towards full sovereignty in Suriname. The country became a republic in 1975, but has remained heavily dependent on The Hague ever since, primarily in the field of development aid. The at times embarrassing parliamentary and governmental interference in Suriname met its counterpart in the continuation of Suriname's strong ties with the Netherlands. A crucial factor in this is that since the 1970s the demographic growth of the Surinamese population has been limited to its community in the metropolis.

Much to The Hague's disappointment, the Antilles and Aruba – the latter having split constitutionally in 1986 from the other islands, but not from the Netherlands – turned down the 'gift' of the transferral of sovereignty, despite Dutch promises to guarantee their territorial integrity and to continue extending financial support. Having accepted this state of affairs by 1990, the Netherlands have since hammered home the need for the Antillean and Aruban authorities to model their policies on metropolitan standards – which inevitably led to allegations of 'recolonization'.[14]

From a cultural perspective too the gap was large. However ambivalent and convinced the Netherlands may have been of its own superiority, it recognized the existence of a local 'high' culture in the 'East Indies', but not in the Caribbean. The Indonesian elites maintained their own high cultures, even in areas where they leaned towards the colonial culture, such as education and politics. It is hardly surprising that this limited orientation towards Dutch culture soon faded after

1945. On the other hand, the Dutch perceived the cultures of the Caribbean colonies, however much these were their own creations, simply as inferior variants of the Netherlands model. Although this might have been frustrating for the local elites, who were strongly oriented towards patria, it did not lead to a decisive break. On the contrary, in recent history all strata and ethnic groups in the Dutch Caribbean have become ever more involved with the Netherlands.

This is dramatically expressed by the exodus to the Netherlands which now amounts to more than a third of the populations of Suriname and the Antilles. Herein too lies a significant difference with Indonesia. Between 1945 and the early 1960s some 300,000 'repatriates' from Indonesia took up residence in a mother country most of them only knew from hearsay. The size of the Indonesian community in the Netherlands is similar to that of the Caribbean community. However, what is more important is the effect on population numbers and politics 'abroad': the immigrants and their descendants from Indonesia formed only a fraction of the population of the archipelago. This contrasts starkly with the Dutch Caribbean. Numerically the exodus has been crippling for Suriname and threatens to become so for the Antilles. In addition, the majority of the Caribbean elite was and is educated in the Netherlands, as opposed to only a small sector of the Indonesian elite, which today is on the verge of literally dying out. West Indian orientation towards the Netherlands is therefore far more relevant in every possible dimension.[15]

In general, the Netherlands is inclined to regard the history of West Indian colonialism and its legacies more as a burden than a cause for satisfaction. The Dutch West India Company immediately evokes associations with the slave trade and piracy, whereas the colonial history of the East Indies is thought of and spoken of with a certain degree of pride, however furtively. In 2002, four hundred years after the Dutch East India Company was founded, this anniversary was commemorated, even celebrated, with great pomp by both parliament and crown. To underline the argument made here – and actually disclosing a remarkable inconsistency in the nation's rendering of its own colonial past – it should be pointed out that in the same year a national monument was erected in Amsterdam in embarrassed remembrance of West Indian slavery.[16]

For the Netherlands, Indonesia has remained the most important part of its colonial past. The turbulent development that independent Indonesia has been through over the past few decades, and the way this has harshly confronted the Netherlands with her smallness, has only strengthened this awareness. In comparison, the former Dutch West Indies seem to be increasingly tainted with the stigma of uselessness, of disappointed expectations, of a collection of troublemakers. The recent history of mass emigration and costly, but apparently largely ineffect-ual, development aid has firmly underscored this perception. Ideas to deal with a problematic present are rather too easily linked to an anachronistic view of the history of colonial relations. The high level of interest in the Netherlands for a romanticized colonial past in the East (*Tempoe Doeloe*) and for the painful winding up of colonialism in Indonesia was matched until very recently by complete disinterest in colonialism and its legacies in the Dutch Caribbean. Even a theme like slavery and its comparatively late abolition in Dutch territories was not up for discussion until half a decade ago. Somehow the belief was doggedly maintained that whatever once happened in the Caribbean could never have been very important. This is an ironic paradox. For the population and the cultural representatives of more highly respected Indonesia, the Netherlands is largely irrelevant. Yet for the Dutch Caribbean populations, who are treated with much more scepticism by the Netherlands, Dutch culture is of increasing importance. This is a recipe for tragicomic misunderstandings and Caribbean frustrations.

The cultural divide

In cultural terms the West Indian colonies were a far remove from patria – and from each other. This cultural divide naturally reflects the stark differences between the geographic, economic and demographic char-acteristics of the Caribbean territories, as well as the differences between the Caribbean and the Netherlands. Furthermore, it indicates centuries of Dutch inability, and unwillingness, to accomplish a *mission civilisatrice*. A cautious change only came about at the end of the nine-teenth century, bringing with it unforeseeable consequences for recent history.

Take Suriname. In the first centuries of colonization the bond between the colonial planter class and the mother country was weak. The relationship between Suriname's planters and their slaves was ambiguous, dominated by mutual feelings of dependency, hatred and fear. Between the Surinamese slaves and the metropolitan Dutch there was no conscious common ground and even less direct contact. The two worlds remained apart.

Dutch colonialism in Suriname made barely any attempt to change the situation. In Latin America and the French Caribbean, the slave population was Christianized from the beginning – albeit with ambiva-lent intentions and consequences. An attempt was made, at least on paper, to convert the slaves to the culture of the motherland. This was not Dutch policy in Suriname. Only in the decades prior to abolition were serious attempts made to Christianize the slaves. Even then the most active missionaries in this 'civilizing offensive' were not Dutch, but German Moravians.[17]

The yawning gap between the slave population, the colonial elite and the mother country was not purely a religious one. It went much deeper. The slaves, like the planters a population of migrants, developed their own Afro-Caribbean culture: ways of thinking, religion, music, dance, storytelling, and all kinds of daily customs. Slavery obviously provoked slave resistance, and the Dutch Caribbean certainly had its share. Curaçao had several slave revolts, notably in 1750 and 1795. Suriname's planters faced the continuous marooning of their slaves to the interiors of the tropical rain forests. There, in time, large Maroon communities developed which successfully withstood colonial efforts to re-subjugate them and which at times jeopardized the very existence of the plantation colony as such. Resistance in itself spelt cultural specificity, but by no means can all Afro-Caribbean culture be interpreted only as a mode of resistance.

All over the Americas, through processes of creolization, African slaves and their offspring developed new cultures by adapting cultural 'syntax' and forms brought from Africa to their new condition, with all the challenges and limitations that went with a new material environment and the European domination. In the particular case of Suriname, the Maroons developed their own vibrant cultures very much in the margins of colonial society. But slaves too in this colony of so few Europeans developed their own social and cultural capital in an environment in which the colonial elite had made little impact. The legacies of this culture are still visible and audible today, for instance, in popular music. Like the Cuban *son montuno,* the Surinamese *kaseko* is a creolized phenomenon, a new creation through which both African and European elements resonate. Yet the Spanish presence in Cuba, and hence its mark on Cuban culture, had an altogether stronger impact, as is obvious from Spanish Caribbean music, inter alia. However, European elements can also be detected in the Surinamese *kaseko*: the wind instruments, for example, are borrowed from military bands. Yet this genre is above all an *Afro*-Caribbean creation. And what is true of music is true of much more in Afro-Surinamese culture.[18]

This is not in itself unique; other colonies underwent a similar development. However, the situation in Suriname was extreme in that the Dutch did not even manage to get their own language adopted by the population. *Neger-Engelsch* (Negro-English), which had emerged as a contact language between the African slaves and the British planters in the twenty years preceding the Dutch conquest of Suriname (1667), developed into a fully-fledged Creole language. Dutch remained the language of the elite, but they had to communicate with their own slaves in Sranan Tongo. Hence, unlike the rest of the Caribbean, by the time of Emancipation ninety-five per cent of Suriname's population did not even understand the language of its rulers.

On the Antilles the gulf between the local elite and the mother country was even greater. With only slight exaggeration one could say that there was just one 'foreign' country for Suriname, and that was the Netherlands.[19] The cultivated coastal regions were, figuratively speaking, isolated islands which were more cut off from the outside world than the Antilles. 'Cosmopolitan' may be too big a word for Curaçao or St Eustatius in their heyday, but these islands did maintain intensive contact with their immediate surroundings: Curaçao with the Spanish American *tierra firme*; 'Statia' (St Eustatius) with the British colonies in North America, which would soon declare themselves independent; and both with the surrounding French, Spanish and British islands. The Netherlands did not play a prominent role in any of this.[20] And because trade relations with the mother country were limited, the distance between them remained great in other respects too.

The Netherlands had never intended to turn the Caribbean colonies into foreign pendants of its own culture, but the result that began to take shape during the first centuries of slavery was highly peculiar. The slave population of the islands had virtually no contact with Dutch culture. Its language and culture were different, as was its religion. Little attention was paid to Christianization on the Windward Islands, while on the Leeward Islands an ironic situation arose. Insofar as the slave population there turned to Christianity at all, it was to Catholicism they had been converted to by Spanish priests. Ironically again, Catholicism had precisely been one of the reasons why the Dutch had rebelled against the Spanish at home and journeyed to these far-flung regions in the first place.

The islands' elites had less in common with Dutch culture than their West Indian counterparts. While the local elite in Suriname did speak Dutch, this was far less common on the islands. On the Leeward Islands the languages mainly spoken were Spanish, Portuguese and Papiamentu, whereas English was the vernacular on the Windward Islands. The white population of Curaçao comprised a Jewish and a Protestant sector, both of which were subdivided into an elite and a lower stratum. The Jewish group had its own cultural and religious position which was tolerated by the colonial authorities. This group was prominent on the island, but participated only to a limited extent in Dutch culture. The Protestants' background implied more commonality with the Netherlands and hence some sort of natural affinity with the administrators sent out from Holland. Yet Latinization occurred in this group too, leading them to integrate more fully into island society and the surrounding countries. This inevitably led to an estrangement from Dutch culture.

The Dutch Caribbean colonies in this respect again had little in common with each other, far less in fact than the colonies of other powers in the region. Language differences were a major factor. The language of the colonial authorities in Suriname, the Leeward Islands and the Windward Islands was Dutch – it could not be otherwise as the governors and other figures in authority were sent from the Netherlands. The children of the local elites were, of course, largely educated in Dutch, even if only in preparation for a serious education back home. Yet where the local elite in Suriname spoke Dutch among themselves, on the islands this was far less often the case. Even at this time there was no Dutch language community in the Caribbean; rare among the elite, it was non-existent among ordinary people. Papiamentu was spoken on the Leeward Islands; Creole English on the Windward Islands; Sranan Tongo, Amerindian or Maroon languages were spoken in Suriname.

This is not to say that this language difference was the crucial barrier inhibiting contact within the Dutch Caribbean. In fact, until the twentieth century there was hardly question of physical contact at all between the inhabitants of the different parts of the 'West Indies', a notion that only had meaning from a Dutch point of view anyway.

An absurd scenario

Thus, new worlds developed thousands of miles from the home country. Colonies which prior to the arrival of the Europeans had been worlds unto themselves, were now remade as Dutch creations and in the end came to be dominated by Africans and Asians. Dutch in name, these colonies were distinct from the mother country in most respects. The Netherlands had hoped to grow rich from this region, but failed. Some individuals managed to accumulate fortunes, of course, but in the end the financial balance was less than prosperous, despite the high expectations.

Looking back over the history of the Dutch Caribbean today it is hard not to be cynical. On the one hand the phenomena of the slave trade, slavery and contract labour are now regarded with shame, outrage or incomprehension. On the other hand, at the end of the twentieth century, the effects of colonization to date are well known: the persistent ambivalent emotions between the descendants of the colonizers and the colonized; for the moment at least, the debacle surrounding Suriname's independence; the likelihood of the further disintegration of the six Netherlands Antilles, after Aruba's split from the scene now a fragile 'entity' of five; the fact, only recently and hesitantly accepted, that these micro-states are unable to survive without a lifeline – to this day the umbilical cord joining them to the Netherlands. This entire history is redolent of classical tragedy.

But why this history? Why colonization? Why the build up of populations of slaves and indentured workers? Why was a line not drawn sooner under a colonial adventure which generated so little in material terms, was so deplorable in moral terms, and which in other respects has left such a frustrating, though fascinating, legacy? It is easy to ask these questions with hindsight, but not as easy to provide adequate answers. In part an explanation has to be sought in the fact that many individual colonists and managers did make their fortunes. One of the outcomes of this was that the colonies retained something of the image of Eldorado and consequently a history of expectations that were consistently set too high and inevitably bred disappointment.

In the course of the nineteenth century the idea gained currency that this particular colonial possession was simply a millstone around the neck of the motherland. Proposals to dispense with the colonies, to sell them to the highest bidder – the most likely being the United States of America – circulated with some frequency. Futile plans. Apart from the dubious moral significance of this particular train of colonial thought, there was no real foreign interest. Hence, the Dutch West Indies remained intact until the 1970s. There were almost no sweet illusions to foster, except perhaps, on the eve of Surinamese independence, the fervently argued, 'progressive' idea that the long-awaited economic breakthrough was conditional upon political independence.

Since then reality has shattered even this illusion. It is hard to recall a single dream that has become reality. The balance sheet of Dutch colonialism in 'the West' is utterly delusional. A world that was created to make profits generated mainly ever-growing losses. Hundreds of thousands of lives were sacrificed along the way. In some sort of unsolicited compensation, new Caribbean cultures evolved in which the metropolis had little interest. Politically, this chapter in colonialism left behind a legacy of barely viable countries from which the Netherlands cannot detach itself to this day, partly because the contemporary descendants of the brutalized colonial subjects have good grounds to suspect that a Dutch retreat in the first instance would serve metropolitan interests. An absurd scenario, *lo real maravilloso* Dutch style.

Notes

1 A general and very detailed, but not always systematic or consistent account in English of Dutch Caribbean history is given by Goslinga 1971, 1985 and 1990. Relevant introductions to more limited periods and themes are Van den Boogaart et al. 1992, Boxer 1965, Emmer 1998, 2000, Emmer & Klooster 1999, Israël 1995, Den Heijer 1994, De Jongh 1966, Klooster 1997, and Postma 1990. General introductions to Suriname include Bakker et al. 1993, Buddingh' 1995, Helman 1983, Hoefte & Meel 2001, Van Lier 1971; to Curaçao, Hoetink 1958 and Römer 1979; to the Netherlands Antilles in general, Dalhuisen et al. 1997. See Boxer 1957 and Stols 1971 for the 'prehistory' in Brazil. For the history of New Amsterdam, Jacobs 1999.
2 In Dutch: *'Piet Heyn, Piet Heyn, Piet Heyn zijn naam is klein/Zijn daden bennen groot (bis)/Hij heeft gewonnen de zilvervloot.'* 'Piet Heyn, Piet Heyn, his name is small/ His deeds loom large (bis)/He won the silver fleet.'
3 Figures are taken from Postma 1990:296.
4 Usselinx 1608:[32]. All translations made for this book from the original language of publication, unless indicated otherwise.
5 Herlein 1718: n.p. (Voorberigt). Lammens 1982:138. Williams 1970:34.
6 Hering 1779:57. Well into the twentieth century only one Antillean island, Saba, was described on several occasions in terms redolent of Eldorado. It is striking how the descriptions by Abbé Raynal (1774) and G. van Lennep Coster (1842) of this, the smallest of the islands correspond so closely – particularly since the former never actually visited the island (Hoefte & Oostindie 1996: 35–7, 66–7).
7 Raynal 1774, IV:336. See also Oostindie & Van Stipriaan 1995.
8 See Van Stipriaan 1989, 1993.
9 For slave trade figures and the demographic development of Suriname, see especially Postma 1993 and Van Stipriaan 1993.
10 On ethnic plurality and its consequences, see Chapters 3 and 5.
11 A paradox, not a contradiction. The doctrine of the economic inferiority of bonded labour is rather an anachronistic interpretation inspired by contestable readings of contemporaries such as Adam Smith and Karl Marx, and subsequently enhanced by racist ideas of the inferiority of *black* labourers, rather than an empirically established fact. The idea of a contradiction between economic rationality and the use of slave labour often continues to be supported from the equally anachronistic viewpoint that the slave trade and slavery should be seen as necessary evils and that economic modernity is accompanied by a greater moral sensitivity; both assumptions, however, lack empirical foundations (Boomgaard & Oostindie 1989).
12 On Dutch antislavery and abolition, see the various contributions to Oostindie 1995a, and particularly Drescher 1995.
13 Compare Emmer 1988, 1990, 1996, Oostindie 1993a, Van Stipriaan 1989, 1993, 1995.
14 See Oostindie & Klinkers 2003; also Chapters 4 and 5.
15 The Caribbean exodus to the Netherlands and its consequences is discussed in Chapters 5 and 6.
16 For a comparison between the VOC celebrations and the WIC commemorations, see Oostindie 2003. For a discussion of history and identity in Dutch Caribbean context, see Chapter 7.
17 See Chapter 2.
18 On creolization, see Mintz & Price 1992, Bolland 1992, Van Stipriaan 2000, Trouillot 2001, Price 2001, Yelvington 2001 and the literature discussed therein.

19 On the long-distance routes, America was the most important trading partner after the Netherlands.

20 However, recent research has revealed that trade between the Netherlands and the Antilles (Curaçao and St Eustatius) was more significant than was for a long time believed (Klooster 1998).

2 | Slave, Black; human?

Explaining abolition has long been a central concern in the historiography of the Americas. Not so for the Dutch Caribbean, where the ending of the slave trade was imposed by the British and where slave Emancipation came late but apparently undisputed. In fact, the belatedness of Emancipation was the most remarkable fact about it all. The Dutch government accepted the inevitability of the ending of slavery only in the 1840s; and even then little progress was made. By 1861, two years before Emancipation, the Dutch historian J. Wolbers scorned the lukewarm abolitionists for having forsaken the noble cause. Slavery was still a reality. Yet the abolitionists now slumbered, self-congratulatory for once having contributed to the good cause and deaf to 'the shrill cries of the tortured slaves [as] it became so tedious to hear time and again of those Negroes living so far away'. Subsequent historians have consistently remarked on the absence of a passionate public debate on abolition in the Dutch world. David Brion Davis summed it up with the cursory remark that Dutch Emancipation was 'businesslike'.[1]

The question then seems to be not so much why the Dutch abolished the slave trade and slavery but rather, as Seymour Drescher rightly reformulates the issue, why so late and in so laggardly a manner?[2] Why was Dutch society, with its presumed conscience-stricken tradition of questioning the gathering and deployment of wealth, so little responsive to the abolitionist cause? Short of an immediate answer, suffice it to question here the notion of a chronic Dutch 'embarrassment of riches', and to recall that the Dutch were not unique in their apathy. In the context of the times, the British rather than the other participants in the Atlantic slave system were the exception to the rule. Britain provided the momentum in Dutch abolition by simply imposing the end of the slave trade at the close of the Napoleonic Wars; there was no serious public debate on this issue in the Netherlands.[3]

So, arguably, a study of Dutch decision-making could be confined to a study of the mid-nineteenth-century decades, as indeed most scholars have opted to do. Emancipation may then be explained in the context of international pressure and the economic insignificance of the Dutch Caribbean, and particular the major colony, Suriname, to its metropolis.[4] The timing may be related to the eventual emergence of a modest abolitionist lobby and, indeed businesslike, to the rising income from the Dutch East Indies and the simultaneous substantial decrease in the number of slaves in the Dutch West Indies, a fortunate concurrence which helped the Dutch government to settle the indemnification of the West Indian slave-owners.

This perspective is justified. Even so, one wonders about the development, if any, of Dutch colonial ideologies regarding slavery. Both Davis, in his monumental trilogy, and Gordon Lewis, in *Main Currents of Caribbean Thought*, virtually ignore Dutch and Dutch West Indian ideologies.[5] This contribution attempts to partly fill this gap through an analysis of the contemporary literature on the major Dutch Caribbean colonies, Suriname and Curaçao. In discussing current justifications for slavery and particularly representations of the Dutch West Indian slave, I focus on the influence of the Enlightenment, Christianity and the nature of 'progressive' thinking.

The present overview cannot disclose a rich corpus of writings; in fact, after reading Davis's and Lewis's works one is hard pressed to find anything original in the relevant, predominantly Dutch-language writings. This reading therefore largely confirms established notions about the flatness of the Dutch and Dutch Caribbean debate. Even so, the prolonged absence of any serious abolitionist debates did not imply that the various discourses were static. As time progressed, and as some spokesmen thought of themselves as more humanitarian and forward-looking while others tried mainly to postpone Emancipation, they all developed definitions of slaves and of slavery, and attempted to open new fields of appropriation of the West Indian slave.[6]

Slavery as a non-problem in the Dutch world

When the Dutch established commercial relations with Africa in the late sixteenth century, they were coming from a society where blacks were virtually unknown. Like the British who were equally unfamiliar with blacks, it took them only a few decades to establish a set of mostly negative representations of the African. Initially they attributed less importance to 'blackness' and inherent inferiority as such, focusing on the presumed savagery of the African instead, with paganism and licentiousness as defining features.[7] The subsequent involvement in the Atlantic slave trade and New World plantation economies soon induced Dutch spokesmen to use the whole panoply of justifications, including heredity and innate abasement. Analysis of Dutch writings on these topics does not disclose arguments absent in discourse elsewhere in the Western world. In varying admixtures, blackness, paganism, brutality and sexual lasciviousness came to define the representation of the African, thus helping to justify the slave trade and slavery.

There was no denial of the humanity of the African; blackness, however, became associated with the curse of Noah on Cham and his descendants.[8] The infinite inferiority of the blacks was therefore some-how of God's making, and made it only logical that blacks served whites as slaves, even if slavery as such was not the natural condition of mankind. Enslavement by the Europeans moreover provided the Africans with an opportunity to escape the abasement and cruelty of their uncivilized continent; after all, most slaves sold to the slavers were bounties of war who otherwise would have been killed or abused by their African conquerors. Occasionally mention was made of enslave-ment as an avenue for Christianization; yet in the Dutch world this argu-ment never made it to the mainstream as it did in Catholic Europe.[9] Finally an occasional author such as the medical doctor D.H. Gallandat, in his manual for slave traders, voiced the more down-to-earth justification:

> I will only remark here that there are many occupations which would seem unjustified if they would not be of par-ticular advantage. An argument here may be the Slave Trade, which should be acquitted of all unlawfulness solely because of the benefit it furnishes to the merchants.[10]

Even if the profitability of the slave trade did not come anywhere near the exaggerated expectations, the slave trade continued, and all Dutch colonies in the Americas came to depend on slavery. Both institutions could count on the full support both of the Dutch state and of the reli-gious authorities. By the late eighteenth century, some French and English anti-slavery tracts had been translated into Dutch, yet apparent-ly these did not spark a following. An exhaustive study of Dutch litera-ture discovered only a handful of authors speaking out against slavery up to the early 1790s.[11]

How should we account for this lack of interest, which gives the Dutch a poor showing not only in comparison to the unique British case, but even to the French and the Danes? Some tangible factors may have kept Dutch public opinion from reconsidering. The West Indies' impor-tance to the metropolitan economy was dwarfed by the East Indies, where slavery was of minor significance. Perhaps this could have helped the Dutch to discard the institution; in practice, however, it apparently led them to neglect the Caribbean colonies most of the time. The con-trast with Britain is evident. Moreover, and probably working in the same direction, there was no black presence of any importance in the Netherlands.[12] This too may have helped to postpone serious debates on slavery: the very subject was beyond the Dutch frame of reference. Finally, whereas in the eighteenth century the Suriname Maroon Wars – and two slave rebellions in Curaçao – had occasionally brought the colonies into the spotlight, the nineteenth century was tranquil in terms of marronage and slave rebellions. Consequently, little reminded the Dutch of the reality of slavery in their realm.

But what about vital metropolitan interests or ideologies at stake? As Davis demonstrates, the international anti-slavery ideology derived from various sources.[13] The often anti-clerical Enlightenment philosophers were crucial in opening the debate. However, the abolitionist movement derived much of its operational strength from fresh interpretations of Protestant Christianity. From the late eighteenth century onwards, abolitionism gained further momentum through its inextricable connection with new notions of human progress, industrial capitalism and economic liberalism.

These impetuses were weak in the Netherlands. The Dutch eighteenth century has traditionally been depicted as uneventful, and its cultural ambience as boring; the Dutch Enlightenment supposedly was flat, barely radical, and never far from the mainstream of the Dutch Christian tradition. A scholarly volume on the Dutch Republic in the eighteenth century published in the early 1990s succeeded in presenting a more nuanced picture – yet in spite of its debunking objectives, the overall impression remains much the same. In this context, it seems characteristic that in the sixteen essays on the Dutch eighteenth century and Enlightenment, the issue of slavery was not raised even once. This oversight reflects the eccentricity of the issue in contemporary thought. At the same time, it demonstrates how little subsequent scholarship tends to take attitudes towards slavery as a significant yardstick to measure modernity in the Dutch world.[14]

The establishment of the Batavian Republic (1795–1806) seemed a break with the conservative political traditions. Yet the program of its 'radical' leadership fell short of radicalism regarding the colonies. There was no intention of genuine colonial reform. Even if the radicals had earlier applauded the American Revolution, they were not prepared to see the Dutch colonies as anything but subjected sources of metropolitan wealth. Slavery was virtually ignored. The initial 1796 and 1797 proposals for a new constitution did not even mention the slave trade or slavery itself. Prompted by a few radicals, the National Assembly subsequently did appoint a committee to advise on these matters. The committee's report, however, was anything but abolitionist, and the 1798 Constitution did not consider abolition. In spite of its strong commitment to the French Revolution, the radical 'Patriot' government did not even contemplate duplicating the short-lived French abolitionist policy.[15]

If the Enlightenment did not provide a source of antislavery ideology, neither did religious dissenters. The Protestant Nederlandsch Hervormde Kerk with its dominance in Dutch society and politics remained silent until the 1850s. The influence of Catholicism was negligible. A substantial proportion of the Dutch population – even if not of its political leadership – had remained Catholic after the hard-won struggle for independence from Catholic Spain in the mid-seventeenth century. Yet full Catholic emancipation was accomplished only in the late nineteenth century, and in this process the Catholic leadership had found no expediency in championing anti-slavery policies.[16] As neither denomination created significant dissenting offspring, religious potential for abolitionism was far weaker than it had been in Britain.[17]

What about industrial capitalist ideology? In its 'Golden' seventeenth century, the Netherlands had been a pioneer capitalist state. Commenting on recent debates emphasizing the role of a progressive capitalist mentality in the emergence of abolitionism, Drescher indicates that precisely Dutch society should have been a case in point, but failed to live up to the theory.[18] The implications of the Dutch case for this theoretical discussion are not my main concern here. Yet, it may well be argued that the pioneering quality of early Dutch capitalism had long passed. For one thing, and in striking contrast to its major competitors, during the eighteenth century the commercial and industrial sectors of the Dutch economy actually declined somewhat in comparison to agriculture.[19] Moreover, the question remains whether the early Dutch mercantile capitalist spirit may be put on a par with the later British industrial capitalist esprit. In the Netherlands, significant new industrialization came late, and so did the emergence of a class of clearly industrial capitalist orientation. If we may interpret Liberal British support for abolition partly as an expression of optimism regarding Britain's industrial future, the lack of such support in the Netherlands may also reflect a profound pessimism on the perceived decline of the nation's economy.

Either way, much of what was becoming accepted modern ideology in England, and subsequently in France and the United States, remained far from the Dutch elite's mentality and from colonial ideology. By 1776, Adam Smith in *Wealth of Nations* argued for the economic inefficiency of slavery, hence suggesting that real progress even in the colonies was to be expected from the substitution of free labour for slavery. It took another half century before an isolated Dutch observer wrote on slavery in even remotely similar terms.[20]

In the first decades of the nineteenth century therefore, the intellectual climate in the Netherlands was hardly conducive to raising 'modern' arguments against the established practice of slavery. Only by mid-century did the Dutch elite decide to finally abolish the peculiar institution. By then even the Dutch, struggling to modernize their state and to regain the prestige that had once characterized their nation, had succumbed to the 'peer' pressure of more advanced European neighbours.[21] In the modernizing outlook, the project of regaining respectability and rejoining the concert of progressive nations by necessity implied the dismantling of Dutch West Indian slavery.

The colonial perspective: Suriname

For the authors writing on the major Dutch West Indian colony, Suriname, the absence of a significant metropolitan discourse on slavery implied that there was no urgent need to justify the institution. In a way, this makes the literature more interesting. Not that it was of such remarkable quality. With fine exaggeration, Lewis has argued that Caribbean society 'was marked throughout by a spirit of cultural philistinism probably unmatched in the history of European colonialism', and that the 'planter way of life [was] at once crassly materialist and spiritually empty'.[22] Suriname may certainly be read as a case in point. In the late 1770s, the *Essai historique* decried the colony's intellectual levels, while another author concluded that a man of letters was an exotic plant in Suriname.[23] In the last decades of the eighteenth century, some 'Enlightened' inspiration filtered through to Suriname, resulting in the formation of European-style debating clubs and projects to raise the deplorable educational standards of the colony's free population. Yet slavery did not rank high – if at all – on an agenda which was primarily of a utilitarian character.[24]

With the exception of two major historical studies, the bulk of the relevant literature on Suriname was written by men with direct and often ongoing experience with slavery in that colony.[25] Their writings expressed with some clarity the ambivalence of people dependent on humans to whom they had to deny their humanity. Their perspectives, however racist, testified to a continuous need to come to terms with daily realities. With some justification, Suriname planters blamed metropolitan observers for not having the slightest idea of what life in the colony really was all about. If only they knew what blacks were like!

What *were* they like, according to the colonial authors? The bottom line is that their opinions of the slaves were low. Even so, one observes an increasing differentiation, and an apparently sharp reorientation in the early nineteenth century. The original ideology as expressed in J.D. Herlein's *Beschryvinge van Zurinamen* (1718) held sway up to the early nineteenth century at least.[26] 'The blacks are more

often malicious than of good character, [they are] resentful and obsti-
nate, therefore they need to be castigated frequently.' In terms of
religion, nothing positive can be said: they are: 'Heathen Slaves from
the dynasty of Cham, [living] in a confused amalgam of feelings,
buried in the darkness of ignorance, and curved alleys of innumerable
fallacies'. Experience had taught that it was of no use to convert these
people to Christianity; Herlein quoted a failed convert who explained
'that her [Afro-Surinamese] Religion is far more agreeable to the senses than the Christian [doctrines]; because those People [the Christians]
are more pleased by fundamental arguments than by feelings of amuse-
ment which they despise'. This slave was thus implicitly used to
demonstrate the higher and for blacks unattainable level of principle
and abstraction of the creed of the Nederlandsch Hervormde Kerk.
Otherwise Herlein did not go into any detail to justify the slave trade
or slavery, as he admitted some did. He did not fail, however, to provide citations from the Bible allowing for the use of heathen slaves.
Certainly the Suriname slave was no passive subject, as the uprisings
had revealed, but with consistent and 'righteous' rule ('neither too
cruel, nor too lenient'), the slaves did accept their status.[27]

Over the next century and a half some interpretations remained the
same, others changed. 'Righteous' or 'just' rule continued to be thought
of as the single most important planters' maxim – implying that the
slaves would never rebel against slavery as such, but only against
perceived infringements of a shared code of behaviour.[28] The axiom
apparently lost some of its respectability only by the nineteenth century, even if it remained an implicit assumption in pro-slavery writings.
Few antislavery works addressed the theme explicitly, underlining the
fact that the abolitionist ideology was informed more by European discourses than by an awareness of Suriname realities, however defined.

Well-known stereotypes were replicated when it came to describing the Suriname slaves. George Warren, in 1667, had them 'naturally
treacherous and bloody', J.J. Hartsinck, in 1770, was told that slaves
were mostly 'very lazy, treacherous, cruel, given to theft, drinking and
women'. The best eighteenth-century planters' manual had them cheerful, proud, haughty, and resentful.[29] Yet however denigrating or hostile,
no author denied the essential humanity of the slave; the Christian
dogma of the common origins of all mankind was upheld. Fairly soon,
the rather casual justifications of slavery came to incorporate a time perspective. As Thomas Pistorius explained, Christian charity demanded
'that we treat as humans the slaves, who are human beings too, and
share with us the same Divine Being as their Creator, even though it has
not yet pleased him to shine the holy light of the Gospel on them as he
does on us'.[30]

Yet when would the time be set for allowing the slaves to enjoy the fruits of Christianity? Unlike their counterparts in Curaçao, the Suriname colonists were notorious for disallowing any attempts to convert the slaves. Early on, Moravians had been given permission to spread the gospel among the Amerindian and Maroon populations, but arguably an interest in pacifying these potentially dangerous outsiders served as the prime motivation here. Slaves were not included in the project. Reverend J.G. Kals, in the 1730s, had cried out in vain for spreading the gospel, even if his argumentation included the economic gains to be made. Sporadic metropolitan urgings to undertake Christianization equally fell on deaf ears.[31]

In Suriname, one knew that attempting to convert the slaves was to cast pearls before swine. Hartsinck underpinned the superiority of Creole over African slaves by affirming that the former were 'more civilized, and are willing to confess that it was God who created all things and rules'. Nonetheless, they 'acknowledge that, being petty and sinful creatures, they cannot have access to that God'. The slaves therefore inevitably stuck to their own superstitions. Philippe Fermin, a physician, argued for a measure of charity in dealing with 'a folk that, even if born in slavery, nonetheless consists of humans just like us'. Some slaves did qualify for conversion, he thought. Yet, as this in his view would have to result in manumission, spreading the gospel was not a viable strategy in Suriname. Besides, slavery provided the colonists with a rare opportunity to make fellow men happy.[32]

Others were more outspoken. Anthony Blom summed up eighteenth-century wisdom by simply stating that all efforts at Christianization were doomed to failure and should be discouraged:

> The best Negroes for work are those living according to the Law or Religion of their ancestors, and who have not learned anything from us but working. They are never too stupid to learn to work with the pickaxe and the shovel; and that way they live quietly, and are useful for a plantation.[33]

Therefore, in a paradox not unfamiliar elsewhere in the Americas, the slaves' 'paganism' was accepted as a major justification for slavery; at the same time it was argued that conversion to Christianity, the one route to freedom, was premature. In addition, there was the more down-to-earth argument that without slavery, the colony could not survive.

Preparing for Emancipation

Throughout the eighteenth century, authors had commented on the nature of slavery in Suriname and on the character of the slave without a trace of doubt regarding the justification of the institution. Abolitionism was not even on the agenda. But in the nineteenth century, the abrupt ending of the slave trade and the growing awareness that slavery itself was under crucial attack impelled pro-slavery authors to be more explicit. As by the 1840s planters, travellers, politicians and lobbyists finally engaged in polemics, the debates also gained in authenticity. Old arguments were elaborated in a pro-slavery discourse which ended up just struggling for postponement of the inevitable. The debate also provided an opportunity to establish what slavery had accomplished so far. The planters' lobby came to emphasize the civilizing mission of slavery, mostly avoiding the question as to why slavery, by their own standards, had so far failed to do so. The most significant new element in their policy was a remarkable reversal in attitudes towards conversion – even if partly inscribed in the strategy of playing for time.

At the turn of the century, John Gabriel Stedman, in his famous *Narrative of a Five Years' Expedition Against the Revolted Negroes of Suriname*, had confronted planter society with bitter accusations about its dehumanization; it was not the slaves who should be described as animals. Even if rather than urging for abolition he advocated amelioration of slavery, his views on 'Africans' were relatively favourable. However, as Richard and Sally Price in the preface to their publication of the original 1790 manuscript demonstrate, the editor of the *Narrative* as it appeared in 1796 made sure to substitute denigration for appreciation. The bowdlerized edition of the *Narrative* therefore likens Maroon civilization to African cultures and advances the alleged crudeness of both as an argument against premature abolition of the slave trade.[34]

Only a decade after the publication of the mutilated *Narrative*, the slave trade was outlawed, but the same argumentation served subsequent authors well to demonstrate that the abolition of slavery itself was premature. The barbarity or animality of the slaves remained a common theme. The planters' organization *Eensgezindheid* characterized the slaves as 'Pagans and uncivilized people, mostly devoid of good mores or virtues: everything is inclined to barbarity'. This explained the necessity to rule by force. Similar arguments were still advanced as late as mid-century, yet by then the mainstream argumentation was that precisely slavery should be held responsible for keeping the blacks from attaining full humanity.[35]

The core attributes of the slaves as seen by most nineteenth-century authors were laziness and unreliability, on the one hand, lasciviousness and the absence of an orderly family life, on the other.[36] Abolitionists tended to blame these deficiencies on slavery, whereas pro-slavery ideology moved from the position that these were somehow innate characteristics to the affirmation that only further education through slavery could improve the slaves' ways. Whatever the explanations, the convergence was evident. The opinion of the slaves' actual capacities remained low on both sides. Hence most authors continued to think of immediate Emancipation as an irresponsible act.

In the search for ways to prepare the slaves for freedom, Christianization came to be seen as the central means of socialization. This was a remarkable shift, for as late as 1830 the missionary record was still confined to a century of mostly unsuccessful proselytizing among the Amerindians and Maroons. The choice of conversion was therefore a significant innovation. At the same time, the change of policy was all but straightforward. The initial pleas for spreading the gospel were strictly confined to the so-called 'slave friends'.[37] In the first 'modern' critique of Suriname slavery, juxtaposing ideas echoing Adam Smith and a plea for conversion, G.P.C. van Heeckeren van Waliën scoffed at the planters' 'incomprehensible obduracy' against the conversion of the slaves. By the late 1840s, the Moravian missionary Otto Tank stated that his brethren finally had access to a growing number of plantations. Yet his comments were biting: often the Moravians were only used 'as an instrument, to keep the Negroes in submission and under coercion, as if one foresaw that the means of the whip once will be thought of as insufficient'.[38]

This indeed is what the planters' literature suggests. In the first decades of the century, christening the slaves was at best something for the future; even if subsequently such a policy became more accepted, many continued to deny its feasibility.[39] The slaves continued to be depicted as barbaric; as 'such an exceptional kind of people that in spite of the whip which never allows their backs to heal and in spite of the heavy labour, they will concede to the most aggressive whims if only the director allows them every two or three months an occasion for dancing'; as sharing with the Indian the feeling that happiness equals doing nothing at all; as ignorant and animal-like; as ungrateful, stubborn, devoid of pride, childish, superstitious and mendacious; as wild, too uncivilized to aspire to freedom, and actually benefiting from slavery under civilized Europeans; as mentally inferior and averse to civilization; as 'both morally and physically less sensitive [and] in everything exceptionally less accomplished than most Whites'; as lazy and childish; as understanding freedom as a condition of working little or not at all; as destined to relapse into an animal-like life if emancipated; as generally devoid of intelligence and virtue; as uncivilized, lascivious, and prone to idleness; as 'through a lack of education, lazy and indolent'; and as bound for degeneration after Emancipation, as the examples of the free coloureds, the Maroons and the emancipated slaves of the British and French West Indies demonstrated.[40] And so on, and so forth.[41]

One of the problems for the abolitionists was that they actually shared many of these assessments; the above collection of characterizations draws on both pro-slavery and antislavery writings. Devoted to high principles of natural freedom for all, the abolitionists nevertheless were sceptical about the use the freed slaves would make of Emancipation. They therefore came to stress the benefits of Christianizing not only for the slaves' spiritual salvation, but, also, and perhaps even more, as a means of changing their ways and thereby helping the plantation economy survive once slavery was abolished. The advantages of christening the slaves would be twofold, both in terms of demography and work ethic.

First, the continuous natural decrease of the slave population confronted the plantations with a slowly eroding work force. All agreed that the alleged lascivious life of the slaves – polygamy and venereal diseases were recurring themes – caused low levels of fertility. Conversion implied imposing the norm of the monogamous nuclear family. Hence, christening the slaves would result in improved demographic performance of the slaves and, after Emancipation, of the freed population. This policy was first voiced in 1828 by J. van den Bosch, a prominent adviser to the Dutch Crown sent out on a trouble-shooting mission to the colonies. It soon surfaced in many other works.[42]

Second, the imminent Emancipation faced the planters as well as the colonial state with the agonizing prospect of the freed slaves withdrawing their labour from the plantations – after all, they supposedly suffered from a stubborn leisure preference. Conversion again would be useful here, helping the slaves to accept their fate and educating them to substitute a genuine work ethic for their presumed indolence, thereby facilitating the transition from work dictated by the whip to work guided by intrinsic motivation. As the 'modern' analyst Van Heeckeren stated, Christianizing would not only improve family life and hence reproduction, but equally substitute 'compliance with their fate [and] a better grasp of their duties' for their present 'stupidity and beastly life style'.[43]

The initial burden of Christianization fell on the German Moravians, who since the 1730s had dedicated much effort and many brethren's lives to missionary efforts in the colony. The results had been meagre, but they inspired confidence. As a Dutch Minister of Colonial Affairs summed it up in 1842, 'they preach the Negro not only religion and morality, but also impress industry and obedience to the worldly authorities, and what is more, set the example'.[44] The Moravian brethren had indeed attempted – up to the mid-century in vain – to enhance their acceptability by emphasizing their 'neutrality' in worldly efforts: neither in theory nor in practice did they oppose slavery. As late as 1848, the Moravian leader in Suriname reassured planters that their policy was guided by the axiom that

> When the poor slaves patiently accept the roads whence God leads them, and when they do not complain about this and are complacent, then God will bless them for it and look upon the services that they perform obediently for you gentlemen [the planters] as if they therewith served Him.[45]

From this perspective, the prolonged planters' resistance to conversion indeed testifies to an extremely short-term policy and an unwillingness to tolerate anything which might interfere with the established routines of plantation life.[46]

In the 1850s, the Moravians and, gradually, Catholic missionaries obtained access to all plantations. In theory, religious zeal, abolitionist ideology and sensible demographic and economic policy all converged in the effort of converting the slaves. In practice the results were often discouraging, confirming the suspicions of the stubborn pro-slavery party but equally, and more painfully, the subdued apprehensions the 'slave friends' had felt all along. M.D. Teenstra, one of the leading abolitionists, roundly admitted to serious doubts as to the results of the Moravian missionary effort. The slaves had hearts of stone and generally were 'very insensitive' and 'not accessible for impressions of beauty and virtue'. Two years before Emancipation, the abolitionist historian Wolbers wrote squarely about 'the rigidity of their hearts, [...] the propensity to idolatry, [and] the frivolity that still so often surface in the Negroes'.[47]

Indeed, in these last decades of slavery and those of the transition to free labour, conversion and the imposition of Western norms of respectability, family life and work ethic proceeded with less success than was hoped for.[48] This period must have been agonizing and disillusioning to many abolitionists, who had claimed the slaves would quickly internalize 'correct' standards of respectability. Applying the same yardsticks of civility, the ancient pro-slavery party must simply have found its pessimistic forecasts confirmed: the slaves had not yet been prepared for freedom.[49]

Curaçao: colour over status

In 1863, some 33,500 slaves or 55 per cent out of a total population of just over 60,000 were freed in Suriname. Around 1815, at the time of the abolition of the slave trade, the number of slaves had even been some 44,000, over 75 per cent of the colony's total population. In this perspective, the numerical significance of the Antillean Emancipation pales. The number of slaves freed in 1863 was only some 11,500 or 35 per cent of the 33,000 inhabitants of the Dutch West Indian islands. Both the limited number of inhabitants and the modest proportion of slaves corresponded to the longer run of Antillean history. In the major Dutch West Indian island, Curaçao, only 48 per cent of its 14,000 inhabitants were registered as slaves around 1815. At Emancipation in 1863, this proportion had diminished to 35 per cent out of a total population of 19,000 inhabitants.[50]

Therefore, during the entire period from the abolition of the slave trade to the abolition of slavery itself, in Suriname both the number of slaves and their proportion of the total population – and, by implication, their significance for the local economy – exceeded the corresponding figures for the Antillean colonies by a wide margin. From this perspective, it is only logical that the Dutch debate on abolition, perfunctory as it may have been in any case, gravitated towards the case of Suriname. In contrast to the Dutch East Indies, where slavery may not have been so crucial but the colony as such was, the Dutch West Indian islands were characterized by both a limited significance of slavery within their territory and their own scant relevance to the metropolis.

The most telling illustration of this lack of metropolitan interest is the ending of slavery in Dutch St Martin. When in 1848, the slaves of the French part of the island were emancipated, the slaves in the Dutch half reacted by declaring themselves free. For all practical purposes, the immediate negotiations between the (former) slaves and the powerless local planters and administration confirmed the dismantlement of slavery. Yet as no final settlement – locally nor through Dutch legislation – was accorded, the issue remained unsettled right up to the general emancipation of 1863.[51]

Of the six Antillean islands, Curaçao had traditionally been the most important. From a Dutch perspective – if not necessarily as seen from the other islands – it functioned as the centre of the insular Dutch West Indies. Yet again, it is striking how little the case of Curaçao figured in the debate on the abolition of slavery. Obviously, as its colonial council affirmed as late as 1847, the Curaçao slave owners did not want Emancipation.[52] Yet such statements apparently had little impact. The *Staatscommissie*, or State Commission, installed in 1853 to report on slave emancipation composed a modest volume covering both the West Indian islands and the Dutch settlement in Guinea. While its more voluminous report on Suriname had an accommodating tone towards the planters, the commission's conclusions on Curaçao exhibited little inclination to bear with the objections raised against abolition by the island's slave owners.[53]

A variety of factors explains this lack of metropolitan commitment. First, there was the diminished significance of Curaçao to the metropolis, in both economics and geopolitics. During various periods in the eighteenth century, the tiny island's significance as a centre for slave trading, smuggling and financial transactions had been amazing. However, the abolition of the slave trade and the dismantlement of both the Spanish empire on *tierra firme* and the imperial mercantilism in the region had undermined this function. Moreover, precisely the strong orientation of the local elites on Caribbean and Latin American networks now worked against the interests of those perhaps still hoping to influence metropolitan thinking. The creolized – Latinized – Curaçaoan elite related much less to the Dutch elite than the Suriname plantocracy, with its long-standing, virtually exclusive orientation towards the metropolis. There was no question of easy access through family ties, nor through shared commercial interests. Whereas in the Netherlands the lobby for Suriname interests was weak, a Curaçaoan interest group was nonexistent.

One might want to add the limited number of Curaçaoan slaves as an explanatory factor. Yet this provides space for the kind of two-way reasoning also encountered in the discussion of the relevance of the insignificance of the black population in the Netherlands, or even of the limited importance of Suriname slavery to the Dutch economy. Theoretically, numerical insignificance could cause indifference as all this seemed to matter so little, yet in contrast, it could also have facilitated abolition, as the modest economic costs involved would be so easily compensated for by the moral gratification of 'doing the right thing'.[54] It seems evident that as far as metropolitan mobilization and politics are involved, the latter pseudo-causality applies. Yet within the Dutch West Indies, a difference of sorts may be observed. Whereas in Suriname the local elite contributed to the debate on slavery and abolition, such contributions were conspicuous by their absence on the Antilles.

This failure to speak out for their own interests as slave holders is consistent with a longer tradition of both little literary activity and a predominant interest in regional affairs rather than in the relationship with the metropolis. In comparison to the 'canon' of literature on Suriname dating from the period of slavery, the few scattered publications on Curaçao are poor in quantity and quality. Moreover, virtually all were written by metropolitan authors, many of these only drawing on a visitor's limited experience with the island and its culture. In reviewing this small corpus, a further contrast with the literature on Suriname becomes evident. Whereas authors describing life in the latter, typical plantation society dedicated many pages to the slaves and the planter-slave relation, the focus in writings on Curaçao tended towards observations regarding colour rather than to status. This subtle contrast faithfully reflected the more complex economic and socio-racial structure of the island. In contrast to the typical non-Hispanic plantation colony with its overwhelming slave majority, its small and relatively homogeneous white elite, and its equally small intermediate group of free blacks and coloureds, Curaçaoan society consisted of three substantial segments: the white population, the free blacks and coloureds, and the slaves. The share of the intermediate segment increased uninterruptedly. From a modest 22 per cent in 1789, the proportion of free blacks and coloureds increased to 32 per cent in 1817, 44 per cent in 1833, and over half the total population at Emancipation.[55] Moreover, the white population itself was differentiated both along class and religious and cultural lines.

As H. Hoetink has forcefully argued, this particular structure of Curaçaoan society, combined with the relatively tranquil character of master-slave relations, caused the white segments to worry as much – if not more – about the free Afro-Curaçaoans as about the slaves.[56] As a seasoned expatriate in the Dutch West Indies observed:

> In Curaçao, the [free] coloureds are treated by the whites with far more contempt than in Suriname; yet as to the slaves, the contrary applies; the latter are better clothed and less oppressed on Curaçao than in Suriname.[57]

Consequently, colour even more than slavery is the recurring issue in contemporaries' accounts of elite discourse. Thus, the Reverend G.B. Bosch reported on the white opinion that 'the coloureds were already too pretentious, and that the remaining distinction between the whites and [the coloureds] should be perpetuated as much as possible'. The dominant tendency in Curaçaoan politics, he argued, was the focus on maintaining the colour line, defined as white versus coloured and black, irrespective of status.[58] The civil servant H.J. Abbring wrote about both 'the ridiculous vanity' of the white elites regarding racial purity, the 'arrogant' mulatto aspirations to membership of the white elite, and the general contempt of free blacks and coloureds regarding the slave population.[59]

The imagery of slaves was condescending and informed by paternalism, but generally not as negative as in Suriname.[60] Bosch countered stereotypes regarding the slaves' alleged stupidity, and found them in religious matters 'much less prejudiced and less superstitious than the lower classes in Europe'. Even in his summary of the 1795 slave revolt, he pictured the slaves as 'otherwise tranquil and generous' and led astray only by the dynamics of the moment.[61] Abbring likewise, apart from praising the aesthetic attractiveness of young male slaves, mentioned the slaves' humanness; if they lacked certain virtues, this deficiency only stemmed from their bonded status.[62] M.D. Teenstra, drawing upon his own experience as an agricultural expert in Suriname, thought the Curaçaoan slaves were generally better-looking, more cheerful, educated, and industrious and cleverer than their more oppressed counterparts in the Guianas. Yet somewhat confusingly, he added a reference to the 1789 colonial report by W.A. Grovestins and W.C. Boeij, maintaining that the Curaçaoan slaves shared with the free people of colour a reputation for obstinacy.[63] Reverend S. van Dissel in contrast maintained that 'the character of the nonwhites, in particular of the slaves, [is] generally tranquil, docile, peaceful', as well as industrious.[64] The Catholic vicar M.J. Niewindt, while pleading for more education, underlined that 'the slaves here are no coarse Africans: they know they are humans and realize very well that they should be treated as such'.[65]

The 1853 State Commission finally heard conflicting statements. Not surprisingly, the more negative stereotyping corresponded to the plea for gradual rather than immediate Emancipation, and vice versa. The following discussion between the former governor of Curaçao, J.J. Rammelman Elsevier, and the acting chairman of the commission, J.B. Heemskerk, captures that spirit:

> *R.E.*: Generally, [the Afro-Curaçaoans] are the enemies of order.
> *H.*: So, on Curaçao too, troublemaking seems to be a constant element in the Negro character.
> *R.E.*: They are not averse to working in the fields, but [they are] very stubborn. [...] The Negro thinks, I have to be free, not – where will I work, and how will I make a living.[66]

A Curaçaoan slave owner testified in somewhat more optimistic terms, arguing that the slaves on the island were generally well-tempered and more civilized than slaves in other colonies. The latter observation was repeated in stronger terms by a priest formerly working on Curaçao, J.J. Putman, who concluded, 'The slave wants to be happy too. Better than one thinks, he will know how to help himself. They are not as stupid as some portray them'.[67]

The comparatively subdued and even slightly positive tone of this imagery probably reflected the relatively mild character of Curaçao slavery and the resultant absence of a feeling of continuous besiegement among the slave owners. Two additional factors may be mentioned. First, the positions taken by most authors cited echo their position as outsiders to the domestic economy. Second, the timing mattered. Most sources quoted data from the 1830s and beyond; in this period, even in

Suriname the imagery of the slave as only 'as yet' uncivilized became mainstream and politically convenient.

Still, this is not the complete picture. The unconditional acknowledgement of the humanity of the slaves must have been representative even of the majority of the Curaçao elites who, in stark contrast to the Suriname planters, had tolerated the conversion of their slaves from an early stage. From the second half of the eighteenth century onwards, observers affirmed that all Afro-Curaçaoans, slaves and free alike, were Catholics. Indeed, at Emancipation in 1863, 86 per cent of all *Curazoleños* were classified as Catholic. This is a telling contrast with Suriname, where in 1863 only half the population was 'under the surveillance' of the Herrnhutters.[68]

So at least officially Afro-Curaçaoans, slave and free alike, were Christians, and in contrast to the Protestant or Jewish elites adhered to Roman Catholicism. Several observations follow. The contrast between a strong and until the 1830s successful planter opposition to conversion in Suriname versus the early opposite choice in Curaçao falsifies, most certainly for the Dutch case, the decisive significance of metropolitan culture for the specifics of colonial rule. So does the prevalence, in Curaçao, of Roman Catholicism, in contrast both to the dominant religion in the metropolis and among the local whites, and to the subsequent policy of conversion through the efforts of the Protestant Herrnhutters in Suriname.

Why then the early Christianization, and why precisely Roman Catholicism? The answer to the first question is somewhat speculative. The fact that the colonists had not heeded the repeated urging of the Dutch West Indies Company to convert the imported slaves to Protestantism is not remarkable; at this early stage, there was no difference between the two major Dutch colonies. What is puzzling is the subsequent tolerance towards external, and in the context of the times even somewhat antagonistic – Spanish, Catholic – missionaries. Historical contingency certainly played a role. The peculiar location of Curaçao, just off *tierra firme*, facilitated the continuation of Spanish missionary efforts which had begun in the pre-Dutch era, that is, around 1500 until 1634. Apparently, once the initial Catholic zeal had downplayed the apprehension that conversion would provoke rebelliousness among the slaves, the local elites found a continuation of this practice expedient, and perhaps even inevitable.

Two additional motives may have been of significance. First, judging from factors such as the high level of manumission and the remarkable positive demographic growth of the slave population, Curaçaoan slave owners did not face the chronic labour shortage which as late as the 1850s made Suriname planters reluctant to lose time destined for productive work to the possible indirect benefits of missionaries' visits. Finally, the gradual creolization of the Curaçaoan elites into a Hispanic

Caribbean orbit may have made them more familiar with the Catholic nations' practice of 'Christian' slavery.

The contrast with Suriname indeed suggests how far apart the two worlds were. Following the more conventional wisdom reigning among the Protestant colonizing nations, Suriname planters had not seriously considered the experiment of conversion until the last decades of slavery. Arguably, their very late and opportunistic change of attitude would eventually demonstrate the short-sightedness of their ancestors, and the good judgement of their Curaçaoan peers.

To some extent, the choice of Roman Catholicism again followed from Curaçao's specific colonial history and its proximity to Spanish America. Prior to the Dutch take-over in 1634, and true to their colonial logic, the Spanish had made some efforts to Christianize the native population. In the subsequent period, priests from Caracas and Coro continued to make regular visits to the island. This Spanish domination was tolerated well into the eighteenth century; only after mid-century did the initiative pass to Dutch missionaries and, subsequently, congregations. In a way therefore, the later Dutch mission only continued a pattern set by the Spanish.[69]

Yet there was more to the choice of Catholicism. With some justification, contemporaries emphasized the extreme religious tolerance of the colony. As for the whites, Protestants, Sephardic and Ashkenazic Jews all openly confessed their own religion while fully tolerating the other creeds. Moreover, even when the position of both Catholicism and the Jewish faith was still subordinated to Protestantism in the Netherlands, the Protestant Curaçaoans and the local colonial administrators had always welcomed the Roman Catholic missionaries and their activities among the slaves and free Afro-Curaçaoan population. But notwithstanding the further benefits of the proverbial religious tolerance, the hegemonic and pacifying dimension to these policies is obvious. Thus, as early as 1708, a Catholic priest wrote in his diary 'the Governor ordered me to instil in the slaves obedience and loyalty to their masters'.[70] And as for the choice of Catholicism, Reverend Bosch remarked:

> Upon my arrival in Curaçao, it struck me enormously that the visitors to Catholic churches were of another colour than the Protestants, as if for humans colour of skin influenced religious creed; from half an hour's distance I could already notice from someone's appearance to which church he belonged.
> [...]
> However, after spending some years in Curaçao, I understood the true reason why Protestants have reserved their

> own churches here for people of white skin, a reason of
> more significance than the [presumed] appropriateness of
> the Roman church for ignorant people. This [rationale] is,
> namely, a colonial policy of contempt of people of black and
> brown skin. The larger one made the distance between
> whites and [nonwhites], the more one denigrated the latter,
> the stronger and longer, one thought, would colonialism
> remain in place [...].[71]

Religious tolerance and the conversion of the non-white population may
thus have mutually reinforced one another; yet at the same time, the
specific option for Roman Catholicism as the religion of the nonwhites
served as a mechanism for upholding both the slave-free and the colour
divisions. As such, religious distinction would outlive slavery and per-
sist until today.

Whatever the logic behind this double tradition of religious divide
and rule, Roman Catholicism as such, and the Catholic clergy in particular, were of particular significance in the final decades of slavery in the
Dutch West Indian islands. This impact remained ambivalent. On the
one hand, and for obvious reasons, the Catholic clergy had traditionally
emphasized its neutrality in worldly affairs, particularly regarding the
slavery issue, and its pacifying role. The first Catholic vicar, Niewindt,
repeatedly argued that Catholic instruction was fundamental as a means
to secure order in the colony. In 1828, he wrote to the governor, 'what
is better suited to control the slaves, to keep them subordinated, to make
them loyal in their service, than the influence of Religion'? Later, he
also emphasized the crucial significance of religious instruction with a
view to an orderly transition to freedom.[72] In his testimony before the
1853 State Commission, the Catholic priest Putman again affirmed this
view, adding that earlier slave revolts had been enacted in a period
'when the slaves had not yet acquired that understanding of Religion
which today has such a blessed influence among them'. The commission indeed concluded that conversion 'has contributed in no little
measure to augment the susceptibility of the slaves for freedom'.[73]
Likewise, after Emancipation on the first of July 1863, governor J.D.
Crol explicitly thanked Niewindt's successor J.F.A. Kistemaker for the
Catholic Church's assistance in the orderly enactment of full abolition.[74]

On the other hand, a handful of clergymen, among whom again
Niewindt, ended up adopting a stance far more critical of slavery and
slave owners than the Herrnhutters in Suriname had ever ventured to
express. Not surprisingly, their objections were informed by their own
civilizing agenda, and were therefore particularly directed against
obstacles raised by individual slave owners to religious instruction and

formal marriages among slaves. Anyway, the explicitness of their argument reflected the growing strength and in the end the crucial significance of the Catholic Church in the social fabric of Curaçao during the last decades of slavery.

But perhaps another observation is of more relevance to the debate on Dutch slave Emancipation, and the absence of a significant Curaçaoan perspective in the metropolitan debate. Much in contrast to the debate on Suriname, the available sources on Curaçao suggest a rather low-key concern about both the transition to free labour, and freedom as such. The little concern voiced regarding possible social upheaval after Emancipation corresponded to the social fabric and mentality of Curaçaoan slave society. The limited number of slaves involved as compared to the already extant non-white free population may have helped to perpetuate the white elite's preoccupation with race and colour rather than juridical status. The belief that the slave population would remain in the Catholic church's fold after Emancipation added to white confidence that the transition to freedom would not jeopardize their own privileged position or their very safety. The long socializing tradition of Christianity in Curaçao indeed paid off for the white elite, a tangible reward for their traditional 'tolerance'.

The lack of anxiety regarding post-slavery labour mainly reflected the poor profile of the Curaçaoan economy, and particularly the marginality of productive slavery in the local economy. Again, the report of the 1853 State Commission is instructive.[75] The commission concluded that the present situation of an excess of labour supply over its demand would be perpetuated after Emancipation. As moreover the arid and densely populated island provided little room for subsistence peasant agriculture, the freed slaves would be forced to seek employment for a daily wage. In fact, the real problem was not, as in Suriname, how to keep the former slave force engaged in plantation work, but rather how to provide enough work for both the actual free population and the soon to be emancipated slaves. Both the slave owner H. van der Meulen and the priest Putman thought that this objective was virtually beyond reach. They anticipated and even applauded an alternative strategy, already apparent among the free Afro-Curaçaoan population: emigration to Venezuela.

Post-Emancipation agendas

If the case of Curaçao provides some interesting insights, the bottom line remains its relative insignificance to the general debate on Dutch West Indian slavery and its abolition, which in itself never became a major issue in the Netherlands. Absentee owners might for a century or more have had part of their capital invested in Suriname slaves without even once raising a question regarding its moral justification, and get away with it without being frowned upon. Apparently, as late as the mid-nineteenth century the stain of slavery was easily overlooked.[76]

In the end, the Enlightenment and the rise of 'modernity' affected the Dutch attitude towards slavery and blacks remarkably little. The mainstream authors of the pro-slavery movement in the eighteenth century maintained that all mankind originated from the same God. Blacks were humans too, only inferior, indolent, unreliable and lascivious. In the nineteenth century, as abolitionism slowly gained the upper hand, both sides continued to think in much the same terms, only substituting more consistently the evolutionary 'uncivilized' for 'inferior'. The most significant pre-Emancipation change in Suriname was the embracing of conversion, a policy previously deemed useless.

At first sight, it is difficult to perceive an ascendancy of enlightened or modern ideologies here. In its content, the new wave was a confirmation of traditional Christian values. But we may discern 'modernity' in the application of this package deal of religious and social values to a new subject group. The new approach was directly inscribed in a larger policy aimed at assimilating the future free population to European norms regarding work ethics and family life.[77] Of course, the implementation of this policy was remarkable. The conversion of the Suriname slaves was mostly relegated to a German missionary society first, subsequently joined by the Dutch Roman Catholic mission only. In Curaçao, again, mainstream Dutch Protestantism had sought no influence on the slaves whatsoever. Both choices again symbolize the lack of commitment in Dutch political circles and public opinion.

In Suriname, Emancipation in 1863 was followed by a ten-year period of state supervision known as *Staatstoezicht* – again following the British example, but stretching the period of bondage into the 1870s. Metropolitan and colonial observers measured the results by the same yardstick and were not pleased. The effort to transform the former slave population into a rural proletariat catering on a regular basis to the needs of the plantations failed in Suriname as it did elsewhere. By the late 1880s, the plantation sector had come to rely primarily upon indentured labour from British India and the Dutch East Indies, and sugar production had plunged deep below the output during slavery and the *Staatstoezicht*. Moreover, the attempt to discipline the former slaves' family life and to wipe out 'paganism' seemed hopeless. The resilience of Afro-Suriname culture shattered the expectations of previous optimists, and only served to confirm the pessimism of others, both 'progressives' and 'conservatives'.

In Curaçao, the transition to a free labour economy posed a different problem. As the supply of labour exceeded its demand and as few alternatives were available locally, there was no problem of finding means to secure continued plantation labour, but rather of building alternative economic sectors. This challenge would not be effectively met until the late 1920s, when the establishment of an oil refinery redefined the entire economy. In the meantime, in spite of poverty and a lack of opportunities, society remained tranquil. The split between a Catholic Afro-Curaçaoan majority and a Protestant or Jewish white elite remained intact. There is little reason not to accept the contemporary Catholic claim that both the smooth transition to freedom and the subsequent absence of open class conflict owed much to its strong local influence. At the same time, the Catholic church's effort to eradicate 'superstition', 'lasciviousness', and other presumed African traits encountered much the same obstacles as it did in Suriname.

These results could well have contributed to a subsequent rise of Dutch evolutionary, 'scientific' racism regarding blacks as it did elsewhere.[78] That this was hardly the case should probably be explained by the fact that the Netherlands did not partake in the *fin-de-siècle* scramble for Africa, and more particularly by the remoteness of Africa, Afro-America and blacks from the public mind and eye.[79] Meanwhile, Dutch colonial rule in the West Indies moved to a new policy of assimilation, attempting to socialize an increasingly plural population to Dutch standards of respectability.[80]

Notes

1 Wolbers 1861:746. Davis 1984:285. See also Van Winter 1953:61; Kuitenbrouwer 1978:98; Siwpersad 1979:xiv; Emmer 1974, 1980:80; Postma 1990:291–4; Buisman 1992:307–42.

2 See Drescher 1995 and the various contributions to *Fifty Years Later* (Oostindie 1995a) on this issue.

3 Schama 1988. From 1804 to 1816, as a consequence of the Napoleonic wars in Europe, the British occupied the Dutch colonies. The British abolition of the slave trade (1807) applied to the occupied territories as well. This abolition was sanctioned in 1814 and again in 1818.

4 Van Stipriaan 1993 provides the most comprehensive economic history to date of Suriname slavery; see also Van Stipriaan 1989, 1995. From a metropolitan perspective, Suriname was an attractive proposition up to the late 1770s; in the subsequent period up to and beyond Emancipation, the colony fell short of most expectations. In both periods, and increasingly so, the Dutch East Indies commanded far more metropolitan attention and capital. In 1830, the Netherlands imported roughly the same amounts of sugar from Java (the major island of the Dutch East Indies) and Suriname; in 1850, imports from Java were five times higher, in 1860 fourteen times (Oostindie 1989:458).

5   Davis 1966, 1975, 1984; Lewis 1983.
6   Kolfin 1997 is a useful study of the development of pictorial representations of Africans and slaves in the Dutch Caribbean orbit.
7   Van den Boogaart (1982:53–4) provides a thoughtful analysis of these initial representations. He concludes that blackness to the Dutch was no core attribute or as such a symbol of depravity but rather a more neutral distinguishing feature. For the British, according to Jordan (1968), blackness was one of the five core attributes in the perception of the African, the others being heathenism, savagery, beastliness and voluptuousness. Indeed, an early eighteenth-century account of Suriname, however negative its imagery of the slaves, also found the blacks 'rather pretty" and included an engraving of two good-looking slaves, one of each sex (Herlein 1718:94).
8   The association of black with pagan symbols and white with Christianity was half-heartedly overcome in the sensationalist reception of the African convert Jacobus Capitein, a student at Leiden University and author of a Latin tract confirming the 'Cham ideology' and justifying slavery even of christened Africans. Capitein was honoured in a poem underpinning the 'white-washing' of his soul by the workings of the gospel (Oostindie & Maduro 1986:12). On the wider symbolism of blackness, see Davis 1966:447–9, 1984:37–42. On the curse of Cham, see Davis 1984:42–3, 86–7.
9   Cohen 1980:43.
10 Gallandat 1769:3–4.
11 Paasman 1984:98–121.
12 Slave trading in the Netherlands was forbidden as early as the late sixteenth century, and the numbers of slaves accompanying their masters from the colonies to the metropolis was never more than a trickle. This number probably reached a peak in the third quarter of the eighteenth century. Even then, no more than some twenty slaves per year entered the Netherlands, with a roughly equal number leaving; probably there was a significant overlap. Similar migration from the main Dutch Caribbean island, Curaçao, was insignificant. Evidence of blacks in the Netherlands is circumstantial only. The status of slaves brought to the metropolis remained a matter of dispute up to Emancipation (Oostindie & Maduro 1986: 7, 13–7, 155–64). In 1870, a colonial author explicitly linked the virtual absence of blacks in the metropolis to Dutch ignorance regarding the West Indies (Anonymous 1870:777). In contrast, by the 1770s current estimates put the black population in England as high as 20,000 (Walvin 1973:46–7). This figure may have been more in the order of 10–15,000; see Drescher (1987:27–30). Either case, the contrast with the Netherlands is enormous. In the 1760s and 1770s France reacted with xenophobia to an apparently growing but still very modest black presence by simply forbidding free blacks and slaves to enter the country (Cohen 1980:111).
13 Davis 1984. On the ambiguous position of Enlightenment thinkers, see Davis 1966:391–445.
14 Zwager 1980:11–3, 63–4. Jacob & Mijnhardt 1992:23, 204, 212, 220, 227. Mijnhardt (1992), for example, states that 'Montesquieu or Rousseau had little to offer that was relevant to the Dutch situation, except for topoi about the natural equality of humankind or the inalienable rights of the people [...]'. The question whether contemporaries related these topoi to the issue of slavery is not raised. See also Paasman 1984:209–16.
15 The Batavian Republic leaned heavily on revolutionary France. The Dutch radicals were superseded by direct French rule in the so-called Kingdom of Holland (1806–1810), followed by straightforward annexation (1810–1813). During most of the 1796–1813 period, the British held the Dutch colonies in 'protective' occupation. In

1814, the Dutch ceded the colonies of Berbice, Demerara and Essequibo to England, which united them later as British Guiana. The French revolutionary government abolished slavery in its colonies in 1794, a decision which was revoked by Napoleon in 1802. On the colonial policies of the Dutch 'Patriots,' see Schutte 1974:146–9. A first proposal for gradual abolition, co-authored by a French colonial official and a Dutch planter in Demerara, was included in the Dutch translation of Stedman's 1796 *Narrative*, Stedman 1799–1800:148–85. The proposal went largely unheeded.

16 In 1726, the proportion of Catholics in the Netherlands was 34 per cent; in 1775, 36 per cent. Owing to the inclusion of two southern, overwhelmingly Catholic provinces, this proportion rose to 38 per cent in 1809, fluctuating between 35 and 40 per cent up to the 1970s. In 1809, members of the dominant Nederlandsch Hervormde Kerk accounted for 55 per cent of the population; the share of other Protestant denominations was 4.5 per cent. Protestant dissenters did not present a considerable numerical threat to the Nederlandsch Hervormde Kerk before the 1880s – that is, beyond the period under discussion here. All figures taken from Knippenberg 1992:23, 61, 170. Even if the Netherlands was renowned for religious tolerance, the Nederlandsch Hervormde Kerk was the only officially recognized church, and a highly privileged institution. Well into the nineteenth century, active membership was a condition for participation in the national elite.

17 Under pressure of British Quakers, a numerically insignificant but intellectually important movement within the Church, the Réveil, petitioned for abolition in 1842; yet organized action was postponed until the 1850s. Réveil spokesmen in the 1840s found the Quakers too radical, and also shied away from cooperating with Liberal abolitionists (Siwpersad 1979:73–6, 217–20).

18 Drescher 1995 comments on the discussion in *The American Historical Review* (1985, 1987), subsequently reprinted in Bender 1992.

19 Kossmann 1992:20.

20 Van Heeckeren van Waliën 1826. Jacob points to a late eighteenth-century 'Enlightened' vision of industrial progress in the metropolis, but she does not suggest a link to the issue of slavery (Jacob 1992:238–9).

21 Likewise for France: Drescher 1991:733.

22 Lewis 1983:109, 327. See also Davis 1975:184–97. 'As early as the mid-eighteenth century [...] slave societies were acquiring the image of social and cultural wastelands blighted by an excessive pursuit of private profit' (Davis 1984:80).

23 Nassy 1788:5, 1779:83.

24 Nor did colonial reform; see Cohen 1991:94–123. Arguing against the bad reputation of Suriname slavery became a major theme in the literature of the late eighteenth and early nineteenth century. Characteristically, no author took the pains to contradict Voltaire's indictment of Suriname slavery in *Candide* (1759), even if this would have been an easy target in denouncing 'Enlightened' antislavery discourse; see Oostindie 1993b.

25 Hartsinck 1770; Wolbers 1861. J.J. Hartsinck was a servant of the Dutch West Indies Company; his two-volume *Beschryving van Guiana* is based on archival sources, literature and information supplied by Suriname planters and officials. The abolitionist historian Wolbers wrote his voluminous *Geschiedenis van Suriname* on the basis of archival research in the Netherlands. No female authors wrote on Suriname in the eighteenth or nineteenth century; in the *belles lettres*, in contrast, authors such as Petronella Moens, Elizabeth Post and Betje Wolff did publish on issues related to slavery.

26 An expression of the still recent Dutch encounter with Africans, Herlein occasionally deployed the term *Mooren* (Moors) in addition to *Negers* (Negroes), *Slaven*

(slaves), and *swarte* (blacks). The ambivalent *Mooren*, including Southern Mediterranean people, disappeared completely in all later writings on Suriname. In the Netherlands, it continued in use longer. See also Blakely 1993.

27 Herlein 1718:90–121. Citations from pp. 96, 105, 94 and 86, respectively. On a theoretical level, the axiom of just rule had already been formulated early in the sixteenth century by philosophers such as Grotius and theologians like G. Udemans. Their axiom rested on abstract juridical, respectively Christian principles rather than pragmatic grounds.

28 See plantation regulations of 1759 and 1784; Schiltkamp & De Smidt 1973; Pistorius 1763; Hartsinck 1770, I:381, 404, 415, 1770, II:907, 918; Fermin 1770:145–7, 1778:345; Blom 1787:352–5; Stedman 1796. Hartsinck 1770, I:374 cites a leader of the 1763 slave rebellion in Berbice as saying 'that the Christians were rude to them; that they would not endure Christians or Whites in their country anymore, and that they wanted to be the rulers of Berbice; that all plantations were theirs, and that the Christians should cede these plantations to them'. Yet apparently he did not think this rebellious statement to be representative; elsewhere, he reiterated the 'just rule' axioms.

29 Warren 1667:19; Hartsinck 1770, II:906–7. Hartsinck, like virtually all authors, implicitly took the female slaves to be more compliant. See also Blom 1787:330.

30 Pistorius 1763:98; my italics.

31 Kals 1756; Van der Linde 1987; Hartsinck 1770, II:743; Wolbers 1861:265.

32 Hartsinck 1770, II:903; Fermin 1770, I:143, 124, 148. Traditionally, Jews, Christians and Muslims had shared the position that religious conversion did not imply (immediate) manumission (Davis 1984:22).

33 Blom 1787:348. See also Blom & Heshuysen 1786:391–2.

34 Stedman 1796:lxi–lxiv.

35 Eensgezindheid 1804:12; Kappler 1854, I:140, versus Wolbers 1861:775–6.

36 In terms of slave revolts and marronage, this century was far more tranquil than the previous one. The emphasis on the brutality and fierceness of the slave waned accordingly. The Haitian Revolution left only a few traces in the literature on Suriname.

37 Or, before that, of foreign observers. Commenting on his visit to Suriname in the late 1770s, the French official V.P. Malouet blamed the Suriname planters for not christening their slaves and therefore not feeling inhibitions against abuse; this criticism of the planters' policies implied the conclusion that, because of the absence of Christianity, the slaves were 'reduced to animal instinct' (Malouet 1802, III:114). See also Paasman 1984:157–65.

38 Van Heeckeren 1826:78–82, 87–8, 100–2, 127–8; Tank 1848:95. Similar criticism was voiced by the absentee plantation owner G.P.C. van Breugel (Van Breugel 1834:12). On the impact of the Moravians in Suriname, see Lenders 1996.

39 E.g., Eensgezindheid 1804:19–20 and Staatscommissie 1855:294, 302.

40 Citations from Eensgezindheid 1804:12–14; Kunitz 1805:350; Lammens 1823:16; Van Heeckeren 1826:101; Teenstra 1835, II:186; Van Lennep Coster 1836:113–7; Lans 1842:22–3; Teenstra 1842:115, 119; Bosch 1843:147–8, 200–1; Van Emden et al. 1848:11; Hostmann 1850, I:140–1, 1850, II:413; Kappler 1854:56; Staatscommissie 1855:97, 288–90; Winkels 1856:37; De Veer 1861:175–6. One recognizes elements of Elkins's once-celebrated Sambo-type: 'docile but irresponsible, loyal but lazy, humble but chronically given to lying and stealing […] infantile […] talk inflated with childish exaggeration […] utter dependence and childlike attachment' (Elkins 1971:82). For an assessment of 'Sambo' as an ideology, Patterson 1984:96, 207–8, 338.

41 The earlier pragmatic justification – slaves are the only ones able to do the arduous work on tropical plantations – continued to surface, Lammens 1982:191–2; Benoit 1980:63; Lans 1842, II:16–7, 22–7, 30–1. There are interesting parallels here with the enlightened elites' perceptions of the Dutch *vulgus*. See Frijhoff 1992:292–307.

42 Van den Bosch, cited in Oomens 1986:166; Van Heeckeren 1826:87–8, 127–8; Lans 1829:41; Lans 1842:163–5; Lans 1847:79; Staatscommissie 1855:272. See, moreover, Van Lier 1971:72–4, 172–6; Siwpersad 1979:85–7, 161, 185; Lamur 1985:34–43; Oostindie 1989:192–5.

43 Van Heeckeren 1826:87–8, 101–4, 127–8. See also the opportunistic inclusion of conversion in one of the last pro-slavery tracts: Belmonte 1855:60–1, 120.

44 J.C. Baud 1842; in the same vein, J. van den Bosch 1828, and J.C. Rijk 1851; all quoted in Siwpersad 1979:200, 79, 206. Various authors confirmed that conversion would have disciplinary rather than subversive effects; Van Breugel 1834; Bosch 1843:170–3. And, in retrospect, Bartelink 1916:59.

45 H.W. Pfenninger in Van Emden et al. 1848:73. Similarly, Tank 1848:95. Wolbers 1861:720 commented: 'in order to pour the poor slaves a few drops of the plentiful cup of the Gospel, they made the sacrifice of remaining silent, where keeping silent was sometimes really hard'. In exactly the same vein, the above-cited Moravian missionary Tank affirmed that the Moravians had always taught the slaves to accept their status (Tank 1848:95). On an earlier Moravian missionary's socialization towards this conformism, see Riemer 1801:90–4. For a general discussion of the relation between missionary Christianity and the slave-based social order in the Caribbean, see Lewis 1983:199–205.

46 The contrast with the remarkably successful Moravian mission in the eighteenth-century Danish Virgin Islands is noteworthy; Oldendorp 1987. Arguably, the major explanatory factor should be situated in the respective colonizing states. In Denmark, the monarchy and its elites were fervent protagonists of Christianizing, and simply obliged the colonists to comply. As indicated above, the eighteenth-century Dutch elites found no personal or political expediency in spreading the gospel to the colonies. Incidentally, even if the Dutch state had advocated conversion, its influence on the colonists was tenuous well into the nineteenth century.

47 Teenstra 1842:121, 124; Wolbers 1861:810. The militant abolitionist author W.R. van Hoëvell argued for a hierarchy of races in which Africans were situated immediately below Europeans, but above Asians and (the lowest order) Amerindians. Blacks could certainly advance, but not in Africa itself, where nature, climate and isolation combined to form 'a barrier to the progress of civilization' (Van Hoëvell 1854:237–8).

48 In 1830, the Moravians counted less than 1800 converts among the non-white population; by 1861, this figure, according to inflated official statements, had increased to over 27,000, plus 11,000 Catholics; in both years, the total non-white population was barely over 50,000 (Van Lier 1971:173–4). Yet the missionaries themselves expressed strong doubts about the real impact of conversion (Lamur 1985; Oostindie 1989:192–5).

49 Winkels 1856:97, 114; Kappler 1854:56; De Veer 1861; Kappler 1881:10; Siwpersad 1979: 262–70. For similar dilemmas in the British Caribbean, see Green 1976; Turner 1982; Holt 1992.

50 Hoetink 1958:77; *Koloniaal Verslag* 1863. In 1833, slaves accounted for 40 per cent of the 15,000 *Curazoleños*.

51 Even beyond that date, St Martin slave holders and the Dutch administration disputed the level of compensation to be paid to the former. The Hague initially maintained that no payment was required, as the compensation accorded to slave holders else-

where in the Dutch Caribbean could not apply to St Martin, where slavery had been abolished in 1848. The slave holders, in contrast, refused to accept that slavery had really ended in 1848. In the end, a compromise was reached, allowing for compensation but at a much lower level than the price accorded the other territories. See Paula 1993.

52   Raad van Politie 1847, quoted in Lampe 1988:83. A decade later, their spokesman, while admitting the inevitability of full abolition, pleaded for caution and a gradual emancipation (Staatscommissie 1856:253–70).

53   Staatscommissie 1855–56.

54   See Teenstra 1852, II:755–6.

55   Klooster 1998:61, *Koloniaal Verslag* 1863.

56   Hoetink 1958, 1969, 1972. Hoetink convincingly explains the comparatively mild character of slavery in Curaçao by reference to the non-plantation character of the economy, the on average limited number of slaves per slave owner, and the high level of social control on the small island. The 'mildness' of slavery in Curaçao was a recurring theme in writings on the island (Van Paddenburg 1819:75–8, Abbring 1834:84–6, Teenstra 1836, I:169). The obvious comparison was – and still is – with Suriname, with its supposedly extremely harsh slavery; on the pedigree and validity of this reputation, see Oostindie 1993b. On the *hacienda*-like plantation system in Curacao, see Renkema 1981.

57   Teenstra 1836, I:166.

58   Bosch 1829:228, 226, respectively. As to the psychological consequences of the ambivalent position of the free coloureds, he maintained that they easily felt offended, 'as if everything said to them reflects the contempt which their origins and colour inspire' (Bosch 1829:103). See also Teenstra 1836, I:165–7.

59   Abbring 1834:99. Compare Van Dissel 1857:111.

60   Thus G.G. van Paddenburg, while taking the Christianization of the slave population as additional evidence of the mild character of Curaçao slavery, could confirm to his readership that 'The Negroes and coloureds, both free and slaves [...] have far less necessities than we, refined Europeans' (Van Paddenburg 1819:78). Perhaps the most condescending remarks were made regarding Afro-Curaçaoan promiscuity (for example, the Raad van Politie in 1818, quoted in Dahlhaus 1924:406), and the local Creole language, Papiamentu (Van Paddenburg 1819:71–3, Bosch 1829:212–9, Teenstra 1836, I:179). Then again, at least for the language if not for both issues, this criticism implicated the whites as well.

61   Bosch 1829:220–1, 323. During the entire colonial period, two major slave revolts were reported, one in 1750, the larger one in 1795.

62   Abbring 1834:81–2, 85.

63   Teenstra 1836, I:167.

64   Van Dissel 1857:116. Van Dissel uses *kleurlingen*, which is literally coloureds; from the context it is clear though that he means nonwhites in general.

65   Niewindt 1850, cited in Dahlhaus 1924:440.

66   Staatscommissie 1856:232, 243.

67   Staatscommissie 1856:263, 275, 303.

68   *Koloniaal Verslag* 1863, no. 32, Suriname:21–2; no. 43, Curaçao:2. Of the 54 per cent of the total population in the Moravian fold, one-third were not baptized. An additional 6 per cent of the Surinamese were either Baptized Catholics, or aspiring members; these were mostly former slaves too. In 1826, out of 2,829 whites living on Curaçao, 15 per cent were Catholics too. With some justification, Römer-Kenepa (1992:47) argues that this group and its influence in colonial society has been neglected in historiography.

69 Lampe 1988:84, 107–10. Dahlhaus 1924, Goslinga 1956, and Lampe 1988 are the major publications on Catholicism in Curaçao; see also Allen 1992, Römer-Kenepa 1992. At times, Protestant misgivings about the prevalence of Roman Catholicism among the Afro-Curaçaoan population were voiced. See Teenstra 1836, I:174, Dahlhaus 1924:393, 444–5, Goslinga 1956:37, Klooster 1994:291–2.

70 M.A. Schabel, cited in Lampe 1988:36.

71 Bosch 1829:220, 226.

72 Niewindt cited in Dahlhaus 1924:100, 395, and 430–1, respectively. Monsigneur M.J. Niewindt worked on Curaçao from 1824 until his death in 1860, since 1842 as the island's first vicar. In former days, he somehow personalized the Emancipation process in Curaçao (Dahlhaus 1924, Goslinga 1956; for a more balanced discussion, see Hoetink 1958:113–4, 139–43). A similar colonial benefactor did not emerge in Suriname – pride of place, if any, was reserved for King Willem III, who signed the Emancipation bill.

73 Staatscommissie 1856:298 and 26, respectively.

74 Lampe 1988:90.

75 Staatscommissie 1856:9, 25, 30–1, 261–3, 277–8. The president of the commission indeed wondered why slaves were relatively expensive in the island, as the supply of labour far exceeded its demand (Staatscommissie 1856:278). See also Renkema 1981, especially p. 150.

76 Compare Oostindie 1989:362–3.

77 In the same period, 'enlightened' elites in the metropolis embarked on socializing policies for their own proletariat. Actually, the above-mentioned colonial trouble-shooter J. van den Bosch was in the vanguard of that movement as well. Conversely some of the more subtle socializing techniques, such as awarding medals and pecuniary prizes to 'lesser' people for voluntarily rendering outstanding services to the elites, were occasionally applied in Suriname as well (Moes 1845:129–53). See also Davis 1984:121–9, 214–26.

78 Davis 1975:48; Davis 1984:134–6, 277–9; Cohen 1980:98–9, 181, 210–21, 260–2. Ironically, an eighteenth-century Dutch scholar, Petrus Camper, had been one of the first to link phenotype ('facial angle') with race and intellectual capacities; his theory had some acclaim elsewhere in Europe both in the second half of the eighteenth century and again in the 1840s; Curtin 1964:39–40, 366.

79 The absence of 'scientific' racism certainly did not interfere at all with the use of (semi-) bonded labour in both the Dutch East Indies and West Indies well into the twentieth century, nor with routine racism against colonial subjects. On post-abolition 'scientific' racism in Britain and France, see Drescher 1990:440–7.

80 Only in the 1930s and 1940s, Dutch cultural policy in Suriname encouraged the consolidation of ethnic pluralism. Yet educational policies remained firmly modelled after the metropolitan standards.

3 | Stubborn plurality

Over the last few decades, the Netherlands has been confronted with growing ethnic plurality within its own borders, as have most countries in the European Union. For a country that has long boosted a 'centuries-old tradition of tolerance', this rather drastic change has turned out not to be easy. 'Ethnic minorities', which now account for around 15 per cent of the total population, are neatly classified and made the objects of policy-making. Immigrants from the former Dutch East Indies and their descendants, assimilated 'model migrants', have already vanished from ethnic minority statistics. Less integrated minorities, including those from the Dutch Caribbean, are the subjects of state care and, increasingly, concern. A tendency to regard people from Suriname, the Antilles and Aruba as one single group still prevails: culturally other than the Dutch but much the same as one another.

The first assumption, that there are major differences between Dutch and Dutch Caribbean culture, is in certain respects exaggerated. A comparison with migrants from two Islamic countries – Morocco and Turkey – suggests that the divide between Dutch and Dutch 'West Indian' culture is less significant. Yet, the fact that a gulf exists also confirms that the half-hearted mission to 'civilize' overseas was successful only to a limited extent. The second assumption, that of uniformity among Antilleans and Surinamese, is an outright misconception. In terms of both ethnicity and culture the population of the Dutch Caribbean is marked by huge diversity, which obviously reflects the range of patterns of colonization.

This plurality within the Dutch Caribbean is stubborn and has consistently expressed itself in repressed tensions, intolerance and open conflict. However, given the high level of ethnic heterogeneity, we might also establish that the history of the Dutch Caribbean, precisely now that it is in its postcolonial phase, has been remarkably harmonious. The equilibrium might be precarious, certainly in Suriname, but it is evidently controllable. Plurality makes Caribbean society in some respects also more dynamic than Dutch society. Just listen to people constantly switching languages in Aruba: Papiamento, West Indian English, Dutch depending on the company they are keeping. See in Paramaribo how most Surinamese regard themselves in the first instance as belonging to a single ethnic group, but nonetheless move relatively easily in other ethnic spheres. The Dutch, who like to think of themselves as being modern and cosmopolitan, could learn a lot from the dexterity with which this 'code switching' is performed: not simply by understanding that things are very different there, but in particular that people there constantly have to deal with 'others', while clearly managing to keep the ensuing ethnic tensions under control. Closer to home we have learned that things can turn out much more ugly than that.

The ethnic 'pillarization' of Suriname

Caribbean history is a history of migration and the history of the Dutch Caribbean is no exception. Labour migration, which occurred in waves down the centuries, is primarily what has made the Dutch Caribbean as heterogeneous as it is. Consequently the backbone of this chapter, which provides an overview of the role of ethnicity in Dutch Caribbean society, includes frequent references to the socio-economic developments that were set in motion by the migration of labour.

The development of this population growth has to be outlined individually for Suriname and for each of the islands. Before the arrival of the English and the Dutch, Suriname was populated by indigenous Amerindians, in particular the Caribs and the Arawak.[1] Alongside these two groups, which are still the largest, live smaller groups such as the Trio and the Wajana. Whereas European conquest spelled extinction on almost all Caribbean islands, the Amerindians survived colonization in Suriname. After the first few decades of colonial encounters, which alternated between war and armed peace, they were forced to accept the new colonial order. Until well into the twentieth century they kept to the depths of the interior, well away from the colonial world. Their numbers were never large. It is estimated that Amerindians today number around 12,000, possibly about the same as at the time of colonization. However, only a minority now lives in the tropical rainforest. The majority has settled nearer the capital Paramaribo.

Colonization meant the arrival of migrants who pushed back the native population in all respects. Until 1863, when slavery was abolished, these newcomers were Europeans and above all Africans. Both the white and African populations were highly heterogeneous. The most permanent groups among the whites were the Sephardic and later the Ashkenazi Jews; during the time of slavery they had made up one to two thirds of the white population. There were also Dutch, French, Germans and English; a mishmash in which the Dutch formed only a small segment. In the initial phase of colonialism, it was difficult to find enough

Dutch speakers to occupy official posts. The total number of whites was estimated to have been a few hundred in 1675, and between the mid-eighteenth century and the nineteenth century between 2,000 to 3,500. Today the number of 'native whites' is negligible.

The African slaves who were taken to Suriname – around 215,000 between 1667 and 1830 – were probably far more heterogeneous in terms of origin and culture than the whites. The main regions from which they were transported were 'Loango' (South Cameroon, Gabon, Congo and northern Angola), the 'Gold Coast' (Ghana), the 'Windward Coast' (Ivory Coast, Liberia, Sierra Leone) and the 'Slave Coast' (West Nigeria, Benin, Togo).[2] Negative population growth in Suriname during slavery meant that the insatiable plantations demanded more and more labour from Africa. In 1863 the total population of African origin was estimated to be at least 60,000. By this time the population, which consisted mainly of 'Creole' descendants of 'Saltwater Negroes', had become more homogeneous in some respects, and more heterogeneous in others. In these new surroundings, dominated by plantations, African ethnic differences had increasingly lost their significance and a new language emerged: Sranan Tongo. New forms of religious and cultural expression developed which cannot be traced to a single African origin, but which expressed a new, creolized culture. It was not until the second half of the nineteenth century that a hesitant 'civilization programme' was embarked upon through which Christianity, the Dutch language and a Dutch education system were increasingly imposed and to some extent adopted. This offensive was aimed at the 'elevation' of an apparently homogeneous, newly created Afro-Surinamese culture.

However, more or less from the beginning of colonization, the Afro-Surinamese population was divided along yet other lines. Within the borders of the plantation colony there was room for some social differentiation. In vain the colonial authorities had attempted to ban whites from having 'carnal conversation' with their female slaves.[3] By far the majority of whites were men; it was therefore inevitable that they would enter into relations with female slaves. These 'relations' were often fleeting, forced on the women by the white men and were purely sexual. Other relations, where the woman became the man's steady partner, were also affective and less unbalanced, although matrimony was out of the question in this colonial setting. In the eighteenth century this arrangement of concubinage acquired a certain status under the name 'Surinamese marriage'. Preferred female slaves and the children that issued from these mixed relations were increasingly manumitted leading to the gradual emergence of group of 'free coloureds and blacks'. In 1738 their number was estimated at 600, in 1830 it was already around

5,000 and by 1863 the number of 'free people of colour' had grown to over 10,000.

It is telling that these 'coloureds', even though their roots were as much European as African, were always regarded as *Afro*-Surinamese. Over time, in Suriname as in the rest of the New World, an extensive terminology was adopted to enable the colour differences to be named and fixed in a colour hierarchy (*mulat, mesties, kasties, karboeger*). In colonial relations and long afterwards, when there was no longer a judicial distinction between free and unfree, an informal hierarchy remained in effect in which the children of racially mixed relations were given higher status because of their lighter complexion. This mechanism did not disappear with Emancipation, and is still in effect today. However, in the understanding of the role of 'race' and colour in Suriname, this dimension gradually lost its primacy. The emphasis increasingly came to be placed on a more far-reaching, properly *ethnic* heterogeneity, which came to characterize Surinamese society with the arrival of Asian contract workers.

Aside from this social stratification of the Afro-Surinamese population *within* the borders of the plantation colony, a division arose at an early stage through the growth of a second, fundamentally different Afro-Surinamese population group. Slavery implies slave resistance. One form of resistance was the escape from the plantations to the interior of the colony, a phenomenon known as 'marronage' throughout plantation America. Marronage was more significant in Suriname than anywhere else in the Caribbean.[4] The harshness of life under slavery on the plantations presented more than enough reason to rebel. The enormous, largely uninhabited, tropical rainforests offered an opportunity for escape which, although full of risks, in the long term proved to offer a remarkably high chance of survival.

All attempts by the colonial authorities to eradicate the Maroons failed. In the second half of the eighteenth century, Paramaribo found itself obliged to sign a series of peace treaties with the Maroons which, although acknowledging their freedom, also ensured that they remained at a safe distance from the colonial order. At the beginning of the eighteenth century the number of Maroons was estimated to have been 1,000; in 1863 it was 8,000; today it is some 40,000. The Maroon population is by no means uniform. There are six separate Maroon peoples, of which the Saramacca are the largest, followed by the Ndjuka; besides these and others there are the Aluku, who now mainly live in neighbouring French Guiana. Each of these peoples has their own language or linguistic variant and their own distinct culture, despite unmistakable similarities.

The abolition of slavery accelerated the demise of the plantation economy. Confronted with the probability that many, perhaps the majority, of the former slaves would no longer want to work on the plantations – at least not under conditions acceptable to the planters – the colonial authority elected to organize a new migration of labour. Following the example of the surrounding Caribbean colonies, they first arranged the immigration of Chinese and British Indian contract workers. Thereafter a specifically Dutch element was added in the form of contracting of workers from the Dutch East Indies. The number of Chinese contract workers was insignificant, even though this group formed the vanguard of a Chinese enclave in the country which remains important to this day. Between 1873 and 1917, some 34,000 British Indians were taken to Suriname; between 1890 and 1938, another 32,600 East Indians. Thirty-four per cent of the first group returned to the land of their birth, while only twenty-two per cent of the Javanese repatriated.[5]

Although the British Indians were shipped from Calcutta, they originated from a large recruitment area, mainly North-west India and Benares (now Varanasi). They spoke different languages including Bhojpuri, Adwahdi, Hindi and Urdu. Although most came from the lower castes, a small minority were from higher castes. In terms of religion, the majority was Hindu, a minority Muslim. Colonial society, and above all the levelling environment of the plantations where they served out their contracts, erased many of the social and cultural distinctions within this group. Slowly the British Indians grew towards a new, shared language, Sarnami, largely based on Bhojpuri. As the 'Hindustanis' became more integrated into society, Sarnami was forced to give way to the lingua franca of Suriname, Sranan Tongo, and then to Dutch. While the caste system as such did not survive, the high status accorded the Brahmans at the very least alludes to the social structure of times gone by. In religious terms the Hindustani remained relatively faithful to their traditional beliefs; colonial attempts to convert them to Christianity were relatively fruitless and successes were primarily limited to a small section of the Hindu elite. The Hindustani group continues to consist mainly of Hindus and to a lesser degree Muslims. However, over time the form and probably also the perception of these religions began to deviate from what they had been in British India a century earlier.[6]

The contract workers from the Dutch East Indies came almost exclusively from Java and were Muslim. Javanese Islam, however, had preserved strong Hindu, Buddhist and animist undercurrents from the pre-Islamic period and thus had evident differences from the Islam practised by the Muslims of India, some of which are maintained to this day. To give some ceremonial illustrations, the Javanese Muslims have continued to pray to the West even if Mecca – lying to the West of Java – is located east of Suriname. The 'Hindustani' Muslims in contrast upon arrival in Suriname decided to henceforth pray to the East. The two groups also use different languages for their religious ceremonies: the Hindustani Muslims use Urdu, the Javanese Muslims Arabic and Javanese.[7] Because the relatively homogenous Javanese population remained together longest 'in the districts' on plantations, their integration into Surinamese society took a long time. They too developed their own linguistic variant, Surinamese-Javanese, which only in the last decades has begun to be overtaken by Sranan Tongo and, above all, Dutch.[8] Like the Hindustanis, the Javanese preserved and developed their original religion and many elements of their original culture, even if expanding urbanization and integration has entailed a growing incorporation of the creolized 'Western' culture which is dominant at a national level.

The migration of Asian labour delayed the demise of the plantation sector, but did not save it. The arrival of the first contract workers marked the beginning of a drastic change in the make up of the population as a whole, in part due to the strong population growth among the Asian Surinamese. Of the approximately 450,000 legal and illegal inhabitants of Suriname today, it is estimated that over one-third are Hindustani, twenty-five to thirty per cent Creole, fifteen per cent Javanese, over ten per cent Maroon and three per cent Amerindians.[9] The most recent immigrants, Brazilians, may now account for as much as ten per cent of the total. Excluding the Brazilians, these proportions incidentally also closely reflect the make up of the Surinamese community in the Netherlands today. The remainder of the population consists of smaller minorities of Chinese, Lebanese and Syrian origins, and occasional migrants from other Latin American and European origins. The slowly growing category of Surinamese from mixed backgrounds is usually categorized under one of the major ethnic 'pillars' of society, most frequently as 'Creoles', hence Afro-Surinamese. These in-between groups do not yet form an ethnic pillar in their own right.

The ethnic legacy of plantation agriculture and colonialism in Suriname is one of exceptional heterogeneity. In theories on 'plural societies' in the Caribbean region, Suriname has long been identified as an extreme example of a society in which every ethnic group has maintained its own institutions and where the relations between all these groups are relatively aloof, born more out of necessity than inclination towards one another. Hence the metaphor of a 'pillarized society' consisting of disparate ethnic pillars of unequal widths, which together balance an institutional roof, that in turn represents the state apparatus and social communication in the public domain. The key scholar to develop this concept in the late 1940s was Rudolf van Lier, himself Surinamese with roots in the Jewish-Creole elites.[10]

Pessimists have argued that the profound contrasts between the various ethnic groups were irreconcilable. More optimistic observers preferred to refer hopefully to an increasing willingness among the various ethnic communities – with due regard for the profound differences between them – to work together to build up the country. Eager references have been made to the pragmatic attitude of the leadership of different ethnic groups, which has enabled the leaders to represent the interests of their rank and file in an atmosphere of relative harmony and consultation, in a consensual context, and with mutual understanding and respect for the rights of all ethnic groups to a fair share of the national pie. A term that was coined for this in the 1950s is *verbroederingspolitiek* or 'fraternization politics'.[11]

Antillean diversity

Immigration in the Antilles was less complicated, at least until the twentieth century. By the time the Dutch took possession of the six islands, the indigenous Amerindian population had virtually disappeared. Aruba was the only exception. The islands were repopulated with immigrants. As in Suriname, these were European colonists and African slaves, and both groups were initially strongly heterogeneous. The numbers of blacks to whites was less uneven on the islands than in Suriname. Furthermore, the size of the middle group of free coloureds grew rapidly. Unlike Suriname, in the Antilles there was no large-scale immigration from Asia, which would have greatly increased the ethnic heterogeneity on the islands. In the twentieth century there were movements of migrant workers, but these originated mainly from the Caribbean.

The most important island in terms of physical scale and size of population was Curaçao which, although not a typical plantation colony, initially classically divided along the lines of white-coloured-black, in which 'black' was the equivalent of slave and the middle group of free coloureds was small. However, this soon changed and long before Emancipation in 1863, slaves formed a minority of the population. In 'old Curaçao' colour was as significant a discriminatory criterion in social life as legal status.[12] The white population too was more firmly differentiated than in Suriname. Harry Hoetink distinguishes between two sections, a Jewish group and a Protestant group, each of which can be subdivided into a socio-economic 'high' and 'low' classes. These European groups truly made a home of their own island and the Caribbean surroundings, unlike the white population in Suriname with, in the words of the governor Mauricius, its *animus revertendi* – the longing to return home to the Netherlands. In time the whites of Curaçao became creolized into their Afro-Latino environment: first the Jews, followed by the 'low-class Protestants' and finally even the Protestant elite. Estrangement from Dutch metropolitan culture grew accordingly.

It was not the abolition of slavery, but the arrival of Shell around 1920 that triggered a new course in the island's history. Industrialization and modernization attracted new migrant workers. The population increased massively from 32,000 in 1920 to over 100,000 in 1950. There was a minor influx of Dutch, particularly to take up the higher positions. Shell also attracted Portuguese from Madeira and Ashkenazi Jews from Eastern Europe. However, the great majority of migrants were recruited from the region: Suriname, the Caribbean islands and Venezuela. This pattern remains in place to the present day. Official unemployment may be high, but as long as Curaçao is rightly viewed by the region at large as relatively prosperous, this migration will continue. The same prosperity attracted other smaller groups of immigrants – from the Middle-East, China, India and Pakistan – who found niches for themselves in trade. These minorities play a vital role in the contemporary socio-economic structure of the island. In a broader social context the Portuguese and 'Arabs' are now to a certain extent assimilated, largely at the level traditionally occupied by the whites. Recently arrived Asian minorities keep themselves at a relative remove from the social life of the island. Over the last decade a considerable group of Dutch, attracted by the favourable natural and fiscal climate, have taken up residence on the island; they seem to live alongside rather than in Curaçaoan society.

The 'ethnic' heterogeneity of Curaçaoan society therefore appears extreme. However, one should not forget that the large majority of the island's population, which today numbers about 130,000, is still Afro-Caribbean or of mixed African-European origins. This also typifies what continues to be the most important 'ethnic' issue in this society: the deeply embedded presence of a 'colour class' hierarchy. Under the influence of half a century of rapid modernization, the role of objective criteria in social stratification have come to weigh heavier, particularly with regard to education and socio-economic position. 'Colour', however, remains an essential criterion, as does the issue of whether someone is a *landskind* (a native of the land) or not. Together these dimensions make the hierarchy exceptionally complicated.[13]

Take the position that recent Afro-Caribbean migrants occupy in Curaçaoan society. Based on levels of education, socio-economic achievement and, now, their long presence on the island, many Afro-Surinamese hold good positions with corresponding status. However, even they cannot escape the ever active mindset that thinks in terms of colour caste. Moreover, people in this group complain that even the second or third generations backgrounds are still frequently rebuffed as not being true *landskinderen*. Recent Caribbean migrants – uneducated labourers, housemaids – are still largely left dangling beneath this hierarchy: no Dutch passport, badly paid, and practically no access to government benefits. And – with the exception of many Spanish-Caribbean women, who are therefore also more highly valued by many Curaçaoan men – being black, is still not an asset in this predominantly *Afro*-Caribbean society, even today.

Aruba was eternally in second place in the political structure of the Netherlands Antilles, once appositely baptized by The Hague as 'Curaçao and dependencies'. However, in 1986 the island acquired an independent position within the Kingdom of the Netherlands. The break was above all with Curaçao, which Arubans not only experienced as an inefficient and interfering master, but, moreover, as ethnically 'different', if not 'inferior'. Recent research has shown that slavery, and therefore also blacks, *do* form a part of the entire colonial history of Aruba, something that was previously not willingly acknowledged.[14] Nevertheless, this Afro-Antillean element on Aruba was, at least until the 1930s, clearly less significant than on practically all the other Caribbean islands. The Aruban population and culture undoubtedly have much stronger Amerindian roots than any of the other Caribbean islands. Certainly in comparison with Curaçao and Suriname, the proportion of whites and *mestizo* off-spring of whites and Indians was dominant. It is therefore not without grounds that 'native' Arubans often identify more with neighbouring Venezuela or Colombia than they do with Curaçao or the distant Netherlands.

With little significant economic activity, entirely overshadowed by Curaçao and apparently too small to attract outsiders, Aruba was above all a quiet, not to say sluggish place until the 1920s. The establishment of an oil refinery, shortly after Shell had set one up on Curaçao, suddenly propelled the island into the modern era.[15] Within a short space of time, Lago, a subsidiary of Esso, built an enormous industrial complex. In the eyes of the management, the local population presented a too undisciplined and unproductive labour force. Lago was therefore forced to appeal to migrant labour far more than Shell had to Curaçao, where the larger local population was more easily persuaded onto the payroll. This initiated a dramatic growth of the population and economy which in certain respects made Aruba more Caribbean than ever before.

Between 1920 and 1960, the population grew from around 8,000 to 57,000. This increase is mainly attributable to the arrival of large numbers of migrant workers, predominantly from the English-speaking islands: the Dutch Windward Islands and above all the British West Indies. Situated right alongside the refinery, the small industrial town of San Nicolas underwent tempestuous growth. It soon became known as 'Chocolate City', a name that tellingly illustrates how different the black migrant workers were from what Aruba up to that point had regarded as its own. Contemporary opinions vary enormously on the exceptionally sensitive political question of the extent to which the capital, Oranjestad, and San Nicolas have since grown together. Segregation is decidedly less dominant than a few decades ago. As well as English (and Dutch), the second and third generations from San Nicolas also speak Papiamento; the rise of black Arubans to higher positions in government and industry also seems evident. Nonetheless, in a reference to a bridge that connects the road between Oranjestad and San Nicolas, people still refer to the 'authentic' *mestizo* Aruba *pa'bao di brug* (on this side of the bridge) and the 'other', Afro-Caribbean Aruba *pa'riba di brug* (on the other side of the bridge).

The migration of labour to Lago more or less dried up around 1960. Several decades later a new round followed, this time in response to the demand for workers in the emerging tourist industry. Over the last fifteen years this industry has experienced enormous growth. At the point at which large-scale emigration occurred from Curaçao to the Netherlands, Aruba began once again to attract migrant labour like a magnet, thereby further increasing the ethnic heterogeneity of its population. This time the immigrants came mainly from the Spanish-speaking regions and are, to a large extent, illegal. By 2000 the total population of Aruba was approximately 90,000, nearly fifteen per cent of which are recently arrived Caribbean migrants. Aruban schools are now confronted with a massive influx of Spanish-speaking children. This not only creates practical problems in the education system today and in society at large in the future, it is also opening up a new round in the debate about the question of *Ken ta Arubiano?*: 'Who is a true Aruban?'

Over the last few decades St Martin has undergone an even more turbulent development than Aruba. Again a persistent tourist boom led to large-scale labour migration, which in turn bred considerable heterogeneity in the population. The St Martin that arose in the time of slavery was politically exceptional in the region: the north of the island was French, the south Dutch. Slaves were used primarily to work the salt pans. The proportion of white to black was less uneven than was usual in the typical Caribbean plantation colony. The system of slavery in the salt pans allowed individual slaves more room for manoeuvre. But apart from that the story was the same: a socio-racial hierarchy with whites at the top, below them free coloureds, followed by free blacks, with slaves at the bottom. From a Dutch perspective the regional orientation of the islands was exceptional. The whites were predominantly of British origin, the language was West-Indian English.

The abolition of slavery might well have brought liberation for the slaves, but in other respects St Martin changed slowly. Inhabitants of St Martin from all classes became involved in networks of family relations, commercial connections and labour migration initially in the immediate, English-speaking area. But over time they too began to look to a wider region: the United States and, from the 1930s, Aruba. The island's economy repelled more migrant labourers than it attracted.

Tourism made short shrift of that particular St Martin. In the fifty years after 1950 the total population of the French-Dutch island grew from 5,000 to 80,000. This growth came almost entirely through immigration: from the surrounding English-speaking islands, but also increasingly from Curaçao, Haiti and the Dominican Republic. Higher up the social ladder, immigrants also arrived from Europe, the United States and Asia. The composition of the population changed drastically within a single generation. As on Aruba the question of who is a local is now much asked. 'True St Martiners' have more longstanding and hence higher claims on political power and economic privilege. Yet in a sense the question who is a 'genuine' St Martiner loses its significance. In no time at all, the island has been overrun by a migrant population which, although heterogeneous, increasingly overshadows the local population.

St Martin today is therefore remarkably heterogeneous even in the context of the Caribbean. The political divide has little significance for the outside visitor, other than that one notices that French St Martin seems somewhat French – that the French state makes itself felt there – while the Dutch part of the island seems to be a mixture of mainly British-Caribbean and American culture, with a remote trace of Dutch influence. However, this division has radical implications for locals regarding such issues as passports, social services and education provisions. More drastic still is the division between the locals and the rest, particularly the gulf between the prosperous classes of the 'rest' and the large majority of often illegal migrant workers. In this context, nationality is a determining factor which always disadvantages Caribbean labour migrants who, with a bit of luck and hard work, can earn more on the island than anywhere else in the region, but who have few opportunities to break away from the position of outsider.

Ethnicity seems to be subordinate to the criterion of nationality in St Martin. Migrants from nearby British Caribbean islands such as Anguilla, St Kitts or Antigua belong to the same cultural and 'racial' group as the black locals; what distinguishes and divides them is primarily their nationality. Haitians and Dominicans belong – although to differing extents – to the same Afro-Caribbean cultural domain. However, this relationship has almost been obliterated because, apart from having the 'wrong' nationality, they also speak another language and are usually Catholics while traditionally Protestantism dominates the English-speaking isles, St Martin included. Some of the well-off migrants from further afield already possess the national (French or Dutch) passports, but most do not. Moreover, they often come from different 'ethnic' cultures: India, Italy, the United States, the Middle East. These groups are allowed their own niches on St Martin, which is very open in the economic sphere, yet more selective in the social sphere. Economic contribution improves an immigrant group's standing, and can even to some extent make up for a 'wrong' passport and ethnicity.

The three least populated Antilles were until recently isolated and untouched. Little had changed in their socio-political structures since the time of slavery. A rudimentary slavery colony had built up around the salt pans of Bonaire; after the abolition of slavery the predominantly Afro-Caribbean population led a poverty-stricken existence based on small-scale agriculture, fishing and industry. The small local elite was white or light-coloured; the working classes also had some Amerindian blood.

St Eustatius, once known as 'Golden Rock' and centre of an extensive and profitable trading network, was destroyed by the British in 1781 and never recovered. Here too the population is predominantly Afro-Caribbean with a small, lighter coloured elite; without outside assistance, life would be meagre with only limited opportunities for small-scale agriculture, fishing and trade.

What has always made Saba unique is that slavery here never dominated its market gardening- and fishing-based economy. The thousand or so inhabitants still consist of a black group and a white group who have lived a peaceful and, once again, meagre existence alongside one another for centuries. Alongside one another and to a lesser extent with each other; racial mixing has remained very limited up to today.

Two predominantly black societies with the typical Caribbean class-cum-colour hierarchy, one atypical island with two ethnic groups rather than the usual stratification of colour classes. Something the three islands had in common until recently was an almost complete lack of economic development. Bonairean migrant workers went to Curaçao, Windward Islanders – particularly Sabans – were traditionally sailors. Their islands did not attract migrant labourers. The islands' populations barely grew, if at all. Saba has about 1,000 inhabitants, St Eustatius or 'Statia' 1,500 and Bonaire 13,000. Only very recently has this stagnation begun to crack. On Bonaire tourism is rapidly increasing, in a more controlled way than on Aruba or St Martin, but nonetheless with radical consequences. On Statia, too, attempts are being made to increase tourism. Saba is aiming at smaller-scale tourism. But what does 'small-scale' mean to an island with barely 1,000 local inhabitants? The subsidiary of an American medical school, which has been located on the island since the nineties, suddenly increased the numbers with a floating population of a few hundred.

It seems to be merely a question of years before these three Antillean islands become absorbed into the world of tourism. Considering their limited size, it is not likely that such a development will lead to mass migration of labour; the national and ethnic mix of the island inhabitants will primarily change with the constant turnover of tourists. However, this development will also undermine the local populations' sense of who they feel they are. Again the 'intruders' coming to enjoy the tropical beauty of these islands are mainly whites, offspring of the Europeans who once colonized these islands. At times it is hard *not* to reflect on this awkward history as one watches the tourists disembark. And even if one could forget the past, there are always the glaring inequalities of the present which makes these tourist 'encounters', like the colonial ones before, such brutal and thus open invitations for resentment. As Derek Walcott put it in *Omeros*, when pondering the fate of yet another Caribbean island 'selling herself' to modern tourism:

> [...] the village did not seem to care
> that it was dying in its change, the way it whored
> away a simple life that would soon disappear[16]

Colonialism and plurality

The above sketchy view provides an impression of the complex ethnic plurality and internal differences within the Dutch Caribbean. It will by now have become clear that the ease with which the peoples of Suriname and the Antilles are too easily lumped together does no justice to the complex realities. There is no ethnic homogeneity, no overarching ethnic or at least cultural unity, much less a self-evident internal solidarity. The fact that there is no uniform Dutch Caribbean also belies the notion of a 'Mother country' willing and able to model the overseas territories in her own image.

What connects Suriname with the islands and what connects the islands to each other? In reaction to the short-sightedness of subsuming variety into the notion of a uniform 'Dutch Caribbean', the opposite is claimed sometimes. Hence the view that the only thing these former colonies have in common is that they were once colonized by the same country. Yet this view casts too little light on the extent of Dutch influence and, moreover, introduces yet another distortion. Dutch influence, in particular in education, language and administrative positions, did not carry the same weight in all parts of the region. The Windward Islands were far removed from the Dutch realm of influence, the Leeward Islands were somewhat closer, but not as close as Suriname, which developed a more Dutch public culture and language use. However, over the last few years the independence of Suriname has generated more of a distance from the Netherlands, whereas the Netherlands Antilles and Aruba now have tighter administrative links with the Netherlands than ever before. This story is not over yet and the ending is hard to predict. It is evident however that, although the Dutch Caribbean is not really 'Dutch', the shared colonizer did leave a legacy that is here to stay.

In the denial of any kind of Dutch-Caribbean commonality, beyond the 'merely formal' dimension of Dutch colonization, there lies concealed yet another distortion. The history of twentieth-century migration has unquestionably brought the seven disparate parts of the Dutch Caribbean closer together. The prehistory of the Surinamese exodus, then still a traditional migration of labour, was written in prewar Curaçao and continues to the present day. Moreover, around the middle of the twentieth century, many Windward Islanders worked on Aruba and some on Curaçao. Today many thousands of Curaçaoans live and work on St Martin. The relationships forged by these streams of migrants have probably contributed more to a sense of connectedness than the formal network of colonial and postcolonial constitutional relations. Nonetheless, these streams were possible precisely because all those involved were part of the Kingdom of the Netherlands in the first place.

Belonging to the Kingdom was also an essential factor in the migration to the Netherlands. A one-sided metropolitan orientation is shared by the great majority of Surinamese and Antilleans. But the move to the Netherlands has not led to the development of an umbrella Dutch-Caribbean identity on foreign soil. On the contrary, the dominant distinctions in the Caribbean between Surinamese and Antilleans, or between Surinamese from different ethnic backgrounds, have been duplicated almost exactly in the Netherlands.[17]

In these pages I am refraining from engaging in a theoretical discussion of notions of identity and ethnicity. One may object that this is not conceptually particularly refined, but I believe that an intermingling of these concepts does reflect reality. Ethnicity, a notion now increasingly used as a euphemism for discredited terms such as 'race', encompasses a host of assumptions. Under the term 'ethnicity', notions of race and physical, visible features are coupled with suppositions about shared origins, a shared culture, and a shared frame of reference for moral standards. It will by now be clear that there is no ground on which to base the view of Dutch Caribbean inhabitants as a single ethnic group, however inclined outsiders may be to do so. It is also equally apparent that the Surinamese also cannot be regarded as a single ethnic group. Surinamese identity is built up from group identities, each of which has its own specific ethnic component; insofar as such a thing as a Surinamese identity now exists, it does so through the ethnic-specificity of every group being neutralized as much as possible.

It makes equally little sense to regard the Dutch Antilles and Aruba as a single, ethnically homogeneous group. Each of the six islands has its own identity. However, unlike in Suriname, the ethnic dimension of this identity is not a determining factor. The factor that primarily distinguishes the Windward Islands from Curaçao or Bonaire is language and the particular Caribbean environment, rather than ethnicity or, more sinisterly formulated, 'race' or colour. What maintains the divisions on St Martin are issues of nationality, class and status far more than ethnic distinctions. The situation on Curaçao is similar: here a socio-racial and related cultural hierarchy may exist, but ultimately ethnicity in the sense of determining identities and irreconcilable contrasts does not play a significant role. Although on Aruba the question of who may call themselves truly Aruban is freighted with notions of 'race', there is not the ethnic pillarization that exists in Suriname. The fact that skin colour in 'Chocolate City' is black and the language spoken English whereas *pa'bao di brug* skin colour is light and the language Papiamento, is unquestionably what divides Aruba. This does not mean there are fundamentally different cultures. Arubans like the other Antilleans are predominantly Christian and interracial relations are relatively common and are tolerated, even though they may not be popular. In short, there may be a tendency towards the formation of ethnic hierarchies and exclusion, but this is different, and less stubborn, than the ethnic pillarization of fundamentally different cultures in Suriname.

The conspicuous heterogeneity in terms of ethnicity, in the case of Suriname, or colour and culture, in the case of the islands, has been considered by many to be problematic. This includes the nationalists who in the struggle for independence set themselves the goal of overcoming precisely these divides.[18] It is also frequently suggested that ethnic differences and the conceptualization of a hierarchy of races and colours are legacies of colonialism, and that the colonial authorities capitalized on such divisions in order to 'divide and rule'. Much can be said in defence of this view. There is no doubt that thinking in terms of colour hierarchies, with whites at the top and blacks at the bottom, is a legacy of centuries of colonialism and slavery. There is also no doubt that the organized supply of Asian migrants, although in the first place motivated by economics and not ethnic manipulation, considerably strengthened ethnic divisions in a country like Suriname.

On the other hand, this reasoning credits the colonial authorities with too much power and underestimates the internal dynamics of ethnic relations. Moreover, this reasoning in terms of colonial responsibility for past wrongs at times has an undercurrent of reasoning away personal responsibility for the present. Colonialism was, of course, responsible for the entire colonial project in the Dutch Caribbean. Without Dutch colonization there would have been no repopulation of the Dutch Caribbean, no 'black Curaçao', no *mestizos* on Aruba, no *pa'riba di brug* and no *pa'bao di brug*; neither would there have been plantations in Suriname and hence African slaves, Maroons, Asian contract workers and, consequently, perhaps, no colour differentiation and no ethnic tension. However, once these all too obvious observations have been made, more specific questions need to be asked.

Did the colonial authorities systematically play ethnic groups or 'colour classes' off against one another? Examples of this do exist. Take the case of early colonial Suriname. Immediately after the beginning of colonialism, the Dutch began to exacerbate existing divisions among the different Amerindian peoples. They then used them as henchmen in the struggle against the Maroons. Furthermore, the colonial order consistently granted favours to those of lighter colour, to free coloureds and blacks, and also to an elite within the 'slave forces', which in the Afro-Surinamese population led to an increasingly refined hierarchy. To reiterate, the decision to attract Asian contract workers after Emancipation was based on economic considerations, not with a view to stimulating ethnic divisions. However, once they had been confronted with such considerable ethnic plurality, the colonial authorities did help maintain these divisions by exercising a different policy for each group over a long period.

However, it is a misconception to think that the colonial authorities were able to manipulate these ethnic relations at will. There was and is a gaping abyss between Amerindians and Maroons; they regard each other as fundamentally different races. Despite potentially having a common enemy, and despite many individual instances in which Amerindians and Maroons provided one another with shelter, a sense of profound difference always predominated. There was not much need for a colonial policy of divide and rule.

The relation between Maroons and plantation slaves was ambivalent. In the early years the ethnic and cultural divide between the two was relatively narrow. However, Maroon and plantation cultures began to grow apart with the various communities of Maroons each developing their own ways in the interior and slaves increasingly making their particular plantations in a sense their homes, demographically as well as culturally. Again, a common exploiter or enemy does not necessarily make for unity. Maroons attacking plantations were often fought off by male slaves who wanted to prevent them from stealing their provisions and their women. After first investing much to prevent slaves from marooning and to keep Maroons outside plantation territory, in the end the colonial authorities experienced how a degree of ethnic division could be maintained without much effort on their part. And this division has sustained itself to the present day. Urban Afro-Surinamese have a tendency to look down upon the supposedly uncivilized and backwards Maroons. The latter may suffer from discrimination, but they proudly base their identity on the fact that their forefathers successfully stood up to colonial rule and that they have developed their own ethnic cultures since.

If we turn to the consequences of Asian immigration, the conclusion that ethnic divisions have a way of maintaining themselves even without colonial interference seems even more pertinent. The ethnic pillarization of Suriname was initially strongly stimulated by colonial policy. A governor such as J.C. Kielstra (1933–1944) alienated the lighter-skinned Creole elite by – half-heartedly – replacing an assimilation policy with a policy of allowing the Asian population to maintain its own lifestyles, separate from the Creole culture which was becoming more Dutch-oriented. However, following the Second World War, the colonial government returned to a policy of assimilation for all, thus hoping to bridge ethnic differences. This policy was taken on by the Surinamese government both after attaining self-government in 1954 and with independence in 1975. Yet even today, much of public life – such as recruitment for political parties – and, even more so, the private domain, is dictated by the logic of the ethnic divisions inherited from colonialism. That the objective to bridge the ethnic divides still seems so elusive illustrates not only colonial, but also postcolonial Surinamese powerlessness in directing ethnic dynamics.

Similar observations can be made with regard to ethnic issues on the islands. The Aruban struggle for a distinct status, which was partly driven by ethnic sensibilities vis-à-vis Curaçao, was long and doggedly, but ultimately futilely, thwarted by the Netherlands. Insofar as there is cause to regard current 'ethnic' divisions in Aruba as truly problematic, it is in any case clear that this plurality stemmed from a turbulent migration of labour, the consequences of which were barely considered at the time and in which the Netherlands has barely been involved since. This last point is even more relevant to the recent, largely unrestricted migration of labour to St Martin, with all the potential risks inherent in creating new ethnic minorities.

Ethnic cultures

The Dutch Caribbean can boast an attractive but also divisive variety of cultures. None of today's cultures can be understood outside the context of Dutch colonialism and Western culture, and the extent to which these influences affect the different ethnic cultures differs greatly from place to place. It is tempting to envisage the various subcultures of the Dutch Caribbean as points in a continuum with at one pole the most 'authentic', 'Non-Western' cultures and at the other the most 'Western', possibly the most 'Dutch' cultures. In such reasoning the Surinamese Amerindians would be at one end of this continuum. Their native culture predates the arrival of the Europeans by a long chalk and much has remained intact to this day, even though increasing numbers of Amerindians have left the tropical rainforests over the last few decades and virtually all their villages have become connected to modern Surinamese society. What is particularly striking about the oral traditions of the Amerindian peoples, which were recorded not long ago, is the dominance of their cosmology and an utterly unique way of life and thinking which is adapted to the ecological environment of the tropical rainforests. The colonial world occupies a relatively marginal position in this.[19]

Next along the continuum would come the Surinamese Maroons, at less of a remove from colonial and postcolonial culture. Maroon cultural expressions – languages, art, oral traditions, kinship systems, religion and music – are sometimes erroneously thought to be 'purely' African. However, these unique Afro-Surinamese cultures were and are remarkably specific and 'Non-Western', even though urbanization and the expansion of 'Paramaribo' has also increasingly forced open a unique world. Yet even the oldest Maroon oral traditions attest to their constant struggle with the colonial world, which has always been a dominant presence in their cultural universe. This is not only true of the Maroons' crucial understanding of their own history, it is also apparent in far more abstract cultural constructions such as their religion, in which the same antagonism towards the 'city' continues to play in the background.[20]

One step 'further' along the continuum might come the urban Afro-Surinamese population. This population group should then be further classified according to such criteria as education and subcultures partially corresponding with socio-racial hierarchies – a method analogous to those so often used for other Afro-Caribbean societies. After the Maroons come the Creole lower class with its Sranan Tongo language, its belief in an Afro-Surinamese cults such as Winti, whether or not combined with belonging to a Christian church, its matrifocality, and its presumed incomplete assimilation into the world of capitalist *homo economicus*. Finally, the disproportionately light-coloured Creole middle class would be placed at the most 'Western' pole of the continuum; well educated, living in modern families, 'respectable', 'bourgeois', oriented towards the Netherlands or perhaps now also the United States.

The suffocating simplicity, the relentless attribution of characteristics, even the intolerable implication of inevitability, cannot deny this classification system a certain heuristic value and even a certain resemblance to real life. This is also why this continuum not only firmly exists in the literature about Caribbean societies, but also implicitly in the thinking of people in the Caribbean themselves – in Suriname certainly, but equally so on Curaçao, Aruba, Jamaica, Cuba or Guadeloupe.

However, for Suriname especially, unlike the Antilles, social reality cannot be contained within these outlines, even if we were prepared for a moment to accept its sketchy and suffocating nature. All over the region small ethnic minorities – Chinese, 'Arabs', Indians – resist being positioned along a continuum. However, in Suriname the Hindustanis and Javanese are not minorities, but a significant and, when taken together, dominant part of the population as a whole; their cultures by no means also lend themselves to being placed along a simple continuum. In order to salvage anything of this classification we will have to start thinking in terms of a multi-dimensional model in which the polarity of the idea 'Western' can be only one of the axes. Such a matrix would have to do justice to a reality in which there is no uniform coupling of notions of religion, culture in the narrowest sense, kinship and socio-economic orientation.

Hindustanis and Javanese cannot be positioned along a one-dimensional continuum. Descended from the major Asian cultures, only a few have been enticed into the embrace of Christian culture, despite all the efforts of the missionaries. There is little reason to believe that this will be any different in the future. Hindustanis are still very much oriented towards India. For both groups the cultural distance from the – to different extents, but generally Western-oriented – Afro-Surinamese Creole population has remained great. This was also true of the Amerindian population, but unlike these native Surinamese, the socio-economic orientation of the Hindustani and, increasingly, the Javanese populations strongly corresponds with the Western norm.

Thus over the last few decades large sections of the Hindustani and Javanese population have come much closer to the ideal type of Western orientation than the Creole lower class. Among Hindustanis traditional patterns of kinship have evolved, leading to a weakening of the extended family in favour of the 'Western' model of the nuclear family, which is now certainly more deeply entrenched than in the Creole lower class. An obvious assumption is that this socialization has significantly contributed to the persistent socio-economic rise of both groups vis-à-vis the Creole lower class, both in Suriname and the Netherlands. There is no reason to believe that this will change in the near future. In this respect, too, the ethnic plurality of Suriname is a case all on its own, much more than ever was or shall be on Aruba and the Netherlands Antilles.

Creolization and group identity

Long ago the word *vernegeren* (to become like a Negro) was commonly used in the Dutch Caribbean. Today *neger* is still common parlance in Suriname – certainly far more so than in the Netherlands, where *neger* has become politically incorrect – but *vernegeren* much less so. A white man was considered to have become *vernegerd*, or black, if he had adopted too much Afro-Caribbean culture. Later the word was used among the well-educated Afro-Caribbean elites. Anyone who failed to observe the conventions of Dutch culture was accused by his peers of letting himself down, regressing to uncivilized behaviour.

Vernegeren is in fact a specific form of cultural mixing which was severely frowned upon. Today, Caribbean discourse routinely sings the praises of cultural mixing, now baptized as creolization – in a way echoing the concept of *transculturización* introduced in the 1920s by the Cuban anthropologist Fernando Ortiz. Remarkably, in the 1950s the Antillean writer Cola Debrot used precisely the verb *creoliseren* ('to creolize'), long before modern scholars and ideologues of all persuasions appropriated it.[21] Be this as it may, with the concept of creolization the emphasis was once again placed on the gains brought about by cultural cross-fertilization. Creolization has become a reason to admire Caribbean culture, to sing its praises, to hold it up as an example to the world. Just as the population of the Caribbean consisted almost entirely of newcomers, so its culture has been created anew. Elements from Africa, Europe and Asia took root on top of the Amerindian element. No one could leave their own culture intact, everyone had to give up some aspects and further develop others; everyone had to learn to borrow from other ethnic cultures. The result, resounds the 'praise of creolization', was the creation of a completely unique, new hybrid culture.[22]

There are certainly grounds for such high spirits around creolization. The exceptional diversity and cultural dynamics of the Caribbean have been translated into a remarkable literature and – reaching a far larger audience – new musical genres. In the daily life of the Caribbean, one can sense a constant switching of codes; there exists a dexterity in the alternate, sometimes simultaneous operation of different cultural codes, linguistic registers and even languages, which is hard to find in ethnically and linguistically more homogeneous countries. Still, this praise of creolization is also problematic. For one, because it takes an extremely optimistic view of the achievements of Caribbean culture, while disregarding the darker sides of the cultures generated by the process of creolization. Moreover, because this optimistic approach is inclined to deliberately ignore a process of U.S.-style cultural globaliza-tion which has been underway in the Caribbean for decades – that 'U.S. style', incidentally, itself also a product of constant cross-fertilization. And finally because the notion of creolization often suggests a higher level of cross-fertilization than in reality occurs.

Ultimately, the scope of creolization is more limited than many like to believe precisely because the Caribbean is marked by such stubborn plurality. There are, of course, pressing reasons for speaking of a cre-olized culture. There is one cuisine common to many parts of the Caribbean. All Dominicans dance the *merengue*, almost all Haitians adhere to a combination of Catholicism and *voudun*, all Commonwealth Caribbean people speak a West Indian English reflecting their specific, local roots, class and possibly ethnic group. Almost all the people of Suriname speak a variant of Dutch or Sranan Tongo, or both, while the Leeward Islanders speak Papiamentu. These are all cultural elements which have developed in this form only in the Caribbean and which are now part of a shared identity. At the same time there are many other cul-tural elements which are by no means shared by all alike. Some are class-specific elements which have contributed to social stratification in a similar way in almost all societies. But there are also enduring 'eth-nic' subcultures, which maintain the divisions in Caribbean society.

Taking the above into consideration, it is clear that these comments are especially relevant to Surinamese society. Different ethnic groups increasingly share one or two languages, the youth are largely educated in an non-segregated education system, the scale of geographical sepa-ration is diminishing, and the administrative and political structure in principle serves all Surinamese. And yet many people in Suriname still feel themselves to be part of an ethnic group first and foremost, and only in second place, possibly, Surinamese. The Afro-Surinamese habit of referring to one's own group as 'us Surinamese' and to use an explicit ethnic denominator for other groups does not necessarily attest to an unwillingness to accept others as Surinamese. But it does reveal a deep-rooted sense of mutual difference, and for many Afro-Surinamese also to a sense that they have stronger rights, not only in terms of the length of time they have been there, but also because the country is somehow more home to them than to the others.

In the 1960s researchers established that there was little mutual respect between the most important ethnic groups and that interethnic relationships were generally frowned upon; the antagonism between the Afro-Surinamese and Hindustanis was particularly pronounced.[23] Remarkably little research into this subject has been carried out since then, probably because posing these questions has come to be considered less 'correct' in a nation struggling to attain some kind of national unity. However, the little research that has been done and the impressions one gets today suggest that these attitudes are at best changing very slowly. Thus a 1992 survey disclosed a somewhat depressing continuity in the perceptions the various ethnic communities in Suriname have of each other. The most conspicuous positive characteristic of the Afro-Surinamese was 'friendliness', the most negative one a happy-go-lucky attitude. Hindustanis were characterized as hard-working, but prone to alcoholism, intolerance and unreliability. The most highly-rated Javanese characteristic being civilized; the most negative one, again, unreliability. No less remarkable is that almost forty per cent could not decide on either the most positive trait of the Afro-Surinamese or the most negative one of the Javanese.[24]

Arguably the litmus test for ethnic integration is the question of how far ethnic difference plays a part in kinship, in sexual and affective preferences and relations, and especially in the acceptance of interethnic relationships. From this perspective ethnic integration in Suriname still has a long way to go, to the point that one wonders whether this yardstick of integration is not simply too demanding. Again, very little empirical research has been done on this issue. In the 1992 survey cited above, more general questions were asked, and again the outcome testifies to frozen realities. Both Hindustanis and Javanese confessed to a strongly positive attitude towards their own ethnic group. Hindustanis judged the Afro-Surinamese harshly and were mild towards the Javanese. The Javanese were also highly critical of the Afro-Surinamese, and less so of the Hindustanis. The Afro-Surinamese turned out to regard the Javanese in a slightly less negative light than they did the Hindustanis; sadly, their attitude towards their own ethnic community is clearly less favourable than was the case with the other two groups.[25]

Such figures suggest that interracial relations are still frowned upon, and circumstantial evidence strongly supports this view. Even so, inevitably, the proportion of *dogla* or, in the crude Sranan designation, *moksi meti* ('mixed meat') children is slowly increasing. It seems that the Afro-Surinamese community is most open to such mixing, the Hindustani community the least so. The acceptance and frequency of interracial partnerships seems higher in the Netherlands than in Suriname. But this seems to apply mainly to the mutual acceptability of white Dutch and Afro-Surinamese as partners, making for the kind of relations which have a long and not necessarily liberating pedigree in the colonial past. Meanwhile, no matter how successful Hindustani assimilation into Dutch society may be in different arenas, endogamy is still the prevalent norm in this group.[26]

One is therefore inclined to emphasize continuity.[27] Aesthetic preferences and perceptions, and judgements of the social characteristics of the other ethnic groups change exasperatingly slowly, if at all. In order to understand ethnic relations among the Surinamese, it is not enough to find out whether there is a kernel of truth in these ideas and how strong this kernel might be. It is equally important to investigate what mechanisms of ethnic socialization keep these ideas alive. *Vernegeren*, 'going black?' In Suriname the white Dutch play a limited role and they would be wary of using such a charged term. The Afro-Surinamese middle classes also tend to stay away from such denigrating terms today, even if they are concerned about the stubbornness of lower-class Creole characteristics such as matrifocality, Winti and 'hustling', as opposed to Christianity, industrious study and hard work. In this, they echo the earlier Dutch colonial concerns about the Surinamese elite 'going black'. However, today the most common context in which the slur of *vernegeren* is used is probably Hindustani: parents who accuse their son or daughter of not keeping enough distance from their Afro-Surinamese peers and Creole lifestyle ('Boy, you're a black coolie'). In 1953, Munshi Rahman Khan, a first generation Hindustani Surinamese, articulated a sombre vision in his poem 'Changing Times':

> See how morals and standards deteriorate in these immoral times
> Men are leaving their wives and entering into relationships with Creole women
> They fall in love with Creole women and joyously sing their praises:
> Our women are angels, they will transport us to heaven.
> Rahman says: Noble women redeem their ancestors of all sin
> Dynasty, honour, shame, faith and wealth they have destroyed.
> Children born in the dharma are being given names that do not belong to them

Willem, Eddie, Pikinwa, Johan, Keizer, Piet
Johan, Keizer, Piet, what new custom is this[?]
They have destroyed the dharma, the smell of India has
blown away [...] [28]

Such unadulterated nostalgia, such reactionary views, are no longer spoken or written, at least not in public. But on the other hand, 1953 is not that long ago and the question is whether 'Changing Times' is as far removed from the reality of today as a contemporary glorification of colour blindness and ethnic and cultural hybridity. There are as yet few signs of a turbulent new wind blowing through the Hindustani youth of today.

Once again it may be concluded that, in comparison with Suriname, the ethnic divisions on the islands are less tangible. Apart from the differences in nationality, boundaries exist on the islands which indicate shifts in colour and class, and which are considerably less rigid than the lines that divide Suriname. This conclusion can be placed in a broader context. The course of European colonization brought with it the elaboration of an aesthetic hierarchy which throughout most of the Americas introduced a white ideal type as, in the terms of Hoetink, the 'somatic norm'.[29] The white aesthetic ideal at the top, a caricature of ugly blackness at the bottom. Despite worldwide decolonization, Black Power and many other watersheds, this clinging to an aesthetic hierarchy is in all too many respects alive and well. A pitch-black skin colour might still be described in the Caribbean as *color triste*, frizzy hair as 'bad hair', thick lips or a flat nose as ugly, and so on.

Yet in this respect too Caribbean societies differ greatly from one another. This particularly applies to the precise interpretation of the somatic standard and the amount of flexibility with which a society deals with ethnic distinctions. As Hoetink stated in his work on ethnicity in the Americas, Caribbean ethnicity may be defined according to three models.[30] In the Spanish Caribbean, where the ratio of white to black has traditionally been less uneven than elsewhere, and where plantations made a less severe impact, a 'racial continuum' developed in which, certainly in Cuba and the Dominican Republic, a large part of the population falls somewhere between the extremes of white and black. The flexibility with which the distinction can be used is expressed by the high number of interethnic relationships, which further undermine the narrow black-white colour distinction. The somatic norm may still be light-skinned, but there is a high degree of flexibility. This also enables social success to transform the colour hierarchy: 'money whitens'.

A far less flexible ethnic model developed in the colonies of the other European powers where the gulf between black and white was more extreme, the ratio far more uneven and the slowly developing middle group much smaller. White exclusivity remained largely intact in these societies and only 'dissolved', according to Hoetink, because the white elite left the field: by being violently forced out, in places like Haiti; by leaving gradually; or by being absorbed into the light-coloured elite of mixed African and European parentage else-where. In these societies the white elite therefore no longer really existed, or at least not to any significant degree. However, once views on 'race' and colour had taken root they would outlive the physical presence of the whites by a long chalk. A unique third model then emerged in three of the countries in this category – Guyana, Trinidad and Suriname – which imported large numbers of Asian contract workers following the abolition of slavery.[31] This created a second ethnic 'pillar', largely alongside the Creole population. In Suriname there was a third such pillar, the Javanese, which brought about yet another turn in the ethnic dynamics.

Even today there is still little basis for dismissing this three-way division and the associated presumptions about the power of the colour hierarchies and ethnic pillarization. It should also be stressed that in the Caribbean, as elsewhere, aesthetic value is usually linked to a series of presumptions about the attitudes and behaviour of the different 'ethnic' groups. Be this as it may, while Suriname belongs to the third model, the islands – notwithstanding the major differences between them – all fit into the second.

Insofar as a development has become visible, there is reason to conclude that the significance of ethnic difference has crumbled more in this second model than in the third. Developments can be measured against a series of criteria such as religion, culture, historical under-standing and, moreover, kinship systems and an acceptance of interethnic relations, as well as socio-economic orientations and positions. The political dimension – the selection of political parties and leaders on the basis of ethnic preferences – has not been addressed in the above. It may be assumed that politics primarily plays a part as a derivative of the above criteria, even if Caribbean politicians are not always averse to cutely capitalizing upon the emotions surrounding issues of ethnicity and colour.[32]

The conclusion that becomes obvious is that although the hierarchy of black-white or African-European stemming from colonialism is a stubborn one, its significance has to a certain extent declined, particularly over the last few decades. This is especially true of Suriname, where the local white population has long been a negligible group. But, on the islands too, colour consciousness seems hesitantly, but nonetheless increasingly, to be making way for mixed relations. This can in part be simply explained by the withdrawal of the white population. However, a crucial factor also seems to be that the differences in class and education on islands such as Aruba, Curaçao or St Martin may now carry more weight than differences in colour, which ultimately have a weaker 'ethnic' basis. The ethnic plurality of Suriname, however, remains more ingrained and dominant, beginning at the defining level of ethnic preference and exclusion in personal life.

Time and again history teaches us that emphasizing ethnic differences can unleash deep emotions which in turn can be manipulated to achieve completely different ends; in the end, this is equivalent to playing with fire. Leaving aside the exceptions, the leaders of the postcolonial Caribbean states have in general demonstrated their awareness of the dangers of playing the ethnic card too blatantly and extensively. This also generally applies to the Dutch Caribbean.

Ethnic plurality in the Dutch Caribbean is – as almost everywhere in the New World – a stubborn factor in society. The mechanisms at work in daily life, which sustain and possibly strengthen ethnic differences, change at best extremely slowly. The question is not so much whether difference and the conscious or unconscious suppression of differences in ethnicity or colour can be pushed aside, but rather whether it is possible in any way to depreciate their importance. It is hard to answer this question in the affirmative, precisely because the dynamics of ethnic difference are formed and perpetuated, first and foremost, at a micro-level by socialization processes. It is there, in the most immediate environment, that preferences, judgements and prejudices are passed on.

Both Caribbean experience and the more recent sobering lessons to be taken from European government policies for minorities suggest that the possibility of influencing such socialization processes from above is very limited. There is no reason to foist more power on the Dutch Caribbean authorities so that they may enter into the private domains of their citizens. On the other hand, in the process of nation building, for which practically all Caribbean states strive, there is an opportunity to deprive this potentially divisive element in the national identity of some of its importance. Many attempts are being made, but politicians and others who have set themselves the task of defining national identity often find it difficult to distance themselves from their own 'ethnic' group. To differing degrees, this dual loyalty – to the nation and to one's own group – still plays an important part in the predicament of nation building in the Caribbean. The Dutch Caribbean is certainly no exception.[33]

Notes

1   The classic study of the origins of the plural society in Suriname is Van Lier's
     Samenleving in een grensgebied, first published in 1949 and translated into English
     as *Frontier Society* (Van Lier 1971). On ethnic languages in Suriname, see the recent
     atlas by Carlin & Arends 2002.
2   Postma 1990, Van Stipriaan 1993:314.
3   Plantation regulations 1686 (Schiltkamp & De Smidt 1973:168).
4   Price 1976, Hoogbergen 1990, 1992, Scholtens 1994.
5   Van Lier 1971:217–8.
6   See De Klerk 1953, Speckmann 1965, Van Lier 1971, Hoefte 1998.
7   Hoefte 1998:167, 170.
8   See also De Waal Malefijt 1963, Derveld 1981, Grasveld & Breunissen 1990, Hoefte
     1990 and 1998.
9   The official figure for 1998 is just over 422,000 (De Bruijne 2001:33). I have added
     another 28,000, following the widespread opinion that the number of illegal
     Brazilians is dramatically underestimated in official counts.
10 Van Lier 1971. Remarkably, since its first publication in 1949, Van Lier's book and
     vision of the plural society of Suriname was only once fiercely attacked, at the time
     from a rather dogmatic Marxist point of view (Hira 1982).
11 Dew 1978. The metaphor has its roots in Dutch history. From the late nineteenth cen-
     tury until the 1960s, Dutch society was supposedly held together by its own four reli-
     gious and secular pillars – Catholic, Protestant, Liberal and Socialist – which, as it
     were, support the single roof of the state.
12 See the classic 1958 study by Hoetink, *Het patroon van de oude Curaçaose samen-
     leving* and Chapters 1 and 2 in the present book.
13 See Chapter 5.
14 See Alofs & Merkies 1990, Alofs 1996, Verton 1996.
15 See Van Soest 1977, Dekker 1982 and Croes 1987.
16 Walcott 1990:111. On the impact of tourism on the social fabric of small Caribbean
     islands, see Pattullo 1996.
17 See also Chapter 6.
18 See Chapter 5.
19 See, for example, Koelewijn 1987.
20 See among others Price 1983a, 1990, Price & Price 1999, Thoden van Velzen & Van
     Wetering 1988.
21 Debrot 1985:122 (circa 1950).
22 Compare Bernabé, Chamoiseau & Confiant 1989. A recent re-thinking of the con-
     cept of creolization is provided by Price 2001.
23 Speckmann 1963, Van Renselaar 1963.
24 Verberk, Scheepers & Hassankhan 1997:136–7. Survey conducted in 1992, N=1002.
     The 'don't know' category scored only 13.6 and 19.7 % in relation to the positive
     characteristics of Hindustanis and Javanese, and 22.8 % and 15.6 % in relation to the
     negative characteristics of Hindustanis and Afro-Surinamese respectively.
25 Verberk, Scheepers & Hassankhan 1997:136–7, however ,with a much smaller sam-
     ple: Hindustani N=135, Javanese N=51, Afro-Surinamese N=97. See also Mungra
     1990.
26 The norm seems open to erosion though. Choenni & Adhin 2003:61, 88, 174–5, 218.
27 As does a recent 'outsider' analysis: St-Hilaire 2001.
28 Rahman Khan (1873–1972), cited in Van Kempen 1995:82–3. Interestingly, in his
     posthumously published diaries covering the period from his youth in India to his

life in Suriname up to 1943, Khan does not express any strong feelings against the Afro-Surinamese (Hira 2003).

29 See particularly Hoetink 1967.
30 Hoetink 1985.
31 In Caribbean context one may add Belize to this category with its Creole alongside its Amerindian population.
32 See Chapter 5.
33 See Chapter 5, and Baud et al. 1996, especially Chapter 3.

4 | A Dutch model for decolonization?

Over the years it has become commonplace among the Dutch to believe that the Netherlands was dealt a very unfortunate hand in its decolonization process, so much so that this view has become cliché. First there were the unsuccessful, bloody and increasingly futile Dutch attempts to obstruct Indonesian independence as proclaimed in 1945, the aftermath of which still arouses strong emotions, especially in the Netherlands. Then came the issue of New Guinea, where the Netherlands – this time in a slightly different and perhaps more honourable role – once again came head to head with Indonesia and, in 1962, was once again forced to concede. This was followed by the hurried independence of Suriname in 1975 and the notorious golden handshake – an independence that was eventually to produce such disappointing results. Finally there was the failed plan to launch the Netherlands Antilles into independence as a six-in-one micro-state. This policy faltered, culminating in the acknowledgement that the Antilles could neither be kept together as a single entity, nor could they be forced to leave the transatlantic Kingdom of the Netherlands. Indeed, almost nothing in the decolonization process went the way The Hague had envisaged.

From this perspective, the conclusion that the Netherlands was an unsuccessful decolonizer seems justified. One might wonder though whether other colonial powers fared much better. By slightly shifting our angle, we might also remark that this negative evaluation reflects a Dutch inclination to view its role in the world with as much ironic detachment as possible and with an awareness – as guilty as it is contradictory – of both its own failings and its inability to make a difference in the world in the first place. This view, when faced with the obstinacy of reality, all too often inspires the Dutch to a remarkably meddlesome approach in their dealings with others, and particularly with the former colonies.

The 'West Indian' perspective

European colonialism all over the world usually managed to align with the indigenous, colonial elites who, to a certain extent, came to identify

with colonial culture. In most cases it was precisely within the indigenous elite that a countermovement subsequently developed, not infre-
quently fed and directed by an increasing familiarity with the culture of
the colonial power. The classical pattern of the sons of the colonial elite,
returning home after being educated in the mother country, taking the
lead in the resistance against colonialism, also applied to the Caribbean.

For the Dutch Caribbean this pattern only occurred once, and with
much ambivalence, in the radical but short-lived episode of Surinamese
nationalism of the 1950s to 1970s. The contrast with the Dutch East Indies
was in many respects vast, and had its consequences for the course of
decolonization. In contrast to Asia, the colonization of the Caribbean had
entailed the construction of a new society of immigrants. With the exception of tiny numbers of Amerindians in Suriname and Aruba, the Dutch
Caribbean population was a product of colonization. Unlike in Indonesia,
the colonial authorities in the West did not need to take into account an
indigenous elite which prided itself on older rights, which was held in a
certain degree of esteem by the local population, and whose culture also
impacted on the new colonial rulers.[1] The Caribbean elites in contrast saw
themselves primarily as a part of the culture of the motherland, regardless
of how much they became alienated from that culture over time. Besides a
cultural affinity, common economic and administrative interests bound the
colonial elites to the Netherlands. Until well into the nineteenth century,
colonies in the Caribbean were inconceivable without slavery and the local
elites were all too aware of the fact that the motherland offered essential
guaranties for the continued existence of the 'peculiar institution'.

This did not mean that relations between the elites on either side of
the Atlantic were always harmonious. This is borne out by colonial
archives brimming with dossiers on profound conflicts between local elites
and administrators sent from the Netherlands. In practice, the cultural differences turned out to be far greater than had initially been believed. More
importantly, administrative views and economical priorities turned out to
diverge greatly. Most conflicts revolved around such issues as appoint-
ments to the colonial administrative councils, the power of these councils
in relation to the metropolitan governor, levels of taxation, or the responsibility for maintaining order. In short, discussions generally revolved
around the division of profits and expenses of the colonial administration;
there was barely any discord on matters of principle. Local elites judged
the colonial power on the basis of their willingness and ability to maintain
order and, as far as possible, to pick up the bill for doing so. Where eighteenth-century documents from the colonies express bitter criticism of the
Netherlands, they invariably address such issues as excessively high taxation, the inadequate supply of slaves, objectionable interference in the
treatment of slaves, and unfavourable colonial trade regulations.

This only changed in the nineteenth century when the Netherlands, initially with little enthusiasm but gradually with more emphasis, placed the treatment of slaves and subsequently the abolition of slavery on the agenda.[2] To their horror the colonial elites found themselves confronted with a policy that increasingly worked against their interests, or at least against their ideas on how business should be governed. Their lack of power now became painfully obvious. They had no significant lobby within the Kingdom to enable them to set colonial policy. And there were no alternatives outside the Netherlands, at least not ones that they identified.

Independence was not a viable option. There was no mention of trying to follow the examples of the United States, Haiti or Spanish America. The Dutch Caribbean elites were all too aware of how indispensable a reasonably strong mother country was for guaranteeing social order in their colony. They were probably also aware of the limitations the small scale of their society imposed on their economic, administrative or military potential. There was no question of stepping over to another empire in the mid-nineteenth century, or else it was an unattractive alternative. The United States only emerged as a formal colonial power in the region half a century later, and Britain and France had completed their last round of subdividing the Caribbean several decades earlier. The new Spanish-American states, Venezuela in particular, exercised more of a deterrent than an attraction.

Self-appointed spokespeople from the colonial elite allowed there to be no doubt that the West Indian colonies belonged unconditionally to the Kingdom. In 1869, M. Juda in an open letter 'to all those concerned with the future of Suriname' linked the highly relevant comparison with the Dutch East Indies to a rhetorical reminder of the presumed pro-Orange sentiment among his compatriots:

> There is, however, an even more tender bond that binds Suriname to the Netherlands: the love of the Netherlands and her King. This love was most clearly expressed in the horror that prevailed in the Colony when people there learned of the possibility of 'letting go'. The news was received like a funeral announcement. The Surinamese have learned to regard and love the Netherlands as its Fatherland. And that this parent should let go of its child, hand over parental responsibility to another, or leave this child, not yet old enough to look after itself, to its fate?
>
> No, the Surinamese neither could, nor would believe this. The bond that ties Suriname to the Netherlands is hence a tender one.[3]

Not long afterwards, in the same vein the association *Vereniging van Surinamers* wrote:

> Sooner or later you will lose 'the East'. You, who are *considered* to be so outstandingly practical, *be* practical and sell the East before it is taken from you. A possession you can sell, a colony you cannot. The East is a possession, Suriname is a colony.[4]

When rumours began to circulate that the Netherlands wanted rid of 'Curaçao and dependencies', the incensed Colonial Council of the island addressed the Dutch parliament in The Hague, stating that 'the population of the colony...will never voice the desire for Curaçao to be separated from the Netherlands'. One of the signatories, A. Jesurun, explained:

> ...we are Dutch, Dutch by descent, by upbringing, emotionally, and as such the residents of this colony are attached to the Netherlands. Why then wrench loose and break these ties which join the colony to the mother country?[5]

When, in 1879, the subject of selling the colony arose again, A.M. Chumaceiro published another strongly worded indictment against any attempt by the Netherlands to dispose of the Antilles in the brochure *Is Curaçao te koop?* ('Is Curaçao for sale?').[6] This attitude was to continue to set the tone. 'Doctoor' Da Costa Gomez, one of the founders of the modern relations of the Kingdom as laid down in the Charter (*Statuut*) of 1954, described the Caribbean colonies' relation to the Netherlands as a relation within one single nation. This was not the case with the Dutch East Indies, which meant that the development also had to take a different course: 'A development within the state of the colonies of Suriname and Curaçao [sic] into a single entity with the motherland and a development of the colonies and possessions of the State in Asia into a separate state within international law.'[7] In many respects this vision, including the emphasis on belonging to a single, historically evolved cultural community, has been repeated ever since. One of the arguments with which Jaggernath Lachmon, leader of the Hindustani population in Suriname, resisted independence – that Creole 'thing' – to the last possible moment, was that he was fundamentally *Dutch*.[8] In the 1990s, Antilleans and Arubans in their successful attempt to sweep the subject of independence from the negotiation table, reminded their counterparts of the 'Orange sentiment' and the consciousness of a shared destiny with the Netherlands, which was said to be very much alive on the islands.

Meddlesome or absent colonialism?

In this context the colonial elite really had no alternative but to remain within the existing colonial structures and to try in some way to influence the policies that were set in the Netherlands. From the beginning this approach managed to book a few successes, including the postponement of Emancipation until 1863, the enforcement of a considerable compensation claim from dispossessed slave owners, and the establishment of the Government Inspectorate (*Staatstoezicht*) in Suriname.[9] In other respects, however, the colonial elites achieved far less than they intended, starting with the fact that they always received less financial support from the Netherlands than they asked for.

Meanwhile history was taking a slightly different course in each of the colonies. On Curaçao the arrival of Shell in particular confronted the local, predominantly white elite with a frustrating increase in the number of Dutch people who took up key positions in the society. The local elite consequently experienced a relative decline in living standards and prestige, which was made all the more painful by the refusal of the colonial power to award them a dominant position in the colonial government. In Suriname, the constant decline of the plantation sector, and the exodus of the Dutch elite that accompanied it, led to gains in social status for the local Creole elite. But as this elite began with increasing self-confidence to present itself as the representative of the local population, to its chagrin it found itself confronted with a colonial power which was barely willing to accept this claim and which increasingly and emphatically began to highlight the interests of other groups, particularly the later arrivals, the Asian migrants. This pattern changed very slowly, even after the official end of colonialism. Contemporary Dutch criticism of social issues such as poverty among the lower classes in Dutch Caribbean societies to this day generates resentment among the local elites, because of what they consider to be a lack of understanding of local circumstances.

Another, apparently contradictory recurring feature in Caribbean criticism of Dutch colonialism is its resentment of what was and still is experienced as Dutch carelessness and negligence. A direct line runs from the colonial elite accusing 'Patria' of providing insufficient support for the slave trade and too little military backup to crush the Maroons, through the negotiations around the 'Golden Handshake' which launched Surinamese independence, to more recent discussions about the level of financial support the Netherlands should provide St Martin to overcome the devastation of a series of hurricanes. The conviction underlying all these otherwise utterly heterogeneous episodes is that the mother country could and should provide more support than it does. Amidst the aforementioned consternation that arose in 1869 around the rumour that the Netherlands wanted to get rid of the Antilles, an angry Curaçaoan member of the Colonial Council suggested that his island had merely been 'a certain something' with which the Dutch were able to enrich themselves. The Netherlands had also allowed the opportunity to make more of the island to slip: 'I have come to believe that Curaçao in the hands of an Englishman or a Frenchman would be a jewel; in the hands of a Dutchman it is a piece of old iron.'[10]

Seldom has the accusation of the Netherlands' neglect of her Caribbean colonies been so incisively articulated as in the remarkable, 'Multatulian' epilogue to *Zuid-zuid-west* (1926), one of the first publications by Albert Helman, arguably the most important Surinamese author to date:

> And now, gentlemen, listen to the end!...I am sad, because I am born of a land I now see dying, drowning in a bottomless morass... And I dare say to you, pious merchants: the fault is yours. You took possession of this land – I will not say whether justly or unjustly, God alone knows the truth – why does it warrant your love no more, now you cannot speak of Dividends?... Without your love, without the love it is your duty to give – all colonial possession is the voluntary acceptance of a duty! – deliverance will never be possible. For centuries you have been thieves, they say – fairly. But be at least caring thieves, not scoundrels.[11]

This outrage over the Dutch lack of commitment to the Dutch Caribbean has been expressed time and again in various compositions. Usually these were accusations of centuries of exploitation, for which the Netherlands was expected to offer financial restitution. At times there were much more subtle appeals, such as the complaint that the Dutch have unjustly neglected responsibility for a shared cultural heritage.[12]

A final recurring issue has been the paradox of being simultaneously resentful of Dutch interference and aggrieved by Dutch negligence. The contrast is indeed only an apparent one, and to expect anything else would be highly naive. The slave owners of the early colonial period naturally wanted to receive as much financial support from Patria as possible, without, however, paying the price of direct interference in the ways they worked their slaves and kept them under their thumbs. And of course the 'postcolonial' leaders of the self-governing Caribbean would continue to insist upon maximum support with minimum interference from the Netherlands, which all too quickly was – and is – labelled as meddling. It is therefore also unsurprising that the recent history of the transatlantic Kingdom has become a series of skirmishes over the realms of donor and donee, and the borders of consultation, involvement and interference.

Frameworks for colonial policy

To the extent that this more intensive involvement developed at all, it occurred rather late in the day. In fact, if there is a single feature specific to Dutch colonialism in the Caribbean, it might well be this tardiness. Suriname and the other settlements in the Wild Coast were developed as plantation colonies, the Antilles as trading posts. This 'development' was primarily the work of independent entrepreneurs, both individuals and organizations. The most important Dutch organizations in the Caribbean were the West India Company (WIC) which de facto ruled the West Indian Islands and the Sociëteit van Suriname (Society of Suriname). What they shared was a relatively high degree of operational freedom in relation to the Netherlands and a narrow, predominantly managerial interpretation of their duties in the colonies. For the WIC and the Sociëteit, engagement in the colonies went little further than facilitating production and trade, maintaining order, and providing protection against foreign powers and pirates. Neither organization managed to fulfil these roles convincingly. For both the Sociëteit and the WIC, the narrow interpretation of their duties implied an almost complete lack of interest in the colonial subjects, at least insofar as this meant going beyond the realms of power and labour.

The proclamation of the Kingdom of the Netherlands following the Napoleonic wars rang in a new phase in colonial history. Perhaps for the first time since the days of Willem Usselinx, the ideal of an active and relatively comprehensive policy for 'the West' once again gained some currency in the Netherlands. King Willem I himself was a stimulus behind this. The King commissioned Johannes van den Bosch to write a report, not only on the East Indies, of which he had many years' experience, but also on the Caribbean. To this end Van den Bosch, who later would become Governor General of the East Indies, sailed to Suriname in 1828, but did not call in on the islands of the Antilles. In this respect he falls perfectly in line with the still ever-expanding collection of experts who, on the basis of limited observation, believe they are in a position to propose sweeping measures for the Dutch Caribbean.

Back in the Netherlands, he presented his king with a thick report on the state of the colonies and the possibility of taking them in new directions. His proposals for the Caribbean colonies covered many fields, from administrative and economic, to more social affairs. One of

Van den Bosch's administrative measures were adopted, and were as drastic as it was ill-fated: in 1828 the various Dutch colonies in the Caribbean were united under a single overseas territory, with Paramaribo as its administrative centre. A century later such a move would probably never have left the drawing board; had this consolidation been realized, it is likely it would have been effectively undermined by the colonial elite. However, around 1830 all this was still inconceivable. It was therefore through a process of trial and error that it became apparent that the different Caribbean territories had too little in common for them to be efficiently governed from a single centre – even if this was the largest and economically most important colony, it was utterly eccentrically located. The 'West Indies' would remain a term that only held any meaning at all when viewed from the Netherlands.

Van den Bosch's proposals for other areas were more felicitous. His recommendations in the social sphere included improvements to the treatment of slaves, converting them to Christianity and otherwise 'civilizing' them – recommendations which clearly served a purpose within the economics development model he had in mind, but nonetheless in which all colonial subjects were finally viewed as people rather than as objects. In several respects, however, it was already too late to turn the Caribbean colonies into little extensions of the Netherlands overseas. Even if the mother country had been open to the idea of recognizing the predominantly black subjects of the Caribbean as compatriots in foreign places, it would still have been irrelevant. The linguistic situation was fundamentally different. The Sranan Tongo and the other languages of Suriname, the Papiamentu of the Leeward Islands and the English of the Windward Islands had already taken root in local culture. Regardless of all attempts the Dutch have since made, the 'Dutch' Caribbean and the Netherlands still do not belong to a single, undivided linguistic community.

What applied to language also followed for religion and culture in a broader sense. Even a superficial observation of the cultural development of the surrounding Caribbean countries teaches us that the limited presence of Dutch culture is not that exceptional. There is little in the Caribbean that directly reflects the Old World. Insofar as the Caribbean can be regarded as a single cultural sphere, shared cultural features constantly reference the plantations of the New World in which Africa, Asia and Europe all contributed to creolization, to the development of new cultural forms in the entirely new cultural context of the Caribbean plantation colony. However, no other colonial power seems to have begun so late, or to have been so irresolute and unsuccessful as the Dutch in imposing their own culture as the norm on their colonies. The irony is that it has only been in the last few decades that 'Dutchification' has truly taken off – however incompletely and in some respects more to the horror than the joy of a mother country which would have pre-ferred to say farewell to its colonial subjects as if they were just distant relatives.

Despite these very real reservations it must be concluded that the accession of King Willem I and his advisor Van den Bosch brought the first attempt to formulate some form of structured government policy for the Caribbean. With the further institutionalization and moderniza-tion of the Kingdom of the Netherlands, colonial policy too was, step by step, set in an organizational framework. In 1834, a separate Ministry for the Colonies was established. Until the demise of the Netherlands East Indies, the West Indian territories attracted relatively little bureau-cratic attention. Since then, policy for Suriname and the Antilles has graduated somewhat as an issue for political debate, perhaps out of pro-portion with their real significance to the metropolis. Institutionally, West Indian affairs were housed in many different places in the govern-ment bureaucracy. Today, of course, the relations with Suriname pertain to the Foreign Office, even if the country still holds some kind of spe-cial position in The Hague. Symbolically, the policy for the Netherlands Antilles and Aruba was relocated to the Ministry of the Interior in 1998, politely renamed 'Ministry of the Interior and Kingdom Affairs' for the occasion.

The route to the Charter

Until the Second World War, the very existence of colonialism was lit-tle disputed.[13] New solutions to tensions that had existed for centuries between the Netherlands authorities in the colonies and the local elites were constantly sought, leading in the first half of the twentieth century to the first hesitant steps towards a locally-elected 'parliament'. However, the limited number of people eligible to vote and the nomina-tion by the Dutch governor of a number of members, meant that only the local elite was represented in these councils. It was not until 1948 that universal suffrage was introduced in both the Antilles and Suriname.

The Second World War brought about a rupture in the development of colonial relations. The Netherlands and Indonesia were both occu-pied, and although the West Indian territories remained free from German or Japanese assault, they needed the protection of the Allied Forces, especially the United States. The foreign military presence served as a painful reminder of the impotence of the mother country. Administratively and militarily, even economically, the tables had turned. The Curaçaoan and Aruban oil refineries produced a significant amount of the fuel that was so vital for the Allied forces, while the Surinamese bauxite industry produced the raw materials for their aircraft. The 'West' therefore contributed in the most direct way possible to the liberation of the Netherlands – aside from the hundreds of Antilleans and Surinamese who fought alongside the Allied troops. At this time, the Surinamese and Antillean guilders also became linked to the American dollar – a significant symbolic step. The war accelerated the economic development of both countries and strengthened an optimistic self-confidence in the Caribbean territories.[14]

On 6 December 1942, Queen Wilhelmina of the Netherlands made a speech on Radio Oranje from London, which was to enter history as a milestone en route to decolonization. She spoke for the first time of domestic independence for the various territories, of a new future in which there would be more cooperation and instead of imposed Dutch rule, a collective solidarity would henceforth determine the new relations within the Kingdom. Although this was not a whole-hearted recognition of the colonies' right to independence, the Queen did speak of the conviction 'that no political unity and alliance can continue to exist, which is not founded on the voluntary acceptance and loyalty of the vast majority of citizens'.[15]

Extensive discussions had taken place within the cabinet-in-exile in London and between the cabinet and the Queen prior to the delivery of this speech. The speech was in the first instance aimed at improving the Dutch image in the United States, and secondly as a cautious concession towards the Indonesian nationalists. But these concessions were not really made *con amore*. Eventually the speech was to have no real significance for Indonesia. For some time nationalists there had been thinking in terms of independence and by 1940 the will to fully break loose from Dutch rule dominated their thinking. For the Indonesians the speech came too late and offered too little. Moreover, the post-war Dutch armed intervention in Indonesia confirmed the American suspicion that the Netherlands did not know how to take its leave of colonialism.

Wilhelmina's speech has been characterized by Cees Fasseur as marking the end of an era, not as the beginning of a new chapter.[16] This may well be correct for Indonesia, but not for the West Indian colonies – not taken into account in Fasseur's analysis – which faithfully followed the priority Queen and cabinet made of the East Indies and the Dutch role there. For the Dutch Caribbean, the speech *can* be regarded as marking a new beginning. In 1949 the Netherlands found itself forced to recognize that its role as the colonial power in Indonesia was at an end. It was compelled to shift its attention towards the Caribbean. Hence Juda, the *Vereniging van Surinamers*, Jesurun,

Chumaceiro, Da Costa Gomez and all the others were proven right. The East Indies had never become Dutch and now simply resumed its own course, whereas the destiny of the West Indies seemed precisely to be further integration into the Kingdom of the Netherlands.

The transfer of sovereignty to the Republic of Indonesia was signed in 1949. The Charter for the Kingdom of the Netherlands designating Suriname and the Netherlands Antilles as autonomous countries within the Kingdom was proclaimed in 1954. In the intervening five years the transatlantic Kingdom developed into the form it still has today, although Suriname has since seceded and Aruba has acquired the status of a country within the Kingdom. The route to the Charter passed through two relatively uneventful Roundtable Conferences (in 1948 and 1952–54) and a number of measures which prepared the way for autonomy for the former overseas territories. For the first time the Antilles and Suriname could and had to appoint delegations to represent the interests of their countries to the mother country. For the first time the Netherlands had to regard and treat the former colonies in the West as equals, at least formally. In retrospect this process went relatively smoothly.

The chosen representatives of the peoples of Suriname and the Antilles eagerly accepted the final result of the negotiations and the Surinamese parliament even forewent debate 'for the sake of the beauty of the moment of acceptance'; only a small minority of Surinamese nationalists protested. In the Netherlands too the Charter was met with overwhelming assent. Following the fiasco of Indonesia, an amicable decolonization, arranged through collective discussion, was greatly appreciated. And unlike in the East Indies, there was not a lot to lose in the 'West' in the transfer of power ratified in the Charter. With the support of the Antilles and Suriname, the Netherlands immediately set about getting the former colonies removed from the United Nations list of former Western territories that still needed to be decolonized. This obstacle was removed in 1955.

The Charter – still the highest statutory regulation in the Kingdom of the Netherlands, above the Constitution – is a remarkable document. In brief, the Charter defines the Kingdom as consisting of three partners who autonomously set their own domestic policies. Only foreign affairs, defence and Dutch nationality (art. 3), and 'the guarantee of fundamental human rights and freedoms, the rule of law and good governance' (art. 43) are described as overarching responsibilities; the Charter allocates these tasks to the Government of the Kingdom of the Netherlands. A wonderful, but far from watertight construction. In fact the Charter rests upon a remarkable fiction, namely, the fiction of the complete equality of the *de facto* clearly unequal partners in the Kingdom. Its 1954 Preamble reads:

> The Netherlands, Suriname and the Netherlands Antilles, after joint deliberations and having freely declared their willingness to adopt a new system of law in the Kingdom of the Netherlands in which they will *independently* represent their own interests, and will on *an equal footing* take care of the general good and offer each other *reciprocal support*, have decided to lay down the Charter of the Netherlands in the following.[17]

The Charter: pit stop or finish?

In terms of scale, population size, wealth and level of development, in 1954 there was no realistic possibility of the two Caribbean partners protecting the mutual interests of the Kingdom on a truly equal footing with the former colonizer. Even less realistic was the idea that they would provide support to the Netherlands. Fifty years later, this possibility is even more remote. The formulations put forward in the Preamble suggest an equilibrium in power relations and a reciprocity which could and can only be fictitious. The legislator of the Charter seems to have been emphatically led by the spirit of earlier constructions conceived of to keep Indonesia within a Union with the Netherlands. In financial respects the 'reciprocal help and support' has remained a one-way affair. Although it is true that each of the partners was indeed autonomous in its own administration, Suriname, prior to 1975, and the Antilles and Aruba have constantly needed to appeal to the Netherlands government for assistance, or to Dutch experts who have significantly influenced affairs there while working in the service of the islands.[18]

Although the Charter refers to securing shared interests on an 'equal footing', it does not offer this possibility in any formal way. Even today the Kingdom's affairs are represented *de facto* by the Dutch government, supplemented by a Minister Plenipotentiary for each of the two overseas partners; who are thus formally full members of the Dutch Cabinet. However, in practice the cabinets in the Caribbean represented by these ministers have barely any power to reject proposals put forward by the Cabinet of the Kingdom in the Netherlands. Moreover, this Cabinet of the Kingdom is not accountable to a Parliament of the Kingdom – the latter does not exist, or rather, it is the Dutch Parliament that functions as such. This construction, largely based on a faith in mutual understanding and the expectation that differences of opinion would remain limited, worked well as long as relations within Kingdom ran smoothly. As soon as tensions emerged, from the Dutch point of view it became more attractive for the Charter to be terminated by the withdrawal of the Caribbean regions from the Kingdom. In this context, reviewing the statutory regulations was not a priority. However, although it has now been decided that the Kingdom, consisting of the Netherlands, the Antilles, and Aruba shall remain transatlantic indefinitely, increasingly blatant differences of opinion have emerged surrounding good governance and how it is monitored. Consequently, the Charter has inevitably come more under discussion. The phrase 'modernizing the Charter' is quite often used in this context as a mere euphemism for a *de facto* break with the fictional equality spoken of in the 1954 Charter.

Initially the Charter worked more or less smoothly. Those who were involved with it in the 1950s and 1960s gladly refer to the excellent bilateral and tripartite relations at the time. The Dutch in the field felt they had helped to build up Suriname and the Antilles; the first long-term development plans were formulated; the expansion of the education system strengthened the 'Dutch' character of the Caribbean territories; and the Cold War created a context in which the few, mainly Surinamese nationalists, who demanded full independence instead of autonomy, rapidly came to be viewed with suspicion. However, what predominated was indeed a sense of solidarity, at least between the elites, on both sides of the ocean. During a visit to Suriname in 1960, V.S. Naipaul – certainly no fan of radicalism – found himself to a certain extent able to sympathize with Surinamese nationalism, but found their struggle tragic rather than heroic:

> With no inflammatory political issues, no acute racial problem, and with the Dutch Government contributing two-thirds of the money (one-third gift, one-third loan) for the development of the country, nationalism would seem an unlikely and perverse growth. But a nationalism has arisen which is unsettling the established order, proving that the objection to colonialism is not only economic or political or, as many believe, simply racial. Colonialism distorts the identity of the subject people, and the Negro in particular is bewildered and irritable. Racial equality and assimilation are attractive but only underline the loss, since to accept assimilation is a way to accept a permanent inferiority. Nationalism in Suriname, feeding on no racial or economic resentments, is the profoundest anti-colonial movement in

the West Indies. It is an idealist movement, and a rather sad one, for it shows how imprisoning for the West Indian his colonial culture is.[19]

Less than ten years later the genie left the bottle, but not in Suriname, yet. On 30 May 1969, Willemstad, Curaçao, burst into flames.[20] A labour dispute ran out of control and led to strikes, a march on the city centre, and looting and burning. Referring to the obligation to stand by each other, the Antillean Governor appealed to the Netherlands for military intervention. The Hague made troops available: first the navy, which was stationed locally, followed by army troops flown in from the Netherlands. In a short time, order was re-established in Willemstad.

A couple of years of smouldering resentment against the established order had preceded this outburst. Even so, 'May 1969' or, in Papiamentu, *'trinta di mei'* came unexpectedly. Antillean society was harshly reminded of the broad divide separating the elite and working classes, a gulf that was as much socio-economic as it was racial and cultural. The Netherlands was equally confronted with the raw facts. The riots were the consequence of conflicts within Curaçaoan society, conflicts which were by no means resolved and on which the Netherlands had or could have little influence: the Antilles were, after all, autonomous in terms of domestic policy. But because things had gone wrong, the Netherlands, following the Charter, had been obliged to intervene. Another military intervention could not be ruled out. This was not a happy prospect. Greatly overestimating the interest in either the Netherlands or the Dutch Caribbean, the Dutch now worried that international public opinion would once again condemn them as it had in the days of interventions in Indonesia.

In the years that followed, things continued to be turbulent from time to time in both Suriname and the Antilles. Meanwhile in the Netherlands a cautious cultural and political shake up was taking place. Among the currents of this domestic 'cultural revolution' was the need to set a new, 'progressive' course in foreign policy. It was widely felt that the Netherlands should become a model country when it came to North-South relations. The least appropriate thing, therefore, was the maintenance of the 'neocolonial' ties of the transatlantic Kingdom. Hence, the independence of the Antilles and Suriname became an important goal for the centre-left cabinet which assumed office in 1973 under of the social democrat Prime Minister Joop den Uyl. When, at the beginning of 1974, the new Surinamese cabinet of Henck Arron quite unexpectedly announced its intention to become independent in the short term, the Dutch enthusiastically agreed. The Netherlands Antilles in contrast made it very clear that they did not want to follow the

Surinamese example – 'as yet'. The Netherlands believed it would suffice to allow the islands a little respite, en route to an inevitable succession from the Kingdom; this illusion was only dropped by 1990.

Before examining the divergent ways in which the decolonization of Suriname and the Antilles took place, I must first address the question of what motivated Dutch policy post-May 1969 regarding the transfer of sovereignty to Suriname in 1975 and in the run up to 1990. What reasons did the Netherlands have for jettisoning the Caribbean territories? The motives are neither surprising, nor noble. Money, migration, the responsibility to intervene when things went wrong, while lacking the instruments to influence events, were the key Dutch concerns surrounding the desired transfer of sovereignty. These were followed – at a distance – by concern about the Netherlands' reputation. As far as finance was concerned, 'the West' had hardly ever lived up to the expectations of classic colonialism, with the colony financing its metropolis. By the twentieth century, the illusion that the mother country would ever profit from its West Indian territories had been buried along with all the other shameful expectations. The steady increase in development aid to Suriname and the Antilles during the period of the Charter had produced positive effects on living standards, but had not led to noticeable developments in terms of economic viability and self-sufficiency, nor had it led to a reduction in the differences in income between the various parts of the Kingdom. In short, the West Indian extension to the Kingdom was relatively expensive to sustain and it was clear that this would not change in the future.

In the meantime, partly as a consequence of the Dutch-styled education system, the Netherlands became an increasingly fixed frame of reference in Suriname and the Antilles, also with regard to living standards. Increasing numbers of Antilleans and Surinamese emigrated to the Netherlands, not so much because they were worse off than other people living in the Caribbean or Latin American – quite the opposite – but because their living conditions contrasted starkly with how they imagined life to be in *their* 'paradise overseas', the Netherlands. The Surinamese exodus, the first to gather momentum, was given added impetus by the threat of '1975' which provoked a last-minute exodus involving almost one-third of the population. In Dutch society too this exodus was met with some alarm, and it is obvious that Dutch politicians, while not really wanting to say so in public, felt Antillean independence to be advisable in part to prevent a second exodus.

The Netherlands' responsibility for good governance in the Kingdom, as laid down in the Charter, came to be experienced as increasingly problematic. How can the metropolis define its policies when it feels that the territories overseas lack good governance and at the same times knows that, according to the Charter, local autonomy has to be respected as much as possible – and will, incidentally, in any event be strongly defended overseas? The Charter had granted the three partners in the Kingdom a high degree of autonomy in relation to domestic policy. May 1969 confronted the Netherlands with the narrow limits of its power to influence the workings of local government and with the obligation to take on the thankless task of intervening to avert or control escalation. Such interventions became increasingly unpopular within the Kingdom. There was the additional risk of damaging the Netherlands' international reputation. Front-page news in the international press around 30 May 1969, with photographs of military patrols on the streets of Willemstad, undermined the progressive image the Netherlands liked to present of itself. This was yet another consideration that strengthened the Dutch politicians' desire to relinquish 'the last remains of the tropical Netherlands'.[21] Understandably many Dutch politicians worried about more *trinta de mei's*, the inevitability of further military intervention, and new portrayals of the Dutch as a colonial power.

Ironically, a quarter of a century later it was confirmed that *refraining* from intervening in overseas government could also cast the Netherlands in a negative light. In the 1960s and 1970s this turn in history was perhaps only a theoretical option. Not so today. Why, asked the Americans, the British and the French at the beginning of the 1990s, did the Dutch not intervene more radically against the international criminal organizations that were becoming entrenched in the 'Dutch' Caribbean? The Dutch appeal to the Charter with its outline of autonomy for the Caribbean countries of the Kingdom was considered escapist. The Netherlands with its renewed reputation as a serious player in the Caribbean could not ignore international pressure to exercise its authority. This was not an enviable task for a medium-sized European power with little serious interest in remaining a Caribbean power. But then again, in the 1990s the alternative course of action – of granting the Antilles and Aruba independence – was out of the question.

Money, migration and a responsibility that was difficult to live up to, were the 'hard' motives behind the Netherlands' preference for evacuating the Dutch Caribbean. However, Dutch politicians preferred to defend their insistence on early independence by referring to more noble motives and to 'the wheel of history' which now had no alternative but to turn irreversibly through independence for all former colonies. While other voices were becoming ever louder, both in the Netherlands and abroad, this mantra continued to be repeated for a long time. In the end it was not so much the wheel of history that turned events, but the wheel of politics, the momentum of which led to many years elapsing before the illusion could finally be discarded that decolonization always ends in political independence.

In the meantime, particularly after 1975, arguments against independence were expressed with increasing vigour both in the Antilles and, eventually, in The Hague. On the islands, free admission to and right of abode in the Netherlands, together with the certainty of belonging to a prosperous and stable Kingdom were, and are perceived as crucial and decisive advantages of non-sovereignty. Today more than ever before, migration to the Netherlands and the emergence of transnational communities has reinforced the sense of connectedness. The option of independence has almost no support on any of the islands, while The Hague acknowledges that it cannot enforce independence. The real question is therefore: *If* the Charter does not work satisfactorily, would it not be possible to improve it without souring the bonds of the Kingdom?

Suriname: a frustrated showcase of decolonisation

Before turning to this question, it is useful to analyse the post-independence history of Suriname. The Republic became independent almost thirty years ago.[22] Sadly, sovereignty has brought few of the benefits promised by its supporters, and has exceeded many of the gloomy predictions made by its opponents. This is made all the more bitter in view of later developments within the transatlantic Kingdom. The fiasco surrounding the Republic of Suriname contributed significantly to the revision of Dutch decolonization policy regarding the Netherlands Antilles and Aruba. A transfer of sovereignty along the Surinamese model had previously been presumed inevitable. Around 1990 however, the Netherlands had openly accepted that its former colonies may also exercise their right to self-determination by choosing to maintain constitutional ties within the Kingdom. In this way the more cautious parts of the West Indies profited from Suriname's audacity. Note, however, that this 'profit' entailed a dramatic stepping up of Dutch interference in domestic issues.

The drama of the Republic of Suriname is measured against many criteria: the exodus, economic collapse, the decline of the constitutional state and the political dramas. Having begun with people voting against independence with their feet, emigration grew into a phenomenon of proportions as unexpected as it was undesired, even though lessons could have been learned from the history of the British West Indies. The number of inhabitants in Suriname today – legally, some 420,000 – has only grown by about 50,000 since 1970. Conversely, the size of the Surinamese population in the Netherlands – including the second and third generations – has increased from 30,000 to more than 320,000. Thus, since 1970, the Surinamese population has grown mainly on the European side of the Atlantic.[23]

This exodus was of course related to the Surinamese' fears of an uncertain future, and to the economic and political collapse; factors which not only augmented each other, but which were also exacerbated by the exodus. Living standards entered an unbridled decline, the excessively large state sector continued to crumble without being offset by sufficient growth in the private sector. Among the few sectors that continue to experience growth in the young republic, the 'grey' and 'black' markets turned out to be horribly present: drug trafficking, money laundering and illegal gold-digging. Generous remittances from the Surinamese community in the Netherlands have helped to offset the immediate consequences of the collapse of legal production. Even so, Suriname today has a much lower standard of living than in 1975. To make things worse, the income gap has increased, and there are ominous signs of growing divergence in income levels between the different ethnic groups, with the Afro-Surinamese increasingly lagging behind.[24]

We have to add to this the unfortunate political history of the Republic of Suriname. First there was paralysis and suffocating clientelist politics in the first five years after independence. Then, in 1980, there was a military coup followed by seven years of military regime under Desi Bouterse. Among the abuses perpetrated by this regime was the liquidation of political opponents in December 1982, which became known as the 'December murders'; civil war in the interior and the massive killings among the Maroons; the growth of drugs crime, condoned or even encapsulated by the state. Then came a hesitant return to democratic government, which all too soon relapsed into many of its pre-1980 shortcomings, followed by a short-lived return of Bouterse to the centre of power. Finally, in 1990, there was a return to democracy. Since then, democracy has continued to function more or less in the sense that elected parliaments and governments have alternated peacefully. Yet despite fulfilling this formal criterion, many feel that the Surinamese democracy is still characterized more by clientelism than by energy and purpose.[25]

It is therefore not surprising that among Surinamese, on both sides of the Atlantic, there has been heated discussion about the possibility of taking a few steps back, towards the constitutional status quo ante. In the early 1990s, supporters of such an about-turn argued for a referendum to be held on Suriname's relationship with the Netherlands, the aim of which was to position this 'regressive' standpoint at the heart of the debate on Suriname. In itself, this was not a new position. Had such a referendum been held in 1974 or 1975, a majority of the population would certainly have rejected independence. But no such referendum was held, not in Suriname and, incidentally, not in any of the other Caribbean countries which had become independent in the post-war period.[26]

In the Netherlands, initial satisfaction with the 'showcase' decolonization of Suriname – once described by the former Dutch Prime Minister Joop den Uyl as the greatest success of his term – made way for deep frustration and uncertainty. By 1990 Dutch policy-makers were also discussing the possibility of a (partial) return to pre-1975 relations. This swing was not that incredible. As long as the Surinamese continue to regard 'abroad' and the Netherlands as almost synonymous – which they traditionally have done more so than the Antilleans and Arubans – so Suriname will remain 'domestic' for the Netherlands. And this conclusion highlights the ever-present tension: however much all parties would like to, they seem incapable of breaking loose from one another.

The worse the situation in Suriname became, the more often it was said that the Dutch simply were incapable of achieving a sound decolonization. This assessment may well depart from the conclusion that the viability of the republic had been drastically overestimated. Certainly Suriname is a large country with a degree of economic potential, but it is also a country that lacks many of the factors needed to truly exploit it, particularly in terms of human capital and institutional solidity. This is not helped by the way the society is structured. The deep ethnic divisions continue to be translated into political structures. The fact that independence itself was widely identified as a 'Creole thing' was only the ominous beginning. Instead of accelerating the process of nation building, independence brought about ethnic polarization and disillusion. The overnight proclamation of a speedy independence in February 1974 provoked panic and an exodus, which not only reinforced existing ethnic tensions and a lack of belief in their own ability, it also robbed Suriname of its most highly-educated classes who were essential to its post-independence development.[27]

Could it have happened any other way? Much has been said in retrospect which unduly disregards the conditions at the time. After May 1969, the Netherlands indeed increased its pressure on Suriname to speedily accept the 'gift' of independence. Financial cost, responsibility with little authority, the stigma of colonialism, and the gradually increasing flow of migration: for the Netherlands the transatlantic Kingdom had become an oppressive burden. It is therefore not surprising that the Den Uyl cabinet reacted with enthusiasm to the unexpected embrace of a speedy full decolonization by Prime Minister Arron's predominantly Afro-Surinamese cabinet. This cabinet had been legally elected, albeit it not with independence as a major issue at the elections. Independence was indeed finally approved of by a majority in the Surinamese parliament, though by the smallest possible majority and, according to many, a 'fixed' one. Could the Netherlands have refused to work with the democratically elected Arron cabinet? A more blatant example of neo-colonial behaviour is hard to imagine and under the conditions of the time would have led to a huge uproar, riots and worse. And so the Netherlands limited itself to relatively modest and powerless negotiations over the conditions for a smooth transfer of sovereignty. Thus a 'golden handshake' was negotiated of 3.5 billion guilders – about 10,000 guilders per capita; adjusted for inflation, around 10,000 euros today –, more than three times the initial Dutch offer. Yet The Hague was not really concerned about the money, which was peanuts from Dutch perspective, even if it was unprecedented in the international history of decolonization. The real concern of the Dutch gradually shifted to the exodus from Suriname and its implications for both countries. The minutes of discussions in the Den Uyl cabinet attest to a remarkably humane approach rather than a xenophobic one, but this made the cabinet no less impotent. In retrospect all that can be established is that although the exodus generated some problems in the Netherlands, these do not compare with the tragic effects it had on Suriname.

Many Surinamese experienced the years 1973–1975 as yet another fatal phase in their country's history. However, the decision was taken and there is very little chance of Suriname ever returning to the Kingdom. Admittedly, this was briefly considered by both sides in the early 1990s, but it is increasingly unlikely that these ideas will ever materialize. Yet for most of the past three decades, neither country has been able to break loose from the idea that the bilateral relations are and continue to be vital for the well-being of Suriname. For many Surinamese, and certainly for politicians addressing their own rank and file, this view continues to be linked to the presumption that the Netherlands still has major economic interests in Suriname. That this notion is patently incorrect does little to detract from people's belief in it. The broadly held conviction in Suriname, that the Netherlands has a secret agenda, has its counterpart in the equally illusory notion that if only the differences of opinion at the level of the two governments could be overcome, the Netherlands would simply be able to develop Suriname through massive infusions of financial aid.

Within this sensitive postcolonial context, the Netherlands has lately been struggling to formulate a policy that is not paternalistic, but which is more consistent and businesslike than was often the case in the past. Dutch policy on Suriname continues to face a dilemma. On the one hand Suriname has gradually come to figure as a schoolbook example of a failed development relationship in which the expectations placed on the donee's abilities were set too high and the donor was too inconsistent in the demands it set. With the change of the guard in The Hague, the Dutch Government's engagement with Suriname, which in the past was taken for granted, is bound to decline. On the other hand it is barely conceivable that the Netherlands will truly turn her back on her former colony in the near future, if only because of the increasing political clout of the Surinamese community in the metropolis. The Hague has thus moved not towards a farewell, but rather towards a policy directed at channelling future Dutch aid through international organizations. The Hague's hope is that this will liberate both countries from their suffocating liaison and at the same time improve the quality of aid management. It is not really surprising that this proposal has so far run aground on Surinamese opposition. Despite all the rhetoric surrounding Caribbean integration, most Surinamese politicians take the view that a continuation of intensive bilateral relations offers the best guarantee of keeping the Netherlands stuck in the postcolonial twilight zone that appears to be so advantageous for Suriname.

Thus, although in bad shape and powerless, Suriname will remain sovereign for the time being. Unless, as the late Surinamese intellectual Albert Helman once predicted, Brazil decides to valorize its dormant claims on the country by physically appropriating it.[28] The more the republic seems to deteriorate into a failed state, and the more The Netherlands sees fit to withdraw from its former colony, the more likely this end result becomes. In the short run it will be the policy pursued by Suriname itself that will dictate, if not the course, at least the timing of decolonization and subordinate regionalization of the country. Paramaribo is now aiming at regional integration through CARICOM which is dominated by the Commonwealth Caribbean. Geopolitical realities, supported by the spectacular growth of a Brazilian community within Suriname may well work towards a scenario of subordinate regionalization, ultimately under Brazilian flag.

Perhaps this scenario is still too far-fetched; perhaps it is menacing; perhaps it will in the very long run be not only an inevitable, but even a fortunate outcome. But we do not need to consider this at the moment. The Surinamese and Dutch bilateral agenda for the next decade or so will most likely be dictated by the dilemmas of the past. The experiences of the last few decades unfortunately suggest that it will be a long time before both countries will be able to cast off the deadweight of their colonial past and to deal with each other in an atmosphere of friendly professionalism.

The Netherlands Antilles and Aruba: itching relations within the Kingdom

Unlike their Surinamese colleagues, Antillean politicians of all convictions have stubbornly refused the 'gift' of independence. Whereas the nationalist argument in favour of the Surinamese independence held that balanced economic growth had to be preceded by constitutional independence, on the islands the opposite has always been argued. And, as it turns out, with good reason. After all, in the last 'as yet not fully decolonized' parts of the Caribbean not only are living standards considerably higher, the working of a democratic order and the protection of fundamental civil rights are better guaranteed. Moreover, citizens in these dependent territories are free to take up residence in the metropolis, an option that is not available elsewhere. Independence comes at a high price. This realization only grew on the Antilles and Aruba through the post-independence history of their former partner in the Kingdom, Suriname. Consequently, independence continues to be an ever-receding horizon with very few on the Antilles or Aruba bearing any regrets.[29]

In the 1970s and 1980s the policies of successive Dutch governments were geared towards the six islands of the Antilles becoming independent as a single country. By around 1990 it became clear that this policy had run aground. The newly appointed minister for the Netherlands Antilles and Aruba, Ernst Hirsch Ballin, in his 'Outline for a Commonwealth Constitution' (*Schets van een Gemenebestconstitutie*) wrote that his government was now willing to take independence off the political agenda for the foreseeable future, and that the division of the former Antilles-of-six into two or three countries was unavoidable.[30] With this, something that had long been evident finally became formal policy: the impossibility of further dismantling the Kingdom and of keeping the Antilles together as a single country. It appeared as if the Caribbean countries of the Kingdom had won on all fronts.

One premise of Dutch decolonization policy had always been that by assuming full sovereignty, the Netherlands Antilles and Suriname would finally 'find their real place', hence not in Europe, but in their own region. By definition, decolonization had to follow the classic pattern of colonization: the wheel of history continued to turn and was not to be stopped, let alone turned back. In addition, the Dutch regarded decolonization and the acceptance of full political independence as largely the same thing. This resulted in the paradoxical view that self-determination *should* culminate in the *voluntary* choice for political independence.

On the Netherlands Antilles, politicians either definitively rejected independence, or simply paid it lip service, depending on their ideological orientation. Opinion polls showed unequivocally that the majority of the Antillean population was firmly opposed to independence. The Hague politicians, too, had gradually come to retrace their steps – remarkably, beginning with the Dutch social democrats who had previously been the most fervent advocates of 'full decolonization'.[31] This U-turn became official Dutch policy following the publication of Hirsch Ballin's 'Outline'. The spectre of an imposed independence was swept away, and there is little reason to assume that this will change in the foreseeable future.

If Hirsch Ballin believed at the time that he had succeeded in cutting the Gordian knot, he was deceived. The Dutch U-turn on independence was interpreted by many on the islands simply as proof that they had been in the right from the start. After all, the Antillean position was that self-determination implied the right to chose to continue the ties of the Kingdom. So, what the Dutch regarded as a concession was taken for granted overseas. From the Antillean perspective the real negotiations could now be opened which, first and foremost, would have to address the political and economic restructuring of the Antilles, and the 'modernization' of the re-ratified ties of the Kingdom.

At the time the fragmentation of the Antilles seemed to be the least thorny of the issues. Since the 1930s Aruba had voiced a strong desire to break loose from the rest of the Antilles, especially from Curaçao. The Netherlands had consistently opposed this, precisely with a view to granting the Antilles independence as a single state of six islands. Thus the reasoning was that Aruba or any other island that did not want to remain within the group-of-six would have to pay for this by leaving the Kingdom. However, centrifugal tensions reached a climax in the early 1980s and the Netherlands acquiesced to the Aruban separatist leader, Betico Croes, in 1983. But The Hague did impose one condition: the acquisition of an independent position on 1 January 1986 would have to be followed by the acceptance of full independence ten years later. On Aruba '1996' was viewed as a dictate that was only accepted with much foot dragging in order to secure the fiercely desired separate status within the Kingdom. Predictably, in 1986 Aruba immediately began a new offensive, this time to remove the subject of independence from the agenda.

The withdrawal of this imminent sanction by the Netherlands at the beginning of the 1990s also undermined the viability of the remaining entity, the Antilles-of-five. Hirsch Ballin's 'Outline' had accepted the division of the islands into three countries within the Kingdom – Aruba; Curaçao and Bonaire; and the Windward Islands. But then the political classes of St Martin and Curaçao let it be known that they too aspired to separate status, citing the now privileged Aruba as a precedent. Bonaire, St Eustatius and Saba in turn all intimated that they would prefer to have direct ties with the Netherlands, if a continuation of the group-of-five Antilles turned out to be unattainable.

A definitive fragmentation of the Antilles now seemed inevitable and negotiations to this end with The Hague were indeed begun. However, a round of referendums in 1993 and 1994 brought a surprising turn of events. In defiance of their own politicians, the vast majority of the populations on the five islands voted in favour of the continued existence of the Antilles-of-five.[32] The general election that followed confirmed this decision, but also and especially confirmed that this voting behaviour had primarily been a protest against the sitting politicians. A cabinet under Miguel Pourier set out with the promise of making a new start; restoring Antillean unity was part of this policy. Yet in spite of all good intentions, a decade on one can only conclude that the fervour has died down again and that the further fragmentation of the Antilles is once again looming. It is likely that Dutch policy will consist of a package of concessions to centrifugal tendencies, coupled with more direct administrative relations with the individual islands as the price to pay. This will certainly downgrade the present autonomy they enjoy under the construction of the Netherlands Antilles.

The reason The Hague is interested in more direct relations is obvious. In the 1990s the issue of good governance became more pressing than that of restructuring the five-island nation. Increasingly both Aruba and the Antilles were mentioned in one breath with international crime and failing, even corrupt government. With the relatively lavish development aid – presently over 500 euros per capita a year – and Dutch expertise as its trump cards, the Netherlands confronted the islands with the prospect of ever-increasing interference. From a Dutch perspective, once the subject of independence had been removed from the agenda, the need to put the West Indian houses in order grew correspondingly more urgent – partly because of the need to legitimize the new policy in the eyes of the Dutch public, but also to improve the Netherlands' reputation with the United States and other players in the region.

Thus the Charter which for decades had allowed for the broad autonomy of the Dutch Caribbean now – at least from a Dutch perspective – provided the legal framework for justifying precisely the opposite: intervention and thus the restriction of Antillean and Aruban autonomy. So far the real changes in the Kingdom's relationships have occurred at the level of increased supervision and intervention, not at a constitutional level. There are ample examples of this. In 1993 The Hague forced the central Antillean government to bring the allegedly corrupt administration of St Martin under direct rule, with firm Dutch supervision. Two years later, Aruba narrowly escaped the same procedure, but has since had to allow the implementation of procedures for more transparent government. The central government of the Antilles, faced with a disastrous economic position, was forced to allow not only Dutch, but also IMF supervision in the faltering process of financial and administrative restructuring. Several prominent politicians from Curaçao were recently arrested on corruption charges, and many feel that Dutch pressure played a role in this. There has therefore been a substantial increase in direct assistance to the overseas administrative machinery, and indirect interference in the workings of the judiciary and the maintenance of law and order. Short of constitutional reform, a process is already underway which some – mainly on the islands – criticize as 'recolonization'. Conversely, others – mainly, but certainly not exclusively in the Netherlands – applaud this as a justified and much needed step towards guaranteeing good governance overseas, an objective that was after all laid down in the 1954 Charter.

With independence seemingly not an option, the political situation in the Netherlands Antilles and Aruba is sometimes referred to as one of 'stagnated decolonization'. This interpretation, insofar as it is not already outdated, is at least less relevant to the problems the partners in the Kingdom find themselves confronted with. Stagnation presumes a temporary delay. In fact, amidst a great deal of disagreement, the three countries of the Kingdom at least concur in denouncing a policy geared towards decolonization in the sense of dismantling the transatlantic Kingdom. The Kingdom will no doubt continue to include the Caribbean partners, even if it remains unclear as to how many partners there will be in the end and within what kind of structure. The Netherlands will continue to leave a strong mark on the overseas administrations, more so than it has in the past. Exit decolonization, enter recolonization? This might be putting it too strongly. But certainly, with the agenda for the coming years determined by the search for a new equilibrium between Caribbean and Dutch visions and interests, in real life the centre of gravity is indeed shifting towards the Netherlands. Antillean and Aruban objections are not entirely unfounded. The question is how far this metropolitan reassertion can go.

The most extreme consequence of a Dutch 'return' would be the introduction of a model of rule of the overseas territories analogous to the French Caribbean *départements d'outre-mer*. There is no enthusiasm about that option among Antillean and Aruban politicians – small wonder, some may add cynically; this would not only mean an ideologically painful regression but equally a ruthless undermining of their own power base. But what about the islanders themselves who, particularly in Curaçao, have suffered tremendously from the prolonged economic and political crises since the late 1980s? About five years ago, a large-scale survey was held on all the islands to attain a better understanding of the opinions and expectations of Antilleans and Arubans regarding the present Kingdom and the role of the Netherlands vis-à-vis the islands.[33] Briefly, the survey first corroborated the belief that independence is not a serious option anywhere, with clear majorities everywhere opting for either the status quo or increased Dutch involvement with the islands. The reasons why Arubans and Antilleans prefer strong constitutional ties are evident: firstly, the Dutch passport and right of abode in the Netherlands, followed by the protection of human rights and liberties, and safeguards against external threats on the one hand, and for economic assistance on the other. Immaterial dimensions such as a sense of belonging to Dutch culture carry little weight.

If a clear majority of the islanders favours a continuation of the Kingdom – and substantial minorities on some islands, clear majorities on others would like to see more Dutch involvement – does this mean that they would applaud more direct interference and perhaps even a departmental status? Clearly this is not the case. There is much, perhaps even mainly pragmatism in the Caribbean appreciation of the Dutch presence. When asked whether they feel the Dutch understand and appreciate their local cultures, most tend to answer in the negative. The option of becoming a Dutch province is strongly rejected by clear majorities on five of the six islands.[34]

Constitutionally, the Kingdom has been deadlocked for some fifteen years now. The Charter stipulates than any change needs the approval of all three countries involved. In the past, this implied that no matter how hard The Hague pushed, the Dutch Caribbean countries had a right to flatly refuse to accept independence. Today, some Dutch politicians feel that the only viable alternative to full independence is departmental status. However, this would again require a change to the Charter and hence the approval of the Caribbean political classes, which have been adamant in their rejection of such a path of 'recolonization'. On the other hand, these politicians strongly favour a further dismantling of the Antilles-of-five, a proposition not popular in The Hague. A trade-off seems the most likely outcome, with the metropolis entertaining more intensive, direct relations with the different parts of what was once the six-islands Netherlands Antilles. This certainly would have something of a recolonizing flavour to it, oddly out of place perhaps in the twenty-first century. But then again, what today, and certainly yesterday seemed inconceivable, might well become reality tomorrow.

A Dutch model?

The balance of Dutch decolonization in the Caribbean is remarkable.[35] Suriname is independent, but, much to the reluctance of both parties, still closely tied to the Netherlands. The complete dismantling of the transatlantic Kingdom so desired by the Netherlands has run aground on Antillean refusal, and is now in a converse situation. Just as in Indonesia, the Netherlands has failed in the Caribbean to achieve the goals it once set itself.

In this chapter, almost no attention has been paid to the geopolitical context of Dutch decolonization policy. This is perhaps more defensible in the case of Suriname than for the Antilles, especially the Leeward Islands. In passing I noted the aspirations Brazil is thought to entertain in relation to Suriname, however, these have not played a substantial role to date, and were certainly not an issue around 1975. The same goes for countries like Venezuela or the United States: their policies have generally been based on a desire for stability in Suriname, without entertaining territorial aspirations themselves.

The situation has traditionally been different for the Leeward Antilles, which lie so close to the coast of *tierra firme*. Down the centuries, Spain and later Venezuela have frequently let it be known that they consider the three small islands off their coast to be part of their *patrimonio*. The time when Venezuela disputed the Dutch presence there and Antillean sovereignty now seems to be passed. The subject of neighbouring Venezuela plays no significant part in current discussions of the political relations within the Kingdom. However, in the background, some continue to take this factor seriously into account and precisely in this respect value the protection extended by the Dutch flag. After all, it is not entirely out of the question that some time in the future Venezuela will once more resort to earlier claims.[36]

To conclude, a few comparative remarks on the issue of decolonization discussed above. How did other colonial powers fare in the Caribbean? In around 1900, Spain was expelled from the stage by the United States. Puerto Rico remains a part of the United States, albeit in the anomalous construction of an 'associated state'. In addition Washington literally purchased the U.S. Virgin Islands from Denmark in 1917. Unlike the British and the Dutch, the Americans strongly value these Caribbean territories, mainly for strategic reasons, and have never attempted to give them up. In this respect, American policy is the same as that of the French who, in 1946, accorded their Caribbean possessions the status of overseas provinces, in all respects equal to those in France.

What the United States and France have had in common is the unequivocal authority of respectively Washington and Paris and the uncompromising demand for Caribbean loyalty to the metropolis. They have also shared a remarkable readiness to subsidize their Caribbean territories on a level unheard of not only in terms of development aid world-wide, but also in comparison to the Dutch and British aid to their own Caribbean territories.[37] French policy has been more successful than the Americans' in one respect: without suppressing French-Creole, metropolitan policy has succeeded in ensuring that the French language and culture have become dominant in the overseas provinces. In Puerto Rico, Spanish has remained the undisputed language of the vast majority of islanders, whatever efforts were made to propagate American English. Partly as a consequence of this, Puerto Ricans regard themselves to be at least as much *latinoamericano* as American, if not more.[38]

Post-war British policy was almost as unswerving, but very differently arranged. Britain strove for the complete independence of the British West Indies and for a withdrawal from the Caribbean. The first setback came with the collapse of the West Indian Federation, an association within which the British had hoped the former colonies would collectively accept independence. This did not prevent the British from helping each of them individually towards independence. A second setback was that a handful of small islands turned out not to be prepared to accept independence, a refusal which Britain finally came to accept by the 1990s. Unlike other colonial powers in the region, Britain has been extremely sparing with financial aid – no golden handshakes to smooth independence, and no lavish aid to those staying within the imperial fold. More than either the United States or France, Britain was absolutely clear about the level of autonomy on offer; this has remained very limited for the few islands that did not chose independence. English, with many local, Creole variations, is the undisputed language of the 'Commonwealth Caribbean'. However, in most respects West Indians even in the remaining British Overseas Territories now look more to the United States, a shift that suits the British very well.

How does Dutch decolonization policy compare to these models? In a certain respect it seems to have been the least successful. The Netherlands shared with Britain the goal of 'complete' decolonization, but was far less successful. Moreover, even the formally complete decolonization of Suriname did little to remove the country's one-way orientation towards the Netherlands. The golden handshake may be without parallel, but it failed to achieve the development targets that were hoped for. Meanwhile five decades of Antillean autonomy have clearly shown, at least from the Dutch point of view, the shortcomings of the instruments and results of the Charter. The divide between metropolis and West Indian islands is the more tangible because Dutch is still a foreign language on the Antilles, despite the Dutch-style education system and the exodus to the Netherlands.

However, a few remarks should be made to slightly redress the balance. First and foremost it is significant that the process of Dutch Caribbean decolonization may have been capricious and awkward, but it at least passed peacefully and for the large part harmoniously. It should also be established that although independent Suriname has been going through a profound crisis, from which it has so far not emerged, there is little reason to lay the 'blame' for this primarily on a failing Dutch policy or the 'exorbitant reparations' of 1975. Furthermore, it may also be argued that the pragmatic change of course with regard to the Netherlands Antilles and Aruba, and the wide-ranging support to the islands has borne fruit: despite their many problems these islands are still among the most prosperous and safe parts of the Caribbean region.

In a way, the very remark 'Netherlands was dealt a very unfortunate hand in its decolonization process' betrays a typically Dutch way of thinking and, consequently, a perspective gladly utilized by the elites in Suriname and the Antilles. France has been unabashedly imperious. Britain sent her colonies packing without a dowry to speak of; the standard of living in Britain's former colonies was and is low, and emigration levels are high, even though West Indians have not been welcome to settle in Britain since 1962. The United States has found that despite all its development plans for Puerto Rico, around 40% of Puerto Ricans choose to live on the mainland, particularly in and around New York, rather than on their island, while struggling with their ambivalence and resentment against that 'other side'. The problems of Dutch decolonization do not pale in this context. But the question arises as to whether the Dutch approach was ultimately really as uniquely laborious and unsuccessful as it might seem.

Dutch, Surinamese, Antilleans and Arubans alike have become accustomed to having high expectations of development plans, in which the large amount of aid given by the Netherlands to 'the West' is more or less taken for granted. This habituation has determined Dutch decolonization policy and Caribbean appeals to the Dutch sense of responsibility still have the desired effect, even if a more sceptic metropolitan approach is gaining ground. The former 'colonial subjects' and their champions have known all too well how to strike the right chord. Dutch politics is imbued with strong Calvinist leanings; the clergyman-politician feels this *is* a Dutch responsibility. Good intentions are then translated into excessively high expectations and ill-considered plans. Projects shatter. Then the Dutch merchant wakes up, complaining of 'money being thrown down the drain' on the other side of the ocean: 'there they cut long thongs of other men's leather', as one politician put it in 1869. More recently in the Dutch parliament, the metropolitan Deputy Minister charged with Antillean and Aruban Affairs was poked fun at for being an 'Assistant Santa Claus'.[39]

The clergyman listens and regains his morality, but now in a negative sense. Has that not always been the Dutch problem with 'the West'? There, and only there, the Netherlands is a 'super power'; there, and only there, do the Dutch truly hold sway, even if mainly through digging deep in her pockets. This does not make it easy to maintain a sense of proportion. Certainly, there has been slavery and infinite other colonial injustices. But how much point is there to being eager to repay a debt of honour for something that can never be put right in the first place? And perhaps it is not the present generations that should be compensated, if only because postcolonial, preferential treatment so quickly degenerates into misplaced condescension?

To a certain extent The Netherlands now shares a language with its former colonies in the Caribbean – ironically, mostly with independent Suriname, but to a certain degree also with the islands, at least those leeward. 'Linguistic community' is a big term, but nonetheless one that deserves to be taken more seriously that it has been over the last few decades, even if only because this exotic language isolates the Dutch Caribbean from its surroundings. This applies to the Antilles, but even more so to Suriname. It is this that creates obligations and, perhaps, possibilities.

Notes

1   See Van Doorn 1994:54, 153 and passim; Van den Doel 1998 on the Dutch decolonization of Indonesia. For a comprehensive study of Dutch decolonization in the West, see the three-volume study *Knellende Koninkrijksbanden* (Oostindie & Klinkers 2001). Our study *Decolonising the Caribbean* (Oostindie & Klinkers 2003) provides a succinct analysis of the same history and adds a comparative framework regarding both Dutch decolonization in Indonesia and the policies of France, the United Kingdom and the United States in the Caribbean.
2   See Chapter 2 and Oostindie 1995a, Siwpersad 1979.
3   Juda 1869:4.
4   Suriname 1872:19.
5   Quoted in Renkema 1970:3.
6   Chumaceiro 1879. See also Renkema 1970:1–2.
7   Da Costa Gomez 1935:64.
8   Dew 1978, Meel 1990b, Oostindie 1990:255.
9   Under the regulations of the State Supervision freed slaves had to work for ten years after Emancipation in paid work in the plantation sector. However, there were all kinds of exceptions to this regulation. In practice, the Government Inspectorate proved to be inadequate in binding former slaves to the plantations (Emmer 1993).
10 N. Rojer, quoted in Renkema 1970:4.

11   Helman 1976:111–2. Pseudonym of Lou Lichtveld (1903–1996).

12   See especially Ramdas 1994, 1996.

13   See Oostindie & Klinkers 2003, Chapters 4 and 5 for an outline of prewar Dutch colonialism and the decolonization process up to the proclamation of the Charter (1954).

14   See Van de Walle 1974 and 1975.

15   Quoted in Oostindie & Klinkers 2001, I:36.

16   Fasseur 1995:232–3.

17   Van Helsdingen 1957:189. My emphasis.

18   See Oostindie & Klinkers 2003, Chapter 6 on the 1954–1975 period, particularly the political process leading to the independence of Suriname.

19   Naipaul 1981:164–5.

20   See Verton 1977, Oostindie 1999a, Oostindie & Klinkers 2003, Chapter 6.

21   The phrase, commonplace in Dutch journalism on the Dutch Caribbean, is borrowed from the late Dutch novelist Willem Frederik Hermans (Hermans 1969).

22   See Buddingh 1995, Dew 1978 and 1994, Van Dijck 2001b, Fernandes Mendes 1989, Haakmat 1996, Hoefte & Meel 2001, Jansen van Galen 1995, Meel 1990a, 1993, Sedney 1997, Trommelen 2000.

23   See also Chapter 6.

24   Schalkwijk & De Bruijne 1997, Van Dijck 2001a and 2001b.

25   See also the Chapter 5.

26   Dew 1978:182, Oostindie & Klinkers 2003, Chapter 4.

27   See also Chapter 6.

28   Lou Lichtveld, a.k.a. Albert Helman, cited in *Vrij Nederland*, 4–9–1982.

29   Cf. also Chapter 6 in this book. Further: Domínguez, Pastor & Worrell 1993; Payne & Sutton 1993; Oostindie & Klinkers 2003, Chapter 11.

30   Hirsch Ballin 1990.

31   For an account of the discussions, see Hoefte & Oostindie 1991. For a more elaborate analysis of post-1975 Dutch policies, see Oostindie & Klinkers 2003, Chapter 7.

32   On Curaçao, 73.6% voted in favour of the option to remain within the Antilles-of-five, on St Martin 59.4%, on Bonaire 89.6%, on St Eustatius 90.6%, on Saba 86.3%

33   Representative sample of approximately N=2,500. Survey conducted late 1997 and early 1998. See Oostindie & Verton 1998a for the full version. A lengthy summary and discussion in English is provided in Oostindie & Verton 1998b. See also Oostindie & Klinkers 2003, Chapter 11.

34   Only St Eustatius opted in favour with 54.5%, as opposed to 40.4% against and 5.1% undecided.

35   For a more extensive weighing up of Dutch Caribbean decolonization policies and a discussion of the regional alternatives, see also Oostindie & Klinkers 2003, particularly Chapters 1–3 and 11.

36   See for example Hoetink 1995.

37   For calculations and quantitative comparisons on this issue, see Oostindie & Klinkers 2003, particularly Chapters 1–3 and 8.

38   See Oostindie & Klinkers 2003, particularly Chapters 1–3 and 10.

39   Quoted in Renkema 1970:5 (1869); *de Volkskrant*, 13–12–1996.

5 | Uphill nation building

The contemporary Caribbean differs in a myriad of ways from the region it was in the early 1960s, when a new phase of decolonization swept the region.[1] An increasing economic and political marginalization has negatively affected most of the region. Standards of living, the functioning of democracy, and guarantees of civil rights may still be relatively high in the Caribbean, especially if one were to take the so-called Third World as a frame of reference. However, in the Caribbean, the relevant comparison is not with the 'Mother Continents' of Africa or Asia, or with geographically and historically nearby Latin America, but rather with the old metropolitan centres in Europe and with the dominant new one, the United States.[2] From that perspective, the economic and political development of the last decades has been disappointing. The high hopes of decolonization that were once nurtured contrast sharply with the present sense of uncertainty and conservatism – sometimes bordering on despair – in the smaller countries of the region.

Caribbean decolonization obviously dates back way beyond the post-war period. In a sense, the Maroon communities established in most of the larger colonies during the early eighteenth century prefigured the establishment of independent states. Maroons in Suriname, once a Dutch colony whose authorities had found no other recourse than to pacify the Maroons by way of granting them autonomy, have indeed claimed that their independence dates back to these peace treaties of the 1760s rather than to 1975, when all of the country became a republic. The more conventional approach, however, dates the beginning of Caribbean decolonization to the slave revolution of Saint-Domingue, leading to the proclamation of the Republic of Haiti in 1804. The emergence of this second independent nation of the Americas – the first black state, and the first one to abolish slavery – triggered the hesitant Dominican secession from the Spanish state, started in the 1820s but only fully accomplished in 1865. The remnants of Spanish empire in the Americas dissolved at the turn of the century with the independence of Cuba and the renewed colonization of Puerto Rico, this time by the United States.

Formal decolonization in the region stagnated for the next six decades. After World War Two, the constitutional status of the French and the Dutch colonies as well as Puerto Rico was brought up to date in a liberalizing move which at the same time consolidated and even strengthened these territories' links to their metropolis. Yet around 1960, two major developments seemed to open up new perspectives for the region. The Cuban Revolution seemed finally to fulfil the promises of independence frustrated during the U.S.-dominated period of what would soon be termed the *pseudorrepública*. At the same time, the British West Indies embarked on a route to full decolonization which, after the collapse of the West Indian Federation, resulted in the individual independence of most territories between 1962 and 1983.

In the early 1960s, nationalist avant-gardes in the non-independent Caribbean nurtured high hopes of the benefits of independence. Not only would full decolonization restore dignity to peoples colonized for centuries in an imperialist framework, but there would be more tangible results too. Once in control of their own destiny, the new Caribbean states would be in a better position to ensure sustained economic growth, fuller political participation of the masses, and the development towards a more equitable society. Somewhat ironically in view of its previous role in the region, Western Europe provided a highly influential model of social democracy. There was an awareness of the disadvantages of scale and the limited scope for independent action in a region where few former colonies could ever hope to be more than micro-states. Yet, according to nationalist rhetoric, this should not keep Caribbean populations from accepting the challenge. In the words of the influential West Indian scholar and activist, Lloyd Best: '…what I am arguing is that social change in the Caribbean has to and can only begin in the minds of Caribbean men'.[3]

Four decades on, one cannot escape the conclusion that expectations at the time regarding the economic potential of the region were inflated, whereas the process of marginalization in the world economy was underestimated. The days that, to take the most obvious case, the British West Indies could generate the wealth which made them 'darlings of the empire' had long been gone. Of course, economic growth was achieved. In many parts of the region, per capita incomes improved considerably between 1960 and 2000, as did standards of education and health. Only notorious exceptions such as Haiti and Guyana remained among the poorest countries of the hemisphere. Moreover, most Caribbean economies made the transition from primary to secondary and particularly tertiary sector producers. Yet the industrial and the services sectors have remained volatile. The high unemployment and emigration figures suggest that the economic transition has been partially successful at best, as have been development strategies based on external financing and aid. Radical new strategies such as the Cuban model have proved to be even less rewarding. Many Caribbean policy-makers must have sym-pathized with the desperate characterization of the development process by the former Jamaican MP, the late Michael Manley, as a struggle 'Up the Down Escalator'.[4] The limitations of scale already apparent in the 1960s have continued to haunt planners. Moreover, the ongoing restruc-turing of the world economy left the entire Caribbean in an ever more marginal position within an Atlantic economy itself struggling to retain some of the gravity which had seemed unbeatable decades ago.

From this perspective, it is hard not to characterize the post-war economic development as disillusioning. Moreover, an intra-regional comparison suggests that the very process of decolonization has been a crucial factor. Just over 85 per cent of the Caribbean's 37 million peo-ple live in independent states. The remaining people in the 15 per cent slice live in what are sometimes thought of as 'not yet fully decolo-nized' territories. Standards of living in this last group of countries are significantly higher than in the independent states. This comparison yields only marginally more positive results if the Spanish-speaking Caribbean and Haiti are excluded. On average, living standards in the independent Commonwealth Caribbean and in Suriname too range below the averages in the 'not yet fully decolonized' territories. Jamaica's real income diminished since the 1960s, and is now below the Latin American average. This is not the case in the French *départe-ments d'outre-mer*, nor in Puerto Rico or the remaining British Overseas Territories. The same applies to the non-sovereign Dutch Caribbean. In fact, the contrasting economic profiles of the relatively affluent Netherlands Antilles and Aruba and impoverished Suriname are another dramatic case in point.[5]

There is an equally disturbing political dimension to this equation. The group of non-independent countries is characterized not only by higher standards of living, but also by a better functioning of their democracies, and more guarantees of fundamental civil rights. Again, the oldest independent states (Haiti, the Dominican Republic and Cuba) are the most striking cases in point. In most of the former British West Indies, the Westminster-style democracy functioned remarkably well in spite of the odds against. However, this part of the region has had its notorious exceptions too, in terms of both totalitarianism and corrupt regimes. In Suriname, independence in 1975 provided the conditions not only for economic collapse, but also for hitherto unthinkable politi-cal malaise: a military regime, internal warfare, widespread lethargy and corruption of the civil state. In comparison, and in spite of serious conflicts enacted in virtually all of these places, post-war politics in the non-sovereign Caribbean has been characterized by more moderation and compromise, and certainly by very little violence.

In sum, in a world in which the significance of the Caribbean diminished and in which the individual countries' economic and political viability became ever more dubious, independence proved to be a worrisome accomplishment. It is therefore not surprising that the populations of Puerto Rico, the French *départements d'outre-mer*, the British Overseas Territories, and the Netherlands Antilles and Aruba demonstrate no inclination to take the final – once supposedly 'logical' and inevitable – step to full independence. Moreover as their respective metropolises do not urge them to do so, the status of 'not yet fully decolonized' may best be understood as one devoid of an expiration date.

By the early 1990s, opting for the prolongation of a postcolonial liaison had become a thoroughly respectable means of exercising the right to self-determination.[6] In the Puerto Rican and Netherlands Antillean plebiscites on these islands' constitutional futures, the case for independence won no significant support. In the French *départements d'outre-mer*, the ever stronger encapsulation in metropolitan France has been translated into the virtual disappearance of true *indépendistes*. Intellectual responses range from former *négritude* protagonist, now Martinican mayor, Aimé Césaire's' claim to be fully French by culture to the younger generation's praise of a cultural *créolité*.[7] In the few remaining British territories, an increased metropolitan presence at the expense of the local political elites has not produced a renewed interest in independence. These are evidently worrying parameters for projects of Caribbean nation-building, as is well illustrated by the case of the former Dutch colonies in the region.

The divergent paths of Dutch Caribbean decolonisation

With the loss in the immediate post-war years of its one major possession, Indonesia, the Dutch colonial empire was reduced to Suriname and the six islands of the Netherlands Antilles. Whereas the Dutch had only given up Indonesia after bitter fighting and under strong international pressure, there was not yet a significant political will on either side of the Atlantic to dismantle the remaining 'empire.' There was an awareness, though, of the need to bring relations at least somewhat up to date with the prevailing trends in a decolonizing world. In 1954, after due consultations and without serious objections in either of the three countries involved, the *Statuut* or Charter of the Kingdom of the Netherlands was proclaimed. The Charter served as a constitution for the three member states: the Netherlands, the Netherlands Antilles and

Suriname. In the newly-styled transatlantic Kingdom, the three partners would each be autonomous in domestic administration. All parties agreed to the principle of mutual assistance, should the need arise. Only foreign affairs, defense and the guarantee of 'good governance' – including the functioning of parliamentary democracies – would remain Kingdom matters, and for all purposes would continue to be managed by the Dutch.

In comparison to the previous periods of colonial rule, the Charter was certainly a progressive move. In the decolonizing mood of the day, it was certainly more so than the French solution of 1946, which had made the former French colonies overseas departments. The Charter provided an acceptable arrangement for the political elites of the three countries involved, even if there was no consensus, not even an open debate, as to its status in view of a possible 'fuller' decolonization in the future. The proclamation of the Charter therefore did raise doubts about the continuing asymmetry in transatlantic relations. It took some years of discrete lobbying before the United Nations consented to drop Suriname and the Antilles from its chapter on decolonization. The historical asymmetry in power relations was compounded by the weight of population figures. In the late 1950s, the Netherlands had 11 million inhabitants, as against 190,000 in the Netherlands Antilles and 250,000 in Suriname. The huge differences in demographic and economic potential implied that the principle of mutual assistance would in practice be unilateral only.

In the first fifteen years of its existence, the new-style Kingdom functioned relatively smoothly. Particularly in Suriname, nationalists urged full independence, but this minority could easily be ignored by the leading political elite. Nor did Dutch politicians think of Caribbean independence as more than a distant horizon. Yet all this changed rapidly since the late 1970s – a period of widespread racial contentions in the Americas, from Black Power in the U.S. to disturbances in Caribbean states such as Jamaica and Trinidad & Tobago. In 1969, riots in Curaçao made the Antillean government request Dutch troops to restore order. According to the Charter, the Dutch had to comply with the request, and marines were indeed sent in. The year after, political turmoil in Suriname threatened to provoke another Dutch intervention. Even if a second intervention was averted, these incidents did create an uneasy awareness that under the Charter, the Dutch could virtually be obliged to engage in 'neo-colonial' interventions. The fact that such interventions could well be triggered by local conflicts over which the Dutch – abiding by the principle of its partners' administrative autonomy – had no prior influence underlined this uneasiness. The Dutch political left first urged 'full' decolonization, soon followed by the centre and conservative parties. In the process, two additional motives assumed increasing significance. There was a mounting irritation over the considerable amount of development aid spent yearly without much benefit to the Dutch and without any clear sign that this money actually enhanced the economic viability of the former colonies. Moreover, Dutch policy-makers worried over the increasing number of Suriname migrants settling in the Netherlands.

The Kingdom's political agenda of the 1970s and 1980s was therefore dominated by the debate over 'full decolonization', understood as the attainment of independence in the Dutch Caribbean and consequently the shrinking of the Kingdom to its European kernel.[8] This debate departed from what has long been thought of as the logical model of decolonization. Whereas the former metropolis persistently recommended independence, the erstwhile colonized West Indians were reluctant to accept the 'offer'. In 1975, Suriname did become a republic, but only half-heartedly and, as would soon become clear, at a high cost for all parties involved. There had been no referendum; the majority required in the Suriname parliament was absolutely minimal; and in spite of the extensive development aid which formed part of the independence deal, one-third of the Surinamese left for the Netherlands. Not only has the subsequent history of the country been bleak, but despite its independence, Suriname has continued to perceive the Netherlands as its most likely, if not only partner in efforts to overcome its crises. Dutch efforts to channel the bilateral relations through international institutions such as the European Community, the World Bank, and the IMF have so far run up against the stubborn resistance of its Caribbean counterpart. Likewise, on an individual level, the Surinamese have continued to emigrate in large numbers, legally or not, to the Netherlands.

The Netherlands Antilles, in contrast, consistently and successfully refused to consider full independence at any near stage. The second largest member of the six-island state, Aruba, negotiated its secession from the Antilles as of 1986, and ably managed to win the concession of being a separate entity without complying with the Dutch request to pay the price of independence in return. In the early 1990s, the Dutch grudgingly acknowledged the impossibility of imposing independence on the islands. However, this change of policy has implied a reclaiming of metropolitan influence in Antillean affairs. The new Dutch policy is defended by reference to budgetary problems and evidence of mismanagement, drug trafficking and money laundering overseas, as well as to problems related to the rapid rise of migration to the Netherlands. The formerly uncontested autonomy of the islands has now become both a negotiable issue and, so it seems, a receding horizon. Predictably, the Caribbean partners in the Kingdom in turn have felt unduly overruled by what many see as a 'recolonization'. Indeed, the Dutch position has undermined their post-1954 situation which combined the best of two worlds: autonomy at home, combined with Dutch protection, financial and logistic support, and unrestrained access for all Caribbean citizens of the Kingdom to the metropolis. Since the early 1990s, therefore, the agenda has been dominated by the delicate negotiation of a new balance between the unequal partners in the Kingdom, possibly to be institutionalized in a modernized version of the present Charter.

The exodus and its implications

This disillusioning trajectory of decolonization did not fail to mark the rhetoric of nationalism in the former Dutch colonies, as will be demonstrated below. Yet in this context, it is useful to first discuss the extraordinarily phenomenon of the exodus in more detail. One the most conspicuous characteristics of virtually all modern Caribbean countries – remarkably, irrespective of constitutional status and economic conditions – has been the unprecedented level of emigration. The swelling stream of migrants has dramatically underlined the region's viability crisis, but at the same time confirmed the 'modernity' of the Caribbean and its people's outward-looking frames of reference.[9] The exodus served to alleviate population pressure in densely populated islands. At the same time, however, both the brain-drain and the institutionalization of migration as an economic strategy and a socio-psychological norm have negatively affected the region's potential for development.

A cursory classification of Caribbean emigration patterns by destination would put the French and Dutch Caribbean in one category, with the British West Indies in a second, followed by Haiti and the Spanish-speaking Caribbean in a third. Both French and Dutch Caribbean migrations have been marked by a near exclusive orientation towards the European metropolis. British West Indian migration has been distinctly bifurcated, with both the New World (the United States and Canada) and the Old (Britain) attracting significant numbers of immigrants. Even so, immigrants of British West Indian origin in the U.S. and Canada far outnumber those in England. Migration from Haiti and the Spanish-speaking Caribbean to France and Spain respectively has been limited, focusing mainly on the U.S. instead. Caribbean populations from various countries of departure have significantly altered the face of major American cities such as New York and Miami.[10]

The number of people of Caribbean origin in the Netherlands exceeds 435,000.[11] The sending communities are relatively small; therefore, over one-third of the Dutch Caribbean populations now live in the metropolis. Ironically, one reads more about the effects of this migration to the host country than about the consequences for the sending countries, even if the share of these Dutch Caribbean immigrants in the Netherlands only slightly exceeds 2.5 per cent of the total Dutch population. The watershed in these migratory moves may be located in the past three decades.[12] The estimated population in Suriname was 350,000 in 1975, and it amounts to some 420,000 today, plus perhaps another 30,000 unclassified aliens, mainly from Brazil. In the same period, the Surinamese community in the metropolis increased from 120,000 to over 320,000. Most of the demographic growth of the Surinamese population was therefore concentrated in the Netherlands. Should this trend continue – and Brazilian immigration to Suriname not expand significantly – one could even expect the two poles of the Surinamese transnational community to reach roughly the same magnitude in the near future. The growth of the Curaçaoan community was less dramatic in absolute numbers, but proportionally of the same magnitude. While its size in the metropolis increased from a mere 20,000 in 1970 to 100,000 today, the island's population dropped from over 150,000 to a mere 130,000.

The explanatory factors for this dramatic increase are manifold. In general terms, globalization and an increasing sense of relative deprivation made the Netherlands seem a more attractive place. Both economic and educational motives and an awareness of the social and psychological drawbacks of small scale induced many to leave. As mentioned above, the Suriname exodus was also linked to the attainment of independence in 1975, which implied the termination of free migration by 1980. Strong doubts – in a sad way, a self-fulfilling hysteria – about the economic and political viability of the new republic inspired many to leave before the expiration of the final deadline. Since then, legal and particularly illegal migration from the young republic have continued apace. The country's deep crisis makes people move, no longer just because of *relative* deprivation, but out of sheer poverty and despair.

The more recent, marked increase in Antillean migration, mainly from Curaçao, seems more puzzling. As both the Netherlands Antilles and Aruba are still part of the Kingdom and will continue to be so, political motivations are less relevant. Otherwise, the motivations of Antillean migrants seem to duplicate those of Suriname immigrants: a longing to get away from small scale, and economic and educational pull factors. Even if the standards of living and education in the Antilles compare favourably to much of the region, Dutch standards are rightly perceived by potential migrants to be much higher. In this context, an additional factor is of crucial importance. Caribbean migrations within the region and to the U.S., as well as the initial post-war migration to

Britain, were and are primarily labour migrations. In contrast, Caribbean migration to the Netherlands may partly be explained by the pull factor of an elaborate metropolitan welfare system. There are evident parallels here with migration from the *départements d'outre-mer* to France, and to some extent even with the Puerto Rican exodus to the U.S.

Post-war immigration has thoroughly changed Dutch society. Apart from the Caribbean, the former colony Indonesia and the Mediterranean have been the major senders of migrants, joined since the 1990s by new categories of asylum seekers from Africa and Asia. Dutch from Indonesian backgrounds no longer figure in the statistics of ethnic minorities.[13] Even so some 10 per cent of the Dutch population and even 30 per cent in the major cities comprise so-called ethnic minorities, a proportion which is rapidly increasing. The Netherlands can no longer escape the fact that it has rapidly become a multi-ethnic society, with all the challenges with go with that.

While the general situation of the ethnic minorities in the Netherlands inspires pessimism, the specific data on Antilleans and Arubans and particularly Surinamese allows for a slightly more optimistic assessment. The differences within the overall migrant population suggest that the theoretically relevant assets of Dutch Caribbean immigrants over those from the Mediterranean and elsewhere – a better command of the Dutch language and a closer affinity with Dutch culture – have indeed been advantageous. This applies particularly to the Surinamese. The Antillean immigrants, mainly from Curaçao, perform clearly worse on dimensions such as employment and education and exhibit higher figures for deviancy, in particular criminality. The fact that the Surinamese community has longer roots in the Netherlands is only part of the explanation. Language is a crucial factor here as well, bearing in mind that command of the Dutch is at a much higher level among Surinamese than among Antilleans.

Researchers and politicians have increasingly argued that the Netherlands is witnessing the emergence of an ethnic underclass much along the lines of other European countries, and partly echoing the U.S. experience. Owing to the Dutch welfare system, this ethnic polarization has so far not become as acutely noticeable as it has elsewhere. Relatively adequate housing, health care, education and social security have ensured that unemployment and low educational qualifications are not necessarily translated into substandard living conditions. Unfortunately, these benefits resulting from a long process of 'socializing' capitalism in the Netherlands have also served to conceal the ongoing marginalization of large sectors of the ethnic minorities. The contemporary major cuts in the Dutch welfare system have dramatically exposed the ethnic minorities' heavy dependence on a hand that 'gives', but may well stop doing so.

The growing presence of postcolonial migrants – a 'colonization in reverse' as the Jamaican poet, Louise Bennett, aptly dubbed the phenomenon – has become a sobering challenge to Dutch self-representation as a progressive and tolerant society.[14] The Netherlands may be a country where nationalism is hardly seen as a virtue, but intellectuals used to count precisely a tradition of hospitality among the few identifiable characteristics of the nation. This image is certainly damaged now that Dutch ethnic minorities find themselves exposed to more xenophobia and racism than the country's reputation of tolerance towards newcomers might have led one to expect.

The breakdown of the supposedly ingrained Dutch tolerance towards newcomers, especially hitting non-whites, has inspired a host of studies reinterpreting past and present Dutch encounters with 'Others' in a grimmer perspective.[15] One of questions one may ask in this perspective is whether there is much continuity between racial relations in the former Dutch colonies and in the metropolis itself. There is no shortage of studies demonstrating the importance of racism, ethnic boundaries and often suffocating somatic norms in the Dutch Caribbean, yet the attempt to transplant such views to the metropolitan mentality is complicated.

In the Netherlands up to Word War Two, the small number of non-whites and the Dutch population's general ignorance of the colonial world seem to initially have fostered no less curiosity than racist prejudice. Certainly, early- and mid-twentieth century black migrants encountered an array of ignorant and arrogant reactions to their physical appearance. Yet, as many later recalled nostalgically, there was a sense of 'benevolent curiosity' which could make life rather easier.[16] There is no doubt that over the past decades, with the rapidly increasing numbers of migrants, far more tension has arisen in day-to-day interracial contacts. Yet at the same time, one notices relatively easy interracial contacts, precisely between the Dutch and the Dutch Caribbean migrant population. Impressionistic though the evidence may seem, the significance of interracial mixing is certainly far more important in the Netherlands than, particularly, in the U.S.

From another perspective, what has been the significance of the exodus for nationalism and nation-building in the Dutch Caribbean? From the 1930s up to the early 1970s, migrants in the metropolis were crucial to the development of Dutch Caribbean nationalism, particularly in the case of Suriname.[17] There is little reason to think of today's metropolitan Caribbean communities as a continuation of this tradition. The exodus has seriously undermined the contemporary articulation of nationalism. The very existence of a large and growing expatriate community belies the belief in the former colonies' viability as independent states which underscored earlier stages of Dutch Caribbean nationalism. Of course, the migrant communities have remained in close contact with their Caribbean places of origin. Surinamese opinion-makers and organizations in the Netherlands have influenced Dutch policies during the periods of military rule and the subsequent re-democratization in Suriname. A Surinamese lobby is working in favour of reserving a privileged position of Suriname when it comes to development aid. The vital remittances in money and kind to Suriname testify to the ongoing individual engagement with the Caribbean, as do the fully booked planes to the Antilles. All the same, the focus among the Dutch Caribbean communities is gradually shifting towards the metropolis itself.

Particularly the Surinamese community has gradually relinquished the myth of return. There is a sad paradox here. The contemporary presence of Suriname in Dutch society is stronger than ever, yet whereas this may be a psychological asset to the 'expatriate' community, it is of little avail 'back home'. Instead of being a source of pride and of support to the agonizing process of nation-building, the stronger Caribbean visibility strengthens both the magnetizing force of the metropolis and the shock of deprivation among those who stayed behind. At the same time, the diasporic replication of Suriname's ethnic pluralism has contributed little to a project of nation-building centred around the concept of national unity irrespective of ethnicity.[18]

If one were to take the success of the annual Antillean carnival in Rotterdam as a metaphor of real life, the Antillean experience of recreating and refashioning home culture in a circular fashion seems slightly more encouraging. Precisely the non-independent status of the Antilles and Aruba enables both residents and migrants to engage in a personal and cultural circularity which is denied, or no longer attractive respectively, to their Suriname counterparts. Circumstantial evidence indeed suggests that in the Antillean case, the cleavage between the communities on both sides of the Atlantic is not as wide. The absence of the deep ethnic divisions characterizing Suriname provides an evident first explanation. Most Antillean migrants come from Curaçao, are Afro-Caribbean, and speak Papiamentu as their first language. This congruence makes it much easier to identify both with the rest of the expatriate community and with the sending island. Yet, as will be discussed below, the odds are that the significance of Papiamentu in the diaspora will diminish. In that case, the vital link between both communities will be seriously undermined.

Some final observations again point at a declining significance of the diaspora for Caribbean nation-building. Whether because of an exposure to racism experienced by the Caribbean communities in the Netherlands or rather because of the waning of the 'ideology of return' and the concomitant realization that the future lies in Europe rather than the Americas, there has been a distinct reorientation among Caribbean organizations in the Netherlands from lobbying for Caribbean issues to negotiating concerns about life in the metropolis. Moreover, time works against the consolidation of 'pure' Caribbean cultures in the diaspora. Music and life-style are cases in point. Research among younger generations of Dutch Surinamese suggests that they place higher value on the international styles of the global village than on 'traditional' Caribbean culture, and that metropolitan revivals of elements of Afro-Suriname culture are mainly enacted among the older generations.[19] Again, this leaves Dutch Caribbean projects of nation-building ever more isolated from the diaspora.

The fading rhetoric of nationalism in Suriname

If indeed the project of nation-building in the Caribbean is frustrated by doubts about the viability of independent micro-states and by the extraordinary phenomenon of the exodus, the Dutch Caribbean provides telling illustrations. In the remainder of this essay, I discuss the trajectory of nationalism in both parts of the former Dutch West Indies, with a particular view as to how the divergent paths of decolonization have found rather paradoxical translations in the rhetoric of nation-building.

The present predicament of the Dutch Caribbean and its diaspora is not particularly conducive to the formulation of an assertive nationalism. The failure of Suriname's independence project; the painful trade-off between less autonomy and continued metropolitan assistance imposed on the Netherlands Antilles and Aruba; and the irreversible trend of settlement in the metropolis. These sobering facts have frustrated the aims of nationalism and undermined the project of nation-building. In this ideological malaise, the crisis of the Republic of Suriname continues to be a dominant factor. The philosophy leading to the country's full decolonization had been shared by Suriname nationalists, progressive Dutch politicians, and a handful of Antillean nationalists alike. It implied that political independence was a necessary precondition for economic and cultural development. Shaking off the patronizing Dutch neo-colonialism would provide the necessary impetus for the country to finally take its future into its own hands. Moreover, in the effort towards becoming a nation, the deep divisions of a thoroughly pluralist colonial society would be overcome by a stronger sense of belonging. Independence would therefore enhance Suriname's viability.

Now that this philosophy has sadly been falsified by Suriname's trajectory since 1975, other perspectives impose themselves. First, there is the question of ethnicity. Pre-independence Suriname provided a classroom example of what was then described as a plural society. The ethnic composition of the population reflected a colonial history in which descendants of plantation labour recruits from Africa, India and to a lesser extent Java formed the backbone of society, supplemented with smaller groups of Chinese, Middle Eastern and European origin. Subdivisions mainly based on religion further complicated the picture, also in the political arena. Yet the political system as such faithfully reflected the model of a society in which ethnicity dictates political affiliation. J.S. Furnivall once stated that a 'plural society is in fact held together only by pressure exerted from outside by the colonial power; it has no common will'.[20] Suriname nationalists set out to prove the opposite; those objecting to independence used the argument of ethnic division at least as subscript in their argumentation.

Ominously, the positions in this debate faithfully reflected Suriname's ethnic plurality. The nationalist rhetoric in the 1950s, the call for independence in the 1960s, and its translation into politics in the early 1970s had all been *Afro*-Surinamese projects, nurtured by a small group of intellectuals and only in the last instance embraced by the leading politicians from this group.[21] On the grounds of a lack of confidence in the country's viability and concerns about ethnic relations – the post-independence experiences of neighbouring Guyana were all too well-known – the Hindustani leadership strongly opposed independence. This opposition was only symbolically withdrawn at the point of no return, when the governing coalition dominated by Surinamese of African descent had struck its final deals with their eager Dutch partners. Resentment did not wither, and the subsequent failure of independence has confirmed the earlier, bitter criticism by the Hindustani leadership and its grassroots support regarding what was perceived as irresponsible radicalism.

Since independence and particularly since the mid-1980s, the economy collapsed. The standard of living had been relatively high at independence. Investments financed from the Dutch 'golden handshake' should have resulted in diversifying and strengthening the economy, but instead stimulated mismanagement and corruption. Contemporary Suriname has fallen into the category of the poorest Caribbean countries; most Surinamese live below the official subsistence minimum. Little optimism is voiced today regarding the county's economic viability. At the same time, the political history since 1975 has done little to inspire the population's confidence in its political leadership. The period up to 1980 left a memory of increasing political incompetence, ethnic competition and corruption, which initially provided the military coup with a measure of sympathy. The 1980–1987 years of military rule and internal warfare not only demonstrated the military's incompetence and unreliability as leaders of the nation, but at the same time cast doubt on the traditional political parties' leadership in the return to democracy. The post-1987 period of democratic rule has not put an end to economic decline, whereas the evidence of illegally won wealth amidst growing poverty continues to undermine the legitimacy of the political system. The present political leadership may well nurture resentment against the continued dependence on Dutch support. Yet as this dependence remains in place, the electorate seems to evaluate its leadership's success mainly in terms of its ability to get the Dutch support going again.

There is a tragic ethnic dimension to the crisis of Suriname. In spite of its initial cohesive rhetoric, the military regime did not diminish extant ethnic divisions and perhaps aggravated these. The civil war against specific groups of Maroons soon turned into derisory propaganda, confirming the worst of stereotypes. Whereas initially the military had propagated the heroic struggles of the first Maroons against colonialism as a shining example, now there was a return to tales of primitivism and brutality. As another dimension to the civil war – and perhaps partly engineered by the military – Amerindian ethnic demands became more outspoken, confronting both the civil government and the Maroons, their competitors in the tropical rain forest. The transition to democracy in 1987 may have been guided by an inter-ethnic coalition of the pre-military political parties, each with its own following. Yet underneath this veneer, ethnic affiliation and competition remained prevalent as was evident all through the 1990s and up to this day.

Moreover, ethnic divisions were underlined through the workings of an economy increasingly dominated by the growth sectors of black marketing, drug trafficking, and money laundering. Set in motion in the period of military rule, this powerful underside economy has continued to prosper ever since. Not only did the military leadership enrich itself considerably in the process, further undermining its credibility. The wealth generated through networking with successive governments – both military and civil – has particularly benefited a group of Hindustani businessmen, causing 'ethnic' resentment among the hard-hit Afro-Surinamese population.

Thus, while the militant nationalism of the military was initiated with a nationalist rhetoric of ethnic harmony, in practice little was achieved. Perhaps the most telling case of cynical manipulation of ethnicity by the self-proclaimed nationalist military dates from the 1991 elections. The political party NDP connected to the military faced a coalition of the major ethnically-based traditional parties headed by the Afro-Surinamese Venetiaan. In a cynical effort to win support among the Hindustani and Javanese population, the military – themselves predominantly of African origin – added their own rhyming comment to posters of Venetiaan: *Stemt u op deze baviaan?* (Do you vote for this baboon?).

The exodus finally, with its obvious economic and psychological consequences, has included a disproportionate share of the country's intellectual cadres. Its consequences for nationalist rhetoric are no less evident. It is more than just a passing comment on the sense of distress and lack of confidence in the country's future that the remaining intellectual and political leadership continues to send its children abroad, mainly to the former metropolis. Not surprisingly then, the debate on the future of Suriname is cast in bleak terms, and has increasingly been influenced by the diaspora.

In 1993, a group of authoritative, mainly expatriate Surinamese published a manifesto urging a referendum in Suriname on a possible revision of the relationship with the Netherlands – generally understood as a half-way or full return to pre-1975 Kingdom relations.[22] This plebiscite has not materialized and will not either in the future, if only because Dutch politicians are even less interested in this option today than they were a decade ago. They see no Dutch benefits in what would certainly be interpreted internationally as 'recolonization'. The manifesto itself thus left nothing substantial apart from an eloquent articulation of the profound crisis of Surinamese nationalism. Oblique incantations of national unity and working for progress notwithstanding, the nation seems irredeemably caught in the drama of its decline into a failing state and its ethnic and spatial fragmentation.

The Antilles: ethnicity, race, language

In the Netherlands Antilles and Aruba, the case of Suriname reinforced the awareness of the perils of independence. This sensibility had of course previously inspired the politicians' successful resistance to the 'gift' of full decolonization, and had kept the Antillean electorate from pushing its leaders beyond the line, but the fate of Suriname has made the prospect of future independence even more unattractive. The absence of a serious alternative to the present status precludes a radical nationalist discourse, and leaves the Antilleans and Arubans without much room for manoeuvre vis-à-vis the Dutch. The margins are small indeed. After all, many Antilleans worry about the recent Dutch re-involvement in the Caribbean as some kind of recolonization.

In Curaçao, the main Antillean island, the political response to the renewed Dutch presence was initially characterized by indignation and a defensive attitude. Yet the political elite's attempt to play out the argument of neo-colonialism stood – and stands – little chance of being heeded in a post-Cold War international context. Curaçaoan politicians have come to realize that the new Dutch policy, itself a devastating comment on local politics in the preceding half a century of autonomous rule, leaves them little margin. The political parties' position has been further weakened in the past decade by the electorate's behaviour in elections and plebiscites. Successive unexpected outcomes were widely interpreted as an expression of the electorate's dissatisfaction and lack of confidence in its own political leadership.

Again, the conditions for nation-building and for formulating a persuasive rhetoric of political nationalism are problematic. The lack of an attractive alternative to the present status within the Kingdom is not the only frustration. The crisis of 'traditional' politics is by definition a comment on the shortcomings of autonomous rule, as is the exodus from Curaçao. The tendency among some of the island's political leaders to counter Dutch criticism on alleged mismanagement by referring to differences in cultural style is no convincing rhetorical solution. And the electorate is rather whimsical. In 1994 out of nowhere a new political party (PAR) emerged precisely because it was generally appraised as 'clean'. Yet the same electorate dropped much of its support for the PAR nine years later and voted for the fiercely populist Frente Obrero in spite of – or perhaps even *because* of – its leadership being seriously suspected of fraud. Frente Obrero *has* something of a nationalist appeal. Yet beyond a strictly insular anti-*makamba* (anti-Dutch) rhetoric, there is not much of an ideology there. Moreover, even its own rank and file may enjoy an occasional *makamba*-bashing, but have not expressed the least interest in breaking with the Kingdom. Rather, they would expect the Dutch to provide more financial support, of course without interfering in Curaçaoan affairs. In this hardly realistic objective, Frente's leadership and rank and file do seem to concur.

Thus it seems unlikely that the political system will successfully define an encompassing nationalism. Yet beyond this, there is a deeper frustration. The May 1969 rebellion has routinely been interpreted as the watershed in post-Charter Curaçao. Before that date, so the argument runs, politics was an affair of a small, predominantly non-black local elite. May 1969, in so far as it can be seen as a racial conflict, presumably set the conditions for the emancipation of the black majority, both in politics and beyond. One may well question the extent of this

Afro-Curaçaoan emancipation, particularly in the economy and in private relations – in this respect too, the Curaçao experience parallels the unfinished emancipation elsewhere in the Caribbean. But indeed, since 1969, politics in Curaçao have been dominated by local black leaders, and at the same time the dividing line between administration and its citizenry became increasingly thin – arguably, too thin. As the balance is made up, many feel that post-1969 politics have added to corruption and *clientelismo* rather than to good governance and the fair distribution of opportunities. The PAR in the mid-1990s openly equated the previous decades of Antillean politics with an increasing lack of morality and common purpose.[23] The record of autonomous rule apparently does not provide the strongest foundation for a sense of national pride.

Obviously, there are other and perhaps more significant markers of nationhood and ethnicity than the political ones just mentioned. 'Race' and language seem to have been such crucial markers of ethnicity in Curaçao. Yet there is a crucial difference between the two. Its unique language, Papiamentu, functions as the one element of ethnicity shared by all Curaçaoans. Race or colour, in contrast, provide openings for disconcerting contestations over who belongs to the nation. Crudely, there are two principal ways of defining this belonging, both linked in different ways to history. As the late Antillean scholar René Römer indicated three decades ago, the local population always tended to distance itself from 'newcomers'. The groups coming to the island in the wake of its industrial modernization, thus after 1915, were generally not taken to be *Yu di Korsow*, 'Children of Curaçao'. Race as such was no major criterion in this categorization: Afro-Surinamese immigrants were considered outsiders just as much as Lebanese, Dutch or Poles.

Yet as Römer observed, subsequently a second, more exclusive definition emerged. Some Afro-Curaçaoans began to prefer the term *Nos bon yu di Korsow* ('We, the *good* children of Curaçao') – relating to the black population only. The exclusion of the local whites and those of lighter complexion may be interpreted not as a denial of a common history, but certainly as a *post hoc* castigation for past centuries of slavery, and as a self-confident (post-1969!) claim of belonging to an exclusive Afro-Curaçaoan culture. Römer added that the establishing of this ethnic boundary was partly inspired by 'a poor acquaintance with the history of our island. […] They departed from the erroneous assumption that the blacks had come earlier than the whites'.[24] Probably correct, this observation is at the same time somewhat beside the point. An ethnic group may be defined by a combination of three elements: a shared history (real or supposed); socially relevant cultural or physical characteristics; and shared attitudes or behaviour.[25] The elusive dimension of 'a shared history,' *real or supposed*, is a clue of crucial importance here. The development of a particularly *Afro*-Curaçaoan rhetoric of nation underlines the specificity of what is conceived of the things that really matter – things relating exclusively to the African kernel of Antillean culture.

This rhetoric has not been dropped since. As Aart Broek argues, the concept of *Di-nos-e-ta* ('This is ours') nurtured since the 1970s aggressively asserts this claim of a unique Afro-Curaçaoan cultural heritage which should be valued as the essence of the island's culture – a claim, incidentally, made earlier in virtually the same phrase by Afro-Suriname nationalists.[26] In the 1990s, Curaçaoan intellectuals would still debate this issue in deciding whether the island's history should be written as the past of all of its inhabitants, or mainly (or even exclusively) of its Afro-Curaçaoan majority.[27] Yet at the same time there seems to be little inclination to emphasize 'race' openly, precisely because of its potential damage to the idea of one nation.[28]

In contrast to 'race', language has continued to function as the one element of ethnicity shared by every *Yu di Korsow*. As Benedict Anderson (1983) has demonstrated, definable unique languages can serve as a powerful factor in the creation of the 'imagined community' of the national state, and of ethnic awareness. Both the Curaçaoan Papiamentu and the Sranan Tongo of Suriname emerged in a process in which simultaneously these very peoples, respectively one segment of them, developed. As the languages became institutionalized, they increasingly served as a vehicle for differentiation between insiders and outsiders. Yet in practice and even more so, psychologically, Sranan Tongo continued to be primarily the language of the Afro-Surinamese, less so of the Hindustani and Javanese population groups. Moreover, it did not shed its image of a lower-class language. Therefore, Sranan Tongo has not reached the status of the national language for all classes and ethnic groups. Dutch continues to be the country's official vernacular, and three decades after independence the colonial language – in a recognizably creolized version – is used more than ever before in Suriname.[29]

Papiamentu, in contrast, emerged from a history in which the language was adopted by *all* ethnic groups and classes, and in which it served as the central vehicle not only of communication, but also of affirming a unique identity in counterpoint to the Dutch language and culture introduced primarily through the educational system.[30] The language therefore serves as the most obvious source of nationalist discourse: without even aiming to be, it implicitly serves as such as it is spoken. However, in a new social and economic context, this anthropological marker of nationality and ethnic uniqueness evokes awkward problems of social policy and individual orientation. For most

Curaçaoans, their apparent bilingualism is only an appearance, masking a poor mastery of the Dutch language. One, by now classic, dilemma has emerged as Dutch continues to be the vernacular in education and a requirement for upward social mobility in local society. The dilemma is underlined by the recent upgrading of the Dutch profile in the local scene, but has acquired its most dramatic new dimension as a result of the increasing migration to the Netherlands. The language deficiency in Dutch of the Antillean population in the metropolis is serious – clearly far more so than was the case with the Suriname population – and provides an enormous obstacle to social mobility.

This context confronts the Curaçaoan policy-makers with a formidable dilemma. The political program of a full emancipation of Papiamentu was formulated some decades ago in the heyday of nationalism, and long before migration to the Netherlands had taken its present course. A more extensive use of Papiamentu still ranks high on the agenda of politicians and intellectuals of different backgrounds, and is certainly an obvious issue in the field of nationalist rhetoric. Yet an increased use of Papiamentu in the education system may lead to a further deterioration of the general mastery of the Dutch language – though in all fairness, it should be pointed out that not all experts agree on this. This policy could therefore harm chances for social mobility on the island, and certainly among the migrant population – today, two out of every five Curaçaoans. The stalemate is evident. Promoting the local vernacular is attractive, perhaps even imperative from a nationalist point of view; after all, the dictum that language is the soul of a nation certainly applies to the Leeward Antilles. Yet doing so may seriously damage the social and economic position of the individuals supposedly served by this nationalist stance.

Such dilemmas of course remind one of similar debates in Puerto Rico. One crucial difference is that, even if for Puerto Ricans, and certainly the expatriate communities, a deficient command of English may negatively effect their social and economic position, at least their own Spanish is a major language too, and has increasingly become institutionalized as such in the U.S. By definition, Papiamentu will never have that significance outside its natural locale. The implications should be worrying for Antillean nationalists. The Jamaican intellectual Rex Nettleford has pointed to the social acceptance of Papiamentu as an inspiring example for the future of English Creole languages.[31] Yet one may well wonder whether it is not precisely the postcolonial *status quo*, with its inherent economic and educational benefits, which has so far enabled local politicians to side-step the dilemma of either emphasizing local specificity, or preparing for optimal insertion in an ever more penetrating global economy and culture. Precisely from a nationalist perspective, the dilemma is haunting. As Curaçao, a 'not yet independent' territory, discusses the possibility of upgrading the official use of a language spoken by less than 200,000 people, independent islands such as Dominica and St Lucia, similar in terms of scale and language situation, and equally aware and proud of the cultural heritage embodied in the local vernacular, would not dream of taking such steps at the expense of the English language – '*Konpyouta pa ka palè Kwéyol.*'[32]

These dilemmas seem to have been less prominent for Aruba, with its 90,000 inhabitants the second largest of the Dutch Caribbean islands in terms of population. The island negotiated its own separate status as of 1986, and has recently been accorded full country status within the Kingdom of the Netherlands. All through this process, which started half a century ago, Aruba's significant other was Curaçao rather than the Netherlands. With their more pronounced *latino* roots and their tradition of self-representation as ethnically different from Afro-Curaçao, Aruban nationalists had an obvious case for nationalist discourse.[33] Principles of ethnic differentiation indeed mark many spheres of culture. This applies to the long upheld segregation of the light-skinned local and the black migrant segments of the population, but equally to the advancement of a specific Aruban Papiamento, supposedly slightly more *latino* in spelling and pronunciation, against the Papiamentu of Curaçao.

Now that after attaining its separate status Aruba too has been confronted with a stronger Dutch presence, one does observe slight tendencies towards an anti-metropolitan dimension in local self-definition. Yet beyond the political sphere, Aruban relations with the Netherlands remain comparatively weak. The Aruban community in the metropolis is small in numbers, and the major economic partner has traditionally been the U.S. rather than the official metropolis. As long as these parameters do not change, Aruban politicians may have to struggle with Dutch policy-makers, but will more likely use the rhetoric of other spheres of contention to mobilize their electorate.

The latter observation holds true even more for the English-speaking Dutch Windward Antilles, whose colonial history and post-war economic development have positioned them primarily in the Anglo-American world. As with Aruba, the renewed Dutch involvement has sparked off a new and not necessarily positive awareness of the metropolis. Before his detention on a charge of corruption, the long-term *caudillo* of St Martin, Claude Wathey, indeed mobilized his following on a convenient anti-Dutch masquerade of nationalism. Yet in daily life, the context in which insular ethnicity is elaborated is far more complicated, involving concomitant encounters with the local and metropolitan inhabitants of the island's French half, a by now great number of Curaçaoan 'compatriots', immigrants from various Caribbean islands, and American and European tourists. Again, all this presents a problematic context for national or ethnic self-definition.[34]

Ever since the separation of Aruba, the most complex challenge of nation-building has been the effort of keeping Curaçao, Bonaire and the three Windward islands together in a re-invented Antilles-of-five. The one remarkable highlight in this episode was the outcome of the 1993–1994 plebiscites, in which majorities on all islands in defiance even of their own politicians voted in favour of keeping the five together. While this unexpected voting behaviour partly reflected an open protest against the political elites, it was also related to an awareness of the importance of inter-insular kinship bonds. Whereas during the earlier oil boom Windwarders had flocked to Curaçao and Aruba, now Curaçaoan migrants form a sizeable group on St Martin with its dazzling tourist business. The will to keep the federal Netherlands Antilles afloat in this way probably also reflected the longing to retain the present inter-insular openness. For once therefore the migration phenomenon which has so seriously undermined nation-building in other respects seemed conducive to creating a sense of common inter-island purpose. A decade later, however, one can only conclude that politicians have missed the opportunity and island populations no longer place much value on a truly supra-insular Antillean nationalism.

A Caribbean predicament

The Caribbean contribution to the 'culture of resistance' against colonialism and racism has rightly been applauded for its – in view of the region's small size – amazing impact. From the Haitian Revolution through José Martí, Marcus Garvey and *négritude* to Frantz Fanon and Rasta, the Caribbean has had a resounding voice in the chapters of writing and fighting back to empire. Today the creolization of Caribbean culture is welcomed by many as yet another demonstration of the region's capacity to innovate and to contribute to the global culture of the postmodern world. However, it is difficult not to remark on the increasing fragility of these local cultures, undermined as they are by the bitter fruits of independence and the terrifying demonstration effect of the satellite age, tourism, and the nearby migration outlets.[35]

In this context, nation building continues to be a predicament, as is the search for a wider Caribbean identity. As Nigel Bolland rightly observes, 'Caribbean societies have a desperate need for a coherent national ideology and cultural identity.'[36] Much effort is spent on the forging of 'imagined national communities'. Hence, for example, the omnipresent slogans emphasizing unity, as in 'Out of Many One', 'All o' We is One' and 'Wan Pipel'. Of course, none of this is unique. Though it might appear otherwise today, nationalism and the 'nation' are concepts with a relatively short history, even in Europe. Nor is the predicament of forging national unity confined to the Caribbean – to take but one example, a multi-ethnic Asian state such as Malaysia faces the same challenges and adopts many of the same strategies in response.[37] Yet this is only scant comfort, the more so as the young Caribbean states face so many additional drawbacks, including economic and political marginalization, the exodus, and the fragmentation of the region.

Caribbean nationalisms have been characterized by both an awareness of shared regional identities and a parallel or subsequent practice of insularism. A history of divergent colonial experiences and resulting cultural differences has been of major importance here, but so have – and probably more so – the contemporary realities of differences in scale and economic potential. In spite of earlier optimism, hesitant schemes for sub-regional cooperation, and continuing contemporary efforts such as the recent establishment of the Association of Caribbean States, the post-war period has not witnessed a decisive regional integration. The rhetoric of a Pan-Caribbean identity has foundered on the sad realities of competing islands marketing the same products and services to the same clientele in a situation of cut-throat competition rather than concerted effort. The growing awareness of the volatility of the individual countries' viability has strengthened the trend to value individual life-lines over the insecure prospects of regional integration.

In this context, the absence of a strong pro-independence movement in the remaining American, French and British territories is hardly surprising. Nor is the similar overwhelming desire of the Antillean and Aruban populations to remain within the legal orbit of the former colonial power.[38] Ever since Suriname assumed the agonizing position of providing the counterpoint to the conservative choice, the credibility of a nationalist rhetoric speaking out for full independence has dramatically diminished. The exodus to the Netherlands has only confirmed this predicament.

Dutch Caribbean nationalism today faces the exceedingly difficult task of contesting for a niche in a world increasingly dictated by a U.S.-dominated 'global' culture, struggling on its way with an older metropolitan culture which, contrary to earlier expectations, is as strongly present as ever. The crucial difference with the earlier period of colonialism is that now the link with the Netherlands is actively sought after by large majorities in the former colonies. This explains the agonizingly narrow limits to nationalist rhetoric and practice. Earlier nationalist ideology today painfully borders on the obsolete. Both within the Dutch Caribbean and its metropolitan society, the future seems to lie in the eclectic retention and further articulation of cultural specificities, rather than in a wider politics of opposition to empire. This situation, which is certainly not unique in the contemporary Caribbean, will no doubt continue to inspire debates in which the classic language of nationalism with its illusions of national sovereignty will linger beyond its true lifetime.

Notes

1 I first communicated some of the ideas expressed in this Chapter in an essay for *Caribbean Affairs* (Oostindie 1992) and in my inaugural address as Professor of Caribbean Studies at Utrecht University (Oostindie 1994).
2 In this context, Samuel Huntington's subsuming of the Caribbean within the US-dominated Western cultural sphere clearly makes sense, even if we need not subscribe to the rest of his theory (Huntington 1993a, 1993b).
3 Lloyd Best 1967:28.
4 Manley 1987.
5 Compare Oostindie & Klinkers 2003, particularly Chapter 8 for quantitative data.
6 Maingot 1994:228–49, Oostindie & Klinkers 2003, Chapters 1–3 and 11. Among the good recent overviews of Caribbean development issues and politics, suffice it to mention Aldrich & Connell 1992 and 1998, Clarke 1991, Domínguez, Pastor & Worrell 1993, Knight 1990, Payne & Sutton 1993 and 2001, Ramos & Rivera 2001, Tulchin & Espach 2000.
7 Bernabé, Chamoiseau & Confiant 1989, Burton 1993.
8 For a full discussion of the changing relations within the Kingdom, see Oostindie & Klinkers 2003; see also the previous chapter in the present book.
9 Mintz 1989:37, 328.
10 See also Oostindie & Klinkers 2003, particularly Chapter 9, as well as the next chapter in the present book.
11 The statistics generally used in estimating the magnitude of the immigrant population are tellingly biased though. Anybody born in the Netherlands from at least one non-Dutch parent (in some of the calculations, restricted to a non-Dutch *mother*) is counted among this immigrant population. Therefore, a child born in Amsterdam from a Bonairean mother and a Dutch father and growing up in that city will remain an immigrant for statistical purposes. Figures used in this chapter are based on Oostindie & Klinkers 2003, Chapter 9.
12 In the early 1960s, the total Suriname population in the Netherlands was only 13,000. The same figure applied to the Antillean and Aruban community a decade later. Whereas Suriname and Curaçaoan migration accelerated afterwards, the number of migrants from Aruba, Bonaire and the three Dutch Windward Antilles has remained modest.
13 With the exception of Moluccans who, for historical reasons, are an atypical group.
14 Louise Bennett as cited in Duff 1990:48:
      What a joyful news, Miss Mattie
      I feel like my heart gwine burs'
      Jamaica people colonizin
      England in reverse.
      [...]

> What an islan! What a people!
> Man an woman, old and young
> Jusa pack dem bag an baggage
> An tun history upside dung!

15 E.g., Blakely 1993.

16 Oostindie & Maduro 1986. Cf. the ideas developed by Harry Hoetink on 'exotic minorities' (Hoetink 1973:177–9, 191).

17 Oostindie 1990. This observation obviously applies as well to French Caribbean nationalism, and even, if to a lesser extent, to the British West Indian case.

18 In the Netherlands, the two major ethnic groups of Suriname (those of African and those of Indian descent) are geographically divided among distinct cities, and have tended to organize on an ethnic rather than a national basis. This applies equally to the third largest ethnic group, those of Javanese descent. See Choenni & Adhin 2003:62 for figures on settlement in Dutch cities by ethnic groups.

19 E.g., Sansone 1992.

20 Furnivall 1945:163–4.

21 See Dew 1978, Meel 1990b and 1998, Oostindie 1990, Jansen van Galen 1995 and 2000.

22 *de Volkskrant*, September 29, 1993. See also the writings of the Suriname-born Dutch author, Anil Ramdas (1992, 1994).

23 E.g., the interview with the then Prime Minister for the PAR, Miguel Pourier, in *NRC Handelsblad*, 9–9–1994. Ironically, the PAR was beaten in 2003 by the Frente, the major populist party to have emerged from the May 1969 revolt. It is precisely the Frente leadership which over the years has had to face accusations and indeed courtroom condemnations for fraud.

24 Römer 1974:53; my translation.

25 E.g., *Social Science Encyclopedia* 1985:267–9.

26 Broek 1994:23–6. The name of the Dutch-based Afro-Suriname nationalist organization was *Wie Egie Sanie*, Sranan Tongo for Our Own Things. As these 'things' were all derived from (reconstructions of) an Afro-Suriname past, *Wie Egie Sanie's* program failed to appeal to other ethnic groups (Oostindie 1990:245–50).

27 Huender 1993.

28 In relations with the Netherlands, 'race' or colour are never openly on the agenda, but are often present psychologically.

29 De Bruijne & Schalkwijk 1994:232–3. See Gobardhan-Rambocus 2001 for the history of Dutch education and the role of the Dutch language therein in Suriname.

30 See Van Putte 1999 and Fouse 2002 on the social history of Papiamentu.

31 Nettleford 1990:250; 1988:22.

32 'Computers do not speak Creole.' St Lucian Prime Minister John Compton, quoted in Frank 1993:46. Cf. Frank 1993 and St-Hilaire 2003 on St Lucia, Stuart 1993 on Dominica. Alongside its tributes to local Creoles and dialects, the report of the West Indian Commission, *Time For Action*, equally emphasizes the imperative of continuing and even expanding the use of English in the curriculum of Commonwealth Caribbean education (West Indian Commission 1993:269–71, 306).

33 Alofs & Merkies 1990. See also Chapter 4.

34 Cf. the nationalistic interpretation of St Martin history by Sekou 1996; also Rummens 1991.

35 E.g,. the broad coverage of Caribbean authors in the third chapter of Said's *Culture and Imperialism* (Said 1993); see also Clifford 1988:175–81, Hannerz 1992:217–67. For eulogies of contemporary Caribbean creole culture, e.g., Benítez Rojo 1989, Bernabé, Chamoiseau & Confiant 1989, Nettleford 1988, West India Commission

1993:265–8. For more critical approaches, see e.g. Bolland 1991, Trouillot 1998. Dash (2001:148) writes acidly about 'the triumphalist poetics of creolization and hybridity'.

36 Bolland 1992:64. Perhaps more so than many other scholars, Mervyn Alleyne (2002:247–9) is cautiously optimistic about the ongoing dynamic of Caribbean societies moving from caste-like system based on 'race' and ethnicity to societies in which class takes first place. He adds though that there is still a long way to go.

37 Cf. Anderson 1983 and 1992, Hobsbawn 1990. On Malaysia, see Van Dijk 2003. His quotes from patriotic songs strike many a familiar chord (Van Dijk 2003:38–9): 'No segregation of race, religion, and tradition,/One nation living in peace and harmony.' Likewise: 'Malaysia, fortunate land,/Impelling and beautiful,/Home to various peoples/Living in harmony and happiness.'

38 Oostindie & Verton 1998a; Oostindie & Klinkers 2003, Chapter 11.

The delusive continuities of the diaspora

5 May 1995 was a special day: the Germans had capitulated fifty years earlier, putting an end to five years of Nazi occupation of the Netherlands. The Breestraat (Broad Street) in the city centre of Leiden was the scene of brass bands, old Harleys and jeeps against a background of *tableaux vivants* referring to the Occupation. In between marched war veterans: British, American and Canadian.

I thought of Frank Koulen, who could have been walking there too had he not died ten years earlier. Born in New Nickerie, Suriname in 1922, he died in Terneuzen, a village in the south of the Netherlands in 1985. It seems easy enough to outline his biography. He was born into the Creole working class, into a family of absent men – his sons were the first males in several generations to transmit the family name of Koulen.[1] He was brought up by his grandmother until she died. Then his mother took over the task of raising him, but she died soon afterwards too. Eleven years old by now, he ended up in the Tilburg Lay Brothers' orphanage. The Brothers thought he showed promise and enabled him to learn a profession after completing primary school education. He trained in metalwork, but Suriname did not have much to offer. In 1939, at the age of sixteen, he emigrated to Curaçao to work in the Shell refinery there. Like most of his fellow countrymen, he lived in the Suffisant district, better known at the time as 'Suriname Village'. It was there, not in the Netherlands, that the first chapters of the modern Dutch Caribbean migration history were written.

In 1943 he signed a five-year contract with the navy.[2] The marines were trained in the United States and England before being deployed in the liberation of the Netherlands. In September 1944 they set out for the Netherlands. The offensive was halted just beyond the Belgium border, in Zealand Flanders and was not completed until the spring of 1945. That winter Koulen met a young woman from Terneuzen. They married in 1947. When the first of their seven children was born, Koulen was serving in Indonesia – very much against his will, but still under military discipline – where the Dutch were fighting their last colonial war. In 1949, when he was called up again, he requested to be released from service because of his objections of principle. In the end he was

granted an honourable discharge. The rest of his story is a modest
variation on the rags to riches theme. As a small-scale entrepreneur
and especially as the driving force behind a steadily growing jazz
centre, Koulen made a name for himself in Zealand. In terms of
education and work, his children reached heights which their father
had only dreamed of during his difficult childhood in Suriname. He
revisited his country once, in 1980, but despite his pride in his origins
and his race, it was a disappointing encounter. The much despised
colonialism had come to an end, but he noted with regret that he was
unable to accept what he perceived of as the lethargy and provincial-
ism of life in Suriname.

It is not just my own involvement – Frank Koulen was my father-
in-law – which is my reason for telling this story. I have told it here to
introduce a reflection on the contrast between early Caribbean Dutch
history and today's, and the significance of that prehistory for present-
day migrants. It would be a good thing if biographical sketches like that
of Koulen were typical of Caribbean history in the Netherlands, but as
the title of this chapter suggests, that is not the case. Second, more and
more I have wondered whether an early history like that of Frank
Koulen has any significance at all for the masses of later migrants and
their children. I have grown more sceptical about that as well. And
finally, the existence of different, often contradictory versions of this
very story has gradually helped me to realize how cautious we must be
in interpreting such individual life-stories.

These reflections are the thread running through this chapter. I
have tried to find a solid basis for them by outlining the course of the
historical events and by testing my ideas against the results of a modest
street research among Caribbean Dutch.[3]

Prelude: the slaves

But let us start at the beginning of the story. The history of the
Surinamese and Antilleans[4] in the Netherlands goes back to the earliest
years of colonization. It is the same story that can be told for all of the
Caribbean colonies and their mother countries. The Indians who were
taken to the 'fatherland' as exotic curiosities; the slaves brought along
as servants and status symbols; the colonial elites, who tried to find a
trace of 'refined' living in the Netherlands; and their children, who went
to study there. There were never many of them; in that respect the history of the Dutch Caribbean differs from that of the neighbouring countries. In eighteenth-century England, the number of blacks, mainly from
the West Indian colonies, was estimated to be some tens of thousands.

The relatively large-scale migration of both slaves and free persons from the French Caribbean even led to far-reaching legal restrictions. As for Spain and Portugal, large numbers of Africans were living there long before the *conquista*. This black population was constantly supplemented in a roundabout way through the slaving concerns in the New World.

By comparison, the presence of people from Caribbean or African backgrounds in the Netherlands was negligible. By far the largest proportion of all blacks who arrived there came from Suriname, followed – though a long way behind – by Curaçao. They were few in number. Even at the peak of the Suriname plantation economy, the third quarter of the eighteenth century, hardly more than twenty slaves and a few free coloureds left for patria each year, and the vast majority of them returned later. These figures were even lower during the preceding and subsequent periods. The conclusion must therefore be that, prior to the twentieth century, the presence of blacks from the Caribbean in the Netherlands was negligible. This is even truer of Africans. The contrast with England, France and the two Iberian countries is clear. It is not difficult to explain. While at the time the centre of gravity of the colonial empires of the other European countries was in the Atlantic world, the Netherlands focused on Asia. The Dutch trading posts in Africa and the slave colonies in the Caribbean were always of secondary importance.

What remains of this period are lost trails and a few nice anecdotes. I have collected and described a lot of them, and enjoyed doing so. Nice anecdotes, even though they are often heart-rending – but it is hard to attach any more importance than that to them. The free Indian Erikeja Jupitor, who made a statement with a notary in Amsterdam in 1688 in favour of a soldier who had served in Suriname as an interpreter. The anonymous female slave who was taken to the Netherlands around 1700 and joined the Reformed Church there, but back in her own country seven years later returned to her own belief, as that was 'much more pleasing to the senses'. Quasje, banished from Suriname for trading weapons with the Maroons, but eventually sent back from the Netherlands by a judge who sympathized with Quasje's regret at having had to depart two years earlier, 'leaving behind his wife, children and livelihood'. Free orphans from Paramaribo, who were to receive a Protestant education in the Amsterdam Orphanage and were taught a craft before embarking on the journey back. John Gabriel Stedman's slave Quaco, with whom Stedman was so contented that he took the youth with him to Europe, only to give him away there as a present to the Countess of Roosendaal. The slave Virginie from Curaçao, who waged a bitter struggle on both sides of the Atlantic for her own freedom and that of her children. J.J. Jonas, born a slave, who, 'despite her black colour', developed in the Netherlands to become a 'well-educated Lady, who spoke French as purely and fluently as the best Parisienne and was as fluent in German and English as in Dutch'. The black man skating over the frozen Amsterdam canals, immortalized by the German poet Freiligrath in his poem 'Der Schlittschuh-laufende Neger' (1833).

The transience of these fragments of the past is in sharp contrast to comparable events elsewhere. The English experience is particularly interesting in this connection. The massive presence of West Indian slaves there repeatedly raised the question of whether slavery was acceptable on British soil. This question was answered in the negative in a test trial in 1772. Although this verdict turned out not to have a definitive character, this Somerset case is still regarded as a milestone on the road towards the abolition of slavery in the British West Indies. Moreover, several race riots occurred in this period in British cities. The simple fact that there were so many West Indians in England made it impossible to forget or ignore the slavery issue.

In the Netherlands, on the other hand, the presence of Caribbean slaves was so limited that a clear policy on their status was never formulated. Right up to the last day before the abolition of slavery on 1 July 1863, the few slaves who had been taken to the Netherlands with their masters had no secure basis on which to claim their freedom. Their almost invisible presence meant that the Dutch were confronted even less with the facts of slavery in the Caribbean colonies. Unlike the English situation, the presence of blacks in the Netherlands was hardly visible, devoid of political or social significance, and therefore did not hasten the abolition of slavery.

The exodus and the illusion of continuity

While the arrival of slaves ended by definition after 1863, there was continuity in a different type of migration: that of the colonial elite. In the search for expansion of the narrow colonial horizon, and especially for good education, better-off Surinamese and Antilleans kept on travelling to the Netherlands. The motive remains unchanged today, and is one of the few continuities in over three centuries of migration history. The difference lies in what came afterwards; the return that used to be taken for granted at one time gradually became a receding horizon.

Statistically, this Caribbean history in the Netherlands hardly seems more than a footnote to a larger story. The number of West Indian students who studied in the Netherlands in previous centuries rarely exceeded a handful at any one time. The situation did not change until after the Second World War. By the end of the 1950s there were a few hundred Antillean and particularly Surinamese students; their numbers multiplied in the course of the following decades. All the same, they remained on a modest scale, and the percentage of students among the Caribbean population in the Netherlands actually declined. Seen from a wider perspective, however, the presence of Caribbean students in the Netherlands acquired an enormous importance. By means of their Dutch education, the orientation of the colonial elites was unambiguously attached to patria. Moreover, paradoxically, the experience of a period of study in Europe was eventually to play a decisive role in the development of post-war Surinamese nationalism – and to a lesser degree, the same holds true for Antillean nationalism. More than the awareness of economic and perhaps even constitutional dependence, the inevitability of a period of study in the mother country has left its mark on practically every Dutch Caribbean intellectual. Even the Surinamese nationalism of the 1950s and 1960s, and independence in the 1970s, are unthinkable without the Dutch intermezzo that the protagonists once went through.

During the first half of this century 'other' Surinamese and Antilleans found their way to the Netherlands too on an incidental basis. Enterprising individuals, mainly men, most of them from the Afro-Surinamese working class. They too are a source of wonderful anecdotes. The 'professional Negroes', especially musicians, who skilfully exploited the exoticism of their appearance and their artistic talents, had come a long way since the end of the nineteenth century, when Surinamese could literally be put on display without benefiting from it themselves at all. There were also a few sailors, labourers and clerks. The best known of these migrants is the Afro-Surinamese Anton de Kom. Born in 1898, De Kom went to the Netherlands in 1922. He soon became active in the anti-colonial movement and – in secret – in the Communist Party. As such he was a source of concern to the Dutch authorities. After returning to Suriname in 1932, he was at the centre of serious riots which earned him a compulsory 'repatriation' to the land of the ruler. In 1934 he published his fierce denunciation of Dutch colonialism, *Wij slaven van Suriname* ('We Slaves of Suriname'). This book made De Kom one of the first in the Caribbean – leaving aside Haiti and the Spanish-speaking Caribbean – to rewrite the history of his country from a consistently anti-colonial perspective. A German translation was published almost immediately in Moscow. During the war he worked with the Dutch Resistance, risking his life for the freedom of a metropolis which had denied liberty to his native country. Unmasked, he was arrested and deported to Germany. This remarkable Surinamese died in the Neuengamme concentration camp on 24 April 1945. Most of his relatives – his wife was Dutch – live in the

Netherlands, but it is the university of Suriname which bears his name, a heritage of the period of military rule under Desi Bouterse.

These migrants remained isolated cases with a high curiosity value until the 1960s. Frank Koulen was known as 'the Negro' in the harbour town of Terneuzen – he was the only one there. In 1946 the total size of the Surinamese community in the Netherlands was estimated at 3,000, in 1966 at 13,000. The Antillean component accounted for no more than a few thousand persons. Compared with the next stage, but also compared with what had already been a dramatic emigration from other parts of the Caribbean towards the United States and Britain, the exodus from the Dutch Caribbean was thus very modest in scale. This can largely be explained by the spectacular economic growth of Curaçao and Aruba from the late 1920s on. The oil refineries and all the sectors expanding around them provided a lot of jobs, both for the local population and for immigrants; those with the status of fellow citizens (from Suriname and the Windward Islands) received preferential treatment. The oil boom did not really die out until the late 1960s. Besides, the Suriname economy went through a strong growth period from the 1940s as a result of bauxite. Furthermore, there was a weak labour market in the Netherlands. There was even a clear emigration surplus after 1945. This only changed in the 1960s, but this was the time when the specific recruitment of labourers from the Mediterranean countries started. Unlike the situation in England and France, in the Netherlands hardly any labourers were ever recruited from the Caribbean.

So when an exodus did get under way in the late 1960s, first and above all from Suriname, and later from Curaçao as well, there was not only a change in numbers but also a qualitative change. This was enabled partly because of growing prosperity in the Netherlands and the availability of air transport at ever lower prices. For the first time, travel and settlement in the metropolis became realistic options for many Surinamese and Antilleans. This in turn stimulated chain migration of families and the resulting emergence of a Caribbean community sizeable enough to act as a magnet to those staying behind.

Thus, for the first time, emigration to the Netherlands outstripped migration within the Caribbean parts of the Kingdom. From now on Dutch Caribbean migration was to be extremely unidirectional; the goal is practically always the relatively safe mother country. As for the situation in the Netherlands, the exoticism disappeared, and in a certain sense too the heroism of the prehistory of courageous individuals, musicians, nationalists. The new migrants represented for the first time a cross-section of the societies from which they came. The surplus of men disappeared; the ethnic diversity of Suriname displaced the former Afro-Surinamese preponderance; and most of the migrants were now from the popular classes. Education and work were still a motive for migration. Yet particularly for those not successful in their home societies, the orientation towards Dutch welfare state provisions grew. These provisions were and still are relatively favourable; this, however, soon turned out to be not entirely positive. A part of the current Dutch Caribbean population is dependent on welfare, which keeps them in a paralyzing stranglehold. A comparable ambivalent blessing lay in the continuing growth of the Caribbean Dutch population. The increasing numbers and concentration created the condition for the emergence of 'ethnic' enclaves which functioned as havens in a heartless world. However, it is precisely this new security that is often a major stumbling block on the way to successful integration and upwards social mobility.

In the meantime the Caribbean community in the Netherlands has continued to grow. The Surinamese community today is estimated at over 320,000. The Antillean community, mainly from Curaçao, has increased to the present figure of 115,000.[5] It is typical that the statistics have become not only more refined, but also more problematical in a number of ways. The current practice of classifying the second generation in the statistics as Surinamese or Antillean may correspond more closely to the ideas of their parents and to that of white Dutch than to the feelings of many members of the younger generation themselves.

The growth of the Surinamese population in the Netherlands was most spectacular around the time of independence (1975). Settlement and naturalization in the Netherlands have become considerably harder since 1980, but both illegal immigration and naturalization continues. Furthermore, the share of the second and third generations is growing fast. The Antillean group, mainly from Curaçao, still consists mainly of the first generation, but a second one is emerging. Finally, the constitutional situation has contributed to the phenomenon that, while the migration between Curaçao and the Netherlands is two-directional, the one between Suriname and its former mother country is largely a one-way traffic. This is another depressing result of decolonization, which has not failed to have an impact on Suriname nationalism.[6]

The notion of 'delusive continuity' will now be clearer. There are a number of permanent features of Caribbean migration to the Netherlands. People from the Caribbean came to 'Patria' from the earliest days of colonization. There was always a strong orientation towards the mother country. The Dutch reactions to the predominantly coloured migrants – a subject not yet discussed here – were never free of problems. However, it is the fault-lines which are more significant. The number of migrants has become incomparably larger and their presence is permanent. This has given the diaspora a significance of an entirely different kind, both in the Netherlands and in the Caribbean. The latter point is clear; the failure of the independence of Suriname is closely connected with the exodus, and the island communities of the Antilles too have been profoundly affected by the scale of the emigration. In the Netherlands, the relatively large-scale and far-reaching effects of the Caribbean diaspora was translated into more reserved attitudes towards West Indian migrants.

Events could hardly have proceeded differently, given the rather profound changes which the Netherlands underwent in the post-war period. The first wave of immigration from Indonesia was followed in the 1960s by the predominantly spontaneous influx of migrants from the Caribbean and the migration from the Mediterranean, which was initially organized from the Netherlands. More recently, the 'foreign' population has been enlarged with asylum seekers from various continents. Now that these 'newcomers' account for over ten per cent of the population, the Netherlands is becoming a multi-ethnic society, whether it likes it or not. This is particularly true of the large cities, where more than thirty per cent of the total population and half of the youth is classified as of foreign extraction.

Unfortunately, there are now solid grounds for speaking of the emergence of an ethnic underclass. In terms of a number of socio-economic criteria, the 'foreign' population lags far behind the 'native' population, and although there are large differences within the various ethnic groups, generally speaking the gap between 'foreigners' and 'natives' is wide and not clearly diminishing at best. The fact that this assumes less dramatic forms in the Netherlands than in many other immigration countries is closely connected with the social safety-net which still covers all aspects of life. However, state intervention of this kind has tended to disguise rather than prevent the marginalization of a very large number of new Dutch. With the ongoing contraction of the welfare state, they too are beginning to experience how precarious it is to depend on a hand which can take as well as give.

The situation of the Dutch Caribbean diaspora compares rather favourably to the general condition of so-called non-Western migrants in the Netherlands. There is a fairly large middle class, and according to the main socio-economic indicators the position of Dutch citizens of (partly) Caribbean extraction is clearly more favourable than that of the two other major migrant populations, Turks and Moroccans. Understandably, however, the Surinamese and Antilleans do not compare their situation primarily with that of other immigrants, but with that of the 'native' Dutch – and that picture is less rosy. In addition, there is a degree of xenophobia and racism among the 'native' population; although its actual scale is the subject of debate, it is undeniably more pronounced than it was a few decades ago. This is the background

against which one should view the concern and often anger or disen-
chantment of Caribbean Dutch at life in the metropolis. Materially it
may be a better life than in the Caribbean, but to many it is by no means
satisfying in terms of the new local standards which they have appropriated – not even mentioning the fact that many miss the satisfaction,
appreciation and happiness they had longed to find in 'the paradise of
Orange'.

The situation which arose as a result of the recent large-scale
immigration confronted the Netherlands with 'Others' in an unprecedented way. While Italians were still considered pretty exotic around
1960, since then the borders have been extended (for 'Europeans'), but
on the other hand it has become more difficult for outsiders to become
'Dutch'. Once again, this is much easier for someone from the Antilles
or Suriname than for a Turk or Moroccan – as is clearly shown by
interethnic relations and marriages – but it has indisputably become
more difficult than it used to be. It is this trend which sometimes makes
the older Caribbean migrants so bitter about the present-day situation,
and which makes it virtually impossible for a younger generation of
black Dutch to believe that things really were better 'in the old days'
than they are now.

Interpretations

If the fault-lines are clearer than the continuity of the migration history,
it is natural to ask what that early history still means for the present-day
generations of Caribbean Dutch. There is not much point in raising this
question for the more distant past; the answers are hidden too far back
in time. Of course we can ask ourselves what the experiences were of
the earlier migrants who lived in a 'different' era. One wonders how
they felt in patria, that Surinamese slave, that Curaçaoan child of a *shon*
and his slave girl, those children of the colonial elites? How were they
perceived and treated there? It is substance for speculation, but hardly
anything serious can be said. Travellers from the elites have scarcely left
any paper trail. All that is left of the others are some scattered anecdotes
and the occasional testimony. Only recent history has left a wide trail of
bureaucratic and personal papers in its wake. In addition, the fact that
this is in the imperfect tense, history still in the making, means that
those involved can still have their say.

Some twenty years ago I carried out research on the history of
Surinamese in the Netherlands. My research stopped at 1954 – an arbi-
trary limit except in a constitutional sense.[7] I had many conversations
with older Surinamese who had been living in the Netherlands for years,

sometimes even decades. At the same time my colleague Emy Maduro held interviews with older generations of Antilleans. The results of these interviews did provide some contours of Caribbean life in the Netherlands between the 1930s and the 1960s. In brief, it was a period in which the Dutch hardly came into contact with West Indians or other non-whites. The rarity of such encounters usually had some favourable results. Certainly European culture was permeated by ethnocentrism and a feeling of superiority to the non-West. The Netherlands was no exception in this respect, and this had an effect on the attitude towards coloured migrants. All the same, if encounters took place at all, they were dominated by naivety and curiosity rather than hostility – said our spokespeople. Additional research in press and government archives introduced some clouds to this relatively untroubled sky, but did not substantially alter the picture. Thus, the various interviewees voiced rather nice recollections. 'In general we were treated well, though I can mention some annoying incidents as well. Fortunately they were not very common. In the last instance, it was easier for Surinamese then than nowadays.' And so on, often followed by a tirade against 'some Surinamese' who 'today spoil it for the rest'. My Curaçaoan colleague was told similar stories by her interviewees.

What were these contours? What strikes one today in hearing these stories is the parochialism of the Netherlands in the middle decades of the century – the period of the German occupation of course being a different story in its own right. They related lack of familiarity on the part of the Dutch with 'foreigners', especially if their skin was dark. The continual confusion of East Indians and West Indians. The idea that blacks only lived in Africa and the United States, not in the Dutch colonial empire. The myths and expectations regarding typical black characteristics, from a feeling for music to sexual prowess. The naïve remarks on skin pigmentation ('is it colourfast?'), hair, teeth. And, beside that lack of familiarity, a wide range of attitudes, from quiet fascination to undisguised irritation – though there was more of the former than of the latter, most of the interviewees stressed. 'Benign curiosity?' I sometimes asked, and the interviewee usually agreed.

In retrospect, I have come to realize that it is precisely the parochial, sheltered quality of life in the Netherlands at that time – not implying, incidentally, that present-day Dutch culture is all that cosmopolitan – which helps to explain the predominantly positive tone of these memories. It was apparently fairly easy for a lack of familiarity to make way for acceptance, once the other was recognized as 'one of us'. Despite all the external differences, this was an easy step to take in the case of the migrants from the Dutch Caribbean colonies. They spoke Dutch, the Surinamese remarkably well. They generally belonged to the colonial middle class, with its strongly Dutch-oriented culture. And they could often join subcultures with a certain sense of security. The Catholics from Curaçao picked up the thread again with the Lay Brothers and the Catholic universities in the South, while the Moravian background of the Suriname students made it easier for them to relate to the Protestant Free University. Likewise, Anton de Kom found a setting in the Communist movement which recognized him as being 'one of us'. It was just as natural for the marines stationed in Terneuzen to be assisted by the villagers whom they had just liberated. One of the friendships that it provided in the case of the black but 'nonetheless' Catholic corporal Frank Koulen was that of the butcher. With winter approaching, he requested a girl neighbour to knit the corporal a jumper; she later became his wife. 'Shelteredness' implied a tendency to accept people in the same social situation, or like-minded people in a religious or ideological sense, despite what were initially such dominant differences. This openness created the conditions for a certain predictability and security for all.

This almost idyllic picture has to be taken with a pinch of salt. First, it has to be stated that, no matter how well-intentioned some Dutch might have been, isolation was always among the factors which determined the Caribbean experience. It was not until the 1950s that the Suriname associations gradually began to achieve something of the importance that they had had back in Suriname. In fact, however, it was not until the 1970s in the case of the Surinamese, and the 1980s in the case of the Curaçaoans, that they could boast something of a culture of their own on Dutch soil. Inevitably the earlier isolation had created a sense of loneliness at times, for one more than the next. Yet there must be more to recollect, and that seems to be the most difficult part. Isolation and loneliness cannot be reconstructed from the archives, and the same is true of the feelings of being accepted or not. Interviews with Surinamese or Antilleans can provide some further information on this point, but how much are they prepared to tell a – in my case, white Dutch male – interviewer, how reliable are their memories, and, depending on the positions they adopt today, how eager are they to suppress or magnify their recollections?

My own experiences with this set of problems have made me more sceptical, not so much about the possibility of reconstructing events, nor even about the recording of emotions, but about how to assess them. Every individual life-story, every individual description of what took place or was experienced at some point in time is a construction which not only varies from one individual to another, but is equally dependent on the context in which the recollection is retold, the distance in time from the original event, and the audience that one hopes to reach, or not to reach. Let me try to make this clear with a few remarks on the stories about Frank Koulen. When I was recording his life story in 1984 and 1985, I had conversations mainly with him and with one of his three daughters. After his death in 1985, when I got to know the family better, I was surprised at the divergences between the stories, and started asking myself different questions. I offer them for consideration.

The degree of acceptance by the Dutch is always a key issue, even more than the feelings which are so hard to discuss which this evokes in the 'object'. Nothing seems to be a foregone conclusion. A nickname like 'the Negro' immediately underscores that the white environment could hardly forget about the difference in physical appearance. But hardly is not the same as never. And was 'the Negro' merely a neutral statement, like 'redhead' or 'longlegs', or was it a denigrating or an affectionate term? What was more characteristic: the fact that the white woman wanted to marry this black man, and was allowed to do so, or the fact that various members of her family objected to it? Is it significant that some of the latter soon changed their minds completely? How is one to explain the fact that the various children from this one, tight-knit family – all coloured, unique in Terneuzen at the time – hold such different views on these questions, and have such different memories of their childhood? What is the relation between their present memory and their own later experiences, for some in the Netherlands or elsewhere in Europe and as far away as New Zealand, for others also or predominantly in the highly colour-sensitive Caribbean and the United States? And why does their white mother sometimes recall such different memories?

Perhaps I can answer some of these questions, but here I am simply raising them here to emphasize how careful we must be in interpreting all those individual migration stories. It is patently obvious that there is no single story, but an enormous collection of stories, and that the quest for the 'typical' story is only meaningful in a limited way. Perhaps we may succeed in reconstructing something of a lowest common denominator of experiences; but the feelings which go along with them cannot be reduced to a meaningful collection of experiences of the same kind. What we can and should do, however, is to reflect on ways of doing justice to the highly divergent stories. A first prerequisite in this respect is the recording and analysis of large collections of data and interviews. In turn, this calls for learning to scrutinize those stories for such obvious variables as ethnicity, nationality, gender, generation, class, kinship, length of stay, and degree of success in the new environment. Even then, the most difficult task is still probably that of searching for the space between what is told and what is felt.

One further remark in this connection. Researchers on Caribbean migration tend to concentrate on the migrants, but only in the last resort to write an account in which their experiences and feelings are set within a broader framework. By now we have become aware of the fact that the migrants have their own story. At the same time, however, there is often a tendency to think in classic bipolar terms when it comes to tackling the question of where the 'real' stories are to be found. In this sense the research approach I once adopted now strikes me as naïve. It is a particularly inappropriate approach when we are writing about the early migrants, who in the Netherlands at least (characteristically!) chose white partners almost by definition – were able to choose them more easily than in England and in sharp contrast to the United States – and thus had racially mixed children.[8] It seems advisable to be less doctrinaire than our statisticians in this field, who in their quantifying wisdom polish the racist American principle that white plus black equals black. The statisticians decided on their classification on the basis of honourable considerations, but as historians it is better for us to try to represent life in its actual diversity. This implies, among other things, that we should talk more seriously with the white partners and surroundings, and not be too eager to represent the children as Caribbean while they might feel more British, French or Dutch.

'Circus figures'

In 1986 the Curaçaoan historian Emy Maduro and myself published the first book on Caribbean history in the Netherlands. Published simultaneously with a volume on the history of Indonesians in the metropolis,[9] *In het land van de overheerser II: Antillianen en Surinamers in Nederland, 1634/1667–1954* received a relatively large amount of publicity. Some two thousand copies were sold, a large figure for the Dutch-language market. The reviews, largely by outsiders, and personal reactions, mainly from those involved, were predominantly friendly. Fifteen years ago that all gave the idea of having made a real contribution not only to historiography but even to the awareness and to improving the image of the groups involved.

Nowadays it is easier for me to question my mildly euphoric mood of the time. Who read the book and was satisfied with it apart from a Dutch reading public that had not known anything about this history before? Mainly, I now believe, relatively small groups of Surinamese and Antilleans. First of all, those directly involved, who could now read and get others to read their forgotten history in a narrative which, despite the necessary academic distance, was still quite flattering. The image in which the older generations recognized themselves was that of serious students, hard workers, who were generally well treated but of course did not offer the slightest provocation not to be. They were also satisfied because they were not described as white Dutch, but as people who were proud of their origins and who at the same time could cope perfectly with Dutch-style modernity.

More politically oriented, nationalistic Surinamese and Antilleans could also feel well served by the book. Of course, the title helped, and the book devoted considerable attention to the nationalist victories of the diaspora: the pre-war agitation against racism and fascism, the spectacular career of Anton de Kom, the suffering and resistance during the German occupation, and the post-war political and cultural nationalism. And then there were the sections on the period of accursed slavery which of course once again showed how dependent the slaves were on their masters, but also included stories of clever male and female slaves who, like genuine Anansi/Nanzi figures, against all odds obtained their freedom.[10]

Once out of the warm shower, one begins to realize that not only the distribution of *In het land van de overheerser*, but in a general sense the interest in the subject, has mainly been a matter for a small group of those directly involved, younger intellectuals, and a very limited Dutch public. The absence of any broader or more in-depth follow-up to the book by others is an indication of this. The themes of the few larger publications which did appear suggest the same: a collection of recollections of Anton de Kom, another with fragments from the history of Suriname nationalism in the Netherlands, a work of journalism full of anecdotes on 'the first Negro' in all kinds of obscure parts of the Netherlands, a biography of a Suriname jazz musician who preferred to be presented as a black *American* (even more exotic).[11] Then there was a catalogue of a controversial exhibition on Western images of blacks, in which that theme from *In het land van de overheerser* was treated in more detail and in a considerably more assertive tone, and the much more distanced treatment of the same subject by Allison Blakely, *Blacks in the Dutch World*. The last two studies raise in particular the question of to what extent the cultural expressions analyzed in them really reflect the development of a – monolithic? – Dutch culture, and whether it is reasonable to speak about national reactions to a phenomenon – the presence of blacks, or images of blacks – that was completely marginal in the Netherlands until a few decades ago.[12]

The small number of the other publications and their apparently modest impact confirmed my doubts about the importance of publications of this kind, my own included. What do present-day Caribbean Dutch know about their 'prehistory'? What importance do they attach to it? As part of a larger survey, a non-select group of Dutch of Surinamese or Antillean origin were asked what they knew about that early history.[13] The results confirmed my doubts resoundingly. The vast majority of the interviewees thought that Caribbean history in the Netherlands did not begin until the post-war period. Only a tiny minority knew that Surinamese and Antillean slaves had been taken to the Netherlands in the past. Precisely a small number of highly engaged Surinamese described the early generation as 'a handful of circus figures', a reference to the late nineteenth-century colonial exhibitions with their areas for 'natives', or to the twentieth-century 'professional Negroes'. The prehistory has no point of reference at all to offer for Surinamese of British Indian or Javanese extraction: the diaspora of 'their' group began in the 1970s, and they hardly relate at all to the issues of Creole nationalism. Furthermore, there is no organized transfer of the history of the migrants. In so far as stories are told at all, this is done within a small circle, which is usually ethnically homogeneous. To date, there have been only a few attempts to place the story of the migrants in historical perspective through local television or radio programmes.

The conclusion is hard to avoid. You are not dead until you are forgotten. The history of Frank Koulen and all the other early migrants who remain anonymous here continues as long as their immediate relatives and friends still talk about them. But at the same time their stories – and this is even truer of the stories about the eighteenth-century slaves or nineteenth-century students – no longer appear to hold any interest at all for most Caribbean Dutch today. The actual rupture in the migration history situated around 1970 has left a corresponding mark in the memory of the diaspora.

A multifaceted diaspora

So if in the experience of most Caribbean Dutch the roots of the diaspora only reach back a couple of decades, can we speak of 'history' at all? I am not arguing for a pointless internecine warfare between historians and other social scientists on who is the legitimate 'owner' of the research object. Still, we cannot entirely ignore the conclusion that we are addressing a history that is only just beginning, and that it is by no means clear what direction it is heading in. What is studied in a British Caribbean context is a story covering many generations, a history whose contours have gradually crystallized: the bifurcation towards England and the United States/Canada, the varying degrees of success in both directions, the degree of circularity of the migration, and the differences in behaviour and experiences of the various generations involved.

The Dutch Caribbean diaspora is still lacking in clear-cut contours. There is some clarity as regards which topics are analyzed to death by social scientists, such as social mobility, position on the labour market, and participation in education. The picture that emerges from this research gives grounds for concern in some respects, but at the same time bears witness to large differences within the by no means uniform Caribbean Dutch population group. The ethnicity factor seems – justifiably – to be receiving more and more attention in these analyses. How could it be otherwise? Even where it is possible to carry out more historically oriented research, we cannot get around the fact that the Caribbean Dutch diaspora actually breaks down into widely divergent groups: the Curaçaoans and the Surinamese of Creole, British Indian and Javanese origin live in social spheres which are to a large extent different from one another. In this respect the British West Indian diaspora is considerably more homogeneous, despite the differences in island characters which are so often pinpointed.

A ready illustration of the importance of these ethnic contrasts is furnished by indications that in socio-economic terms, the Hindustani Suriname group is more successful, or at least gaining ground, in comparison to its Creole Suriname counterpart. Obviously, such contrasts are then enthusiastically forwarded by intellectuals from this group themselves.[14] Moreover, with respect to the use of leisure time and affective relations, the disparity which was so typical of Suriname is continued, or even reinforced, in the Netherlands. 'Race' is certainly not the only factor in this process. There is still an enormous gap separating the Afro-Surinamese world from the Afro-Curaçaoan one. The cultural differences between the two groups were traditionally expressed most clearly in the mutual unintelligibility of their individual languages, i.e. Sranan Tongo and Papiamentu. The linguistic choice made in the diaspora could eventually diminish this cleavage, ironically enough as a result of the 'colonial' language. For the time being this process is proceeding at a snail's pace. While Dutch – with all of its variations of Suriname-Dutch – is gradually gaining ground at the expense of Sranan Tongo among Afro-Surinamese, between themselves Curaçaoans in the Netherlands cling to Papiamentu, that one unmistakable mark of their own culture.

In other respects too it is futile to imagine the Caribbean Dutch diaspora as a uniform entity. The shorter duration of Antillean history in the Netherlands increases the orientation towards 'there'. The divergent paths followed by constitutional developments have also had a direct, painful effect on the migration. The continuing 'post-colonial' status of the Netherlands Antilles guarantees Antilleans both a comparatively high standard of living on the islands and the right to freedom of movement between the two parts of the Kingdom and to settle in either of them. It is therefore hardly surprising that there is a large degree of two-way traffic in the case of Curaçaoan migrants. The contrast with Suriname is stark. Not only have the standard of living and the economic prospects there fallen dramatically in the three decades since independence, at the same time independence heralded the end of the possibility of settling freely in either country. The protracted crisis of the republic has meant a virtual drying up of return migration to Suriname. The new constitutional relation also made it more and more difficult to follow the legal route to the Netherlands; hence the increasing number of Surinamese leaving illegally for the former mother country.

Where is home?

How important is 'there' today for Caribbean Dutch, and to what extent do Surinamese differ from Antilleans in the way they think and talk? In 1995, I tried to obtain some insight into these questions by means of street research among just over one hundred Surinamese and Antilleans – no representative sample to be sure, but an indication. When asked where their close relatives lived, more than half replied that these lived mainly in the Netherlands; only half that number replied that most of their relatives lived 'there'. As one would expect, the latter figure was appreciably higher for the Antilleans than for the Surinamese – twice as high, in fact. For these Antilleans, then, the word 'family' still referred primarily to 'there', a stage which the Suriname interviewees passed long ago. Since, however, the balance between the number of Curaçaoans living 'back home' and in the metropolis has dramatically changed and is now more or less at a par with the Surinamese figure, thus presently in the order of 55 to 60 per cent in the Caribbean as against 40 to 45 per cent in the Netherlands.

Of course, the place of residence of the close relatives elicits a natural affinity, and in this sense it is striking to what extent the Suriname Dutch interviewed in the Netherlands were rooted there. However, this does not mean that they had forgotten their overseas relatives and friends. There were no significant differences between the various groups in the frequency of telephone calls; the number of Surinamese who hardly corresponded anymore was high in this sample. Nor were there significant differences in the frequency of visits. On the other hand, the majority of Creole Surinamese in particular indicated that they regularly sent food parcels or money. The considerably better economic situation on Curaçao probably explains why this direct support did not play any significant part in the Antillean Dutch circuit.

Another question is that of the affinity which Caribbean Dutch felt with 'here' and 'there'. Once again, the sample suggested that the Surinamese, especially the younger generation, identified more closely with their new home country than the Antilleans did; but in both cases this orientation remained ambivalent. Further questioning confirmed the obvious supposition that most of them also felt some close affinity with 'compatriots'. In general, they also expressed close affinity with 'compatriots' in the Netherlands; this affinity extended to a lesser extent to Caribbean Dutch from elsewhere. At the same time, however, the orientation of Surinamese and Antilleans in an intimate sphere like that of choice of partner was apparently shifting towards Dutch partners alongside or even in preference to compatriots, a shift confirmed by the impressions one gets from walking down the street today. The little quantitative research available corroborates this impression, with the significant caveat that this applies mainly to Caribbean Dutch from African origins, and for now the least for Hindustani Surinamese.[15]

Finally, the bitter reality of the differences in the standard of living 'there' was directly expressed in the prospects of ever going back. Most of the Antilleans assumed that they would return. This was appreciably more complex for Surinamese. A large majority responded that they would [re]settle in Suriname at some point in the future, but most of the members of this group tied this wish to a number of hard-to-meet conditions. The reality of the migration statistics suggests that they were expressing a wish or a socially desirable reply rather than a genuine option.

The results of this modest sample suggested some clear-cut differences between Curaçaoans and Surinamese. On the other hand, neither gender nor generation seemed to play an important role in this sample, nor did the ethnic background of the Surinamese. While both groups retained a sense of affinity with the country of birth and with fellow countrymen both in the Netherlands and in the Caribbean, there is much less likelihood that the Surinamese desire to return expressed a real option. This difference cannot be explained primarily in terms of a significantly better position of the Surinamese in the Netherlands, but is connected with the troubled situation in Suriname itself. One may expect that the orientation towards 'there' will decrease further among later generations. The fact that this did not emerge clearly from the 1995 survey indicates that the younger Dutch generation of Suriname origin still felt an engagement with their parent's native country, but that at the same time orientation among the older generation of Surinamese had shifted in the direction of *Bakrakondre,* the Sranan Tongo name for 'White man's country'. The fact that this was apparently much less true of the Antilleans is partly due to the more favourable situation on their island.

In addition, it is relevant that the Antillean migration to *Ulanda* started up later and was on a smaller scale – the island still existed for them as the paradise overseas, while the Surinamese lost *their* Eldorado long ago.

In all kinds of gradations, the lives of these migrants, and especially of their children, are still firmly orientated on 'here' and 'there', on a Caribbean background and on the metropolis that never had such a direct significance before. One might be tempted to forget that this orientation has remained remarkably limited. Despite the fact that many have found their feet in the Netherlands, for many others *Bakrakondre* or *Ulanda* has completely failed to offer the opening to social success or personal development. The statistics on the labour market, education, housing, etc., point in the same direction as those on medical consumption or crime: there is still a long way to go, and not only for the late arrivals from Curaçao. Many Caribbean Dutch therefore will deny that the route to the Netherlands was the right one. All the same, the option of a different destination is hardly of any importance. The rather worn metaphor of the umbilical cord linking the metropolis with the former colonies is more relevant than ever. This is striking evidence not just of the time-hallowed intertwining of interests which is so often cited, but equally of the postcolonial 'trap': although the Netherlands may not be an easy destination, it is still the country where there is the best chance of success, and where failure can be concealed the longest.

The Dutch Caribbean case is not an isolated one. Generally speaking, the Caribbean migration to Europe is much more heavily influenced by the attractiveness of what by Caribbean and American standards is an extended welfare state – a magnet which turns out to be a trap now that many of these facilities are being curtailed. This is as true of the West Indians in England and of the *négropolitains* in France as it is of the Dutch Caribbean community. These former colonial subjects enjoy more privileges than other groups of immigrants, such as unconditional citizenship and access to social services. All the same, their situation does not always compare favourably to that of other, less sheltered immigrants. In the case of the United States, the parallel contrast can be drawn between what were generally characterized – until recently at least – as successful West Indians on the one hand versus the Puerto Ricans on the other who have so often been regarded as 'losers', 'ungrateful immigrants' all too dependent on welfare.

The awkward question rears it head: are post-colonial traumatization and metropolitan patronizing perhaps factors which make it difficult for the *nuyoricans* in the U.S., the Jamaicans in England and the Martinicans in France to make full use of what is in theory a relatively favourable starting position? Might the same apply to migrants from the Antilles and Suriname in the Netherlands? Might the frustration of many Caribbean Dutch about the lack of success be connected with unrealistic expectations, the result of a feeling cultivated for generations that everything is better there, and a feeling which became attached to this later on that *Ulanda* or *Bakrakondre* is obliged to provide after having taken for so long? There seems to be a lot to be said for such a hypothesis, and for the conclusion that this attitude not only increases frustration but also has a paralyzing effect. Not just because the discontented stop believing in their own capabilities, but also in the sense that the number of those who decide to seek their fortunes outside the Netherlands is still negligible.[16] For those who fail to seize the opportunities, the protection afforded by the mother country can imperceptibly be transformed into a stranglehold.

Old stories and a new future

The history of Dutch Caribbean migration is marked, not by continuities, but by a fault-line which has emerged in the last decades. Furthermore, there is no single history which unites Suriname and the Antilles. Finally, while the Dutch Caribbean migrants are part of a much larger story about Caribbean migrations, there are hardly any traces of an awareness of this fact. No matter how much has been said about a shared fate, the Caribbean diaspora is still essentially divided, ignorant of and uninterested in the parallel histories.

What does all this mean for the historiography of the Dutch Caribbean diaspora? First of all, it would he incorrect not to differentiate between Antilleans and Surinamese. In fact, it even seems misguided to attribute a single past to the different ethnic groups from Suriname. Another point which should be borne in mind is that the circularity of the migration currents, the continuous come and go of migrants which is so often assumed in studies of the Caribbean diaspora must be critically interrogated and not taken as given. In view of the fact that the divide between the Netherlands and Suriname seems to be growing, it is no longer so natural that historians of the diaspora should continue to let themselves be guided by the ever more mythical idea of the first generations of migrants, as if the transatlantic crossing were to remain a constant two-way traffic. Until recently at least, the Antillean migration history seemed to fit the standard Caribbean pattern better than the Surinamese one-way traffic. But perhaps it is sensible not to accept the cherished ideas on a Caribbean migration movement too readily, as by definition two-directional phenomenon.

The Dutch Caribbean population numbers over 435,000 and will continue to grow. It is bound to become increasingly Dutch, while at the same time creating it own niches in a dominant culture which, partly as a result of the spectrum of migrations, is itself continuously changing. All the same, it is obvious that Caribbean culture in exile is under much heavier pressure than the culture of the 'mother country', no matter how much globalization embraces all cultures. In this sense the commonly voiced belief in the resilience of those Caribbean cultures which even flourish in the relative isolation of the diaspora seems to be overly optimistic. Similar caution should be exercised regarding the belief in the 'transnational family networks' which are supposed to link the Caribbean diaspora with what is too readily labelled 'home'. The prehistory of the current diaspora may go back a long way, but it took a decisive new turn a couple of decades ago. Historians will increasingly have to write a story of detachment from 'there' and the often difficult, often discouraging attachment to 'here'. A lot of this work is already being done by an army of social scientists, but the fact that even many of the liveliest studies lack a sense of history would appear to say something, not only about the researchers and their interests, but also about the low level of interest in the history of the migration on the part of their interviewees.

Still, there are wonderful tales to be told, and they *are* told. When I first recorded stories of this kind almost twenty years ago, I had hardly any idea of their depth and scope, nor of the inevitable, almost systematic distortions, repetitions and clichés they contain. The challenge is undoubtedly to search further for stories, and in the process to raise different, less obvious questions and to make fresh connections. The stories are there, even though the earliest, from before the exodus, are growing more and more scarce. The older generation of Surinamese and Antilleans from the 1995 survey indicated that they did pass on their own life-stories, and that they did find a hearing for these. Historians can help to preserve those stories, but they should do so without romanticizing them. The 'old' stories of isolated migrants in an almost fully white world belong definitively to the past.

Surinamese war veterans have often complained bitterly that their role in the Second World War was never noticed. It is a justifiable complaint, but at the same time this will never change: they were simply too small a group to attract much attention. Their stories run into the dozens only. They are no match for the stories of millions of others in the Netherlands. Only now has that all changed, only now are the Caribbean Dutch a visible group in this Dutch society. But it does not matter to the veterans any more. Their history remains an early footnote to the exodus. A few observers of the 5 May parade may nurture touching memories of a Caribbean migrant, but that history is not the same as the history which is being written today.

Notes

1 The surname was taken to Suriname around the turn of the century by another migrant worker. *Balata bleeder* Samuel Frederik Koulen, born in Berbice in 1881, was recorded as living at Achterstraat 5 in Nieuw Nickerie, although at the time of the census he was 'away (in the forest)', *1921 Census, Nickerie District*. (Balata is a rubber-like substance produced from the latex of the balata tree; the labourers who worked in the interior of the Guyana's to extract latex from the trees were called balata bleeders.)

2 After the German occupation of the Netherlands (1940) and the Japanese occupation of Indonesia (1942), these two Caribbean colonies were the only 'free' Dutch territories.

3 The survey of Dutch Caribbean migration history is mainly taken from Oostindie & Maduro 1986, Oostindie 1988, 1990 and 1995b, Oostindie & Klinkers 2003, Chapter 9, and the literature cited there. For present purposes, I have refrained from giving detailed references.

4 The Netherlands Antilles consisted of six islands until the separation of Aruba in 1986. The Antillean migrants are predominantly from the main island, Curaçao. Therefore, in this text 'Antilleans' and 'Curaçaoans' are used interchangeably.

5 The population in Suriname itself is estimated at 450,000, that from Curaçao at 120,000. More than half of the interviewees in the street survey were unable to provide a reasonable estimate of the number of people 'there', or of the number of their fellow countrymen in the Netherlands.

6 See Chapter 5.

7 In 1954, the *Statuut* or Charter of the Kingdom of the Netherlands was promulgated, granting for the first time a high degree of domestic authority to the two Caribbean partners in what then became the tripartite Kingdom. Suriname became independent in 1975, the Netherlands Antilles and (since its secession from The Netherlands Antilles in 1986) Aruba still function within the same regime. See Chapter 4.

8 Scholars like Mary Chamberlain (1997) and Karen Fog Olwig (1993) rightly emphasize the importance of family networks in the migration process. They do not pay much attention though to the consequences of interracial relations for the family network, which is then by definition no longer exclusively Caribbean (in terms of origin or orientation). This approach may be justified to a large extent in the US or British context, but it is clearly too restrictive for dealing with the French Caribbean and Dutch Caribbean migration history.

9 Poeze et al. 1986. In translation, the title is 'In the Land of the Ruler'.

10 Anansi/Anancy/Nanzi/Nancy – a character in African/Caribbean folklore – is a spider who assumes different shapes and forms to escape from numerous scrapes.

11 Kagie 1989, Oppenneer 1995, Vereniging Ons Suriname 1990.

12 Blakely (1993) has some provocative suggestions in this respect, while Nederveen Pieterse (1990) takes it all to be a matter of course, which is hardly very satisfactory.

13 The interviews, just over 100, were held in Amsterdam, Rotterdam, The Hague, Leiden and Zoetermeer in the summer of 1995. See Oostindie 1998 for Tables.

14 Choenni & Adhin 2003.

15 Choenni & Adhin 2003:61, 88, 174–5, 218.

16 Though a small tributary of the Suriname diaspora has developed in the United States during the last few decades.

7 | Colonial past, contemporary identities

History binds the Dutch Caribbean to the Netherlands. It is a history unknown to most Dutch and one in which few have a genuine interest. Yet in the Dutch Caribbean this same, shared history is very strongly felt and provokes heated emotions. Over the last few decades the discussion about this shared history has frequently been pursued in terms of guilt and atonement. This approach has certainly helped to alert the Dutch to this forgotten and perhaps intentionally silenced part of their history. Representing this history in these terms may also be emotionally gratifying to some who feel they still carry the burden of this past with them everyday. Yet interpreting this past history and its legacies in overly moralistic terms is not particularly fruitful if one is seeking to truly understand it.

What else have people on both sides of the Atlantic still in common, or what can they have in common? How does the colonial legacy still mark national identity in the Dutch Caribbean? Such important questions are less frequently asked. In the post-war period, the existence of a unique Dutch Caribbean identity was constantly postulated. Today, the delineation of this identity continues to be rather unsatisfactory, partly because certain questions seem to be taboo; questions about profound domestic and internal differences, for instance, and the continuing weight of the Dutch legacy. These questions lie at the heart of this chapter. They also bring us to questions of Dutch identity, of that wonderful mix of 'Dutch' and 'Caribbean' that gives Suriname and the Antillean islands such a distinct character, and of the position of the former Dutch colonies within their Caribbean context. What I offer in this closing essay is some reflections on these issues, a sort of wrapping up of the preceding pages, and a postscript written six years after the completion of *Het paradijs overzee* in which I ponder the most recent developments.[1]

Guilt and atonement

Tracing the past of the Caribbean continues to resemble the reconstruction of something that has been irrevocably lost, at least insofar as we are looking for the social history behind the succession of governors, wars, colonial regulations, population numbers, trade figures or production statistics. Yet today we are mainly interested in precisely that which has been irrevocably lost, and about which experts are expected to create a clear, preferably easily understood picture, and to pass judgement. What those experts reconstruct and omit can be used to help young Caribbean states create a genealogy and even an identity.

Sometimes this leads us into murky waters. Is it stubborn misunderstandings, or is it something less naive which repeatedly leads to exaggerations of Dutch involvement in the slave trade and to massive overstatements of the number of slaves taken by Dutch slavers to the Caribbean? Why are some so keen to believe that the building of Amsterdam's canals was made possible due to the exploitation of West Indian slaves, even though the expansion of the city had largely been completed some decades *before* the Antilles or Suriname were even colonized? Why is the myth that slavery in Suriname was the harshest variant in the New World so popular among Surinamese, and why do Curaçaoan historians make such fierce attempts to refute the image of a 'mild' form of slavery on *their* island? Why is it sometimes argued that Hindustani or Javanese contract workers had just as harsh and desperate a lot as the slaves before them? Why are the domestic problems of Afro-Caribbean families today in lower class neighbourhoods such as Seroe Fortuna (Curaçao), Latour (Paramaribo), the Bijlmer (Amsterdam), or Hoogvliet (Rotterdam) so readily blamed on the heritage of slavery?

This and similar, possibly rhetorical questions once again point to the predicament of Dutch-Caribbean nation building, to its postcolonial context which is as depressing here as it is elsewhere in the region. Where there is so much division and discontent about the present, and so much uncertainty about the future, it seems to be the colonial past that offers at least some firm ground in which to anchor national identity. That past figures a mother country which lacked dedication and concern and which, even when not actively colluding in the many excesses, at least turned a blind eye. This provides some kind of foothold for an identity: more so at least than a positively engaging attitude towards the mother country, more than an emphasis of internal divisions, more than an awareness of the continuing exodus. A history of exploitation, maltreatment and heroic resistance offers reassuring possibilities for the formulation of a unique identity without having to pose tricky questions about the present. This is the anti-colonial history that has indeed been passed down through generations of Surinamese Maroons and forms the core of their identity. Something similar was sought by the Surinamese nationalist, Anton de Kom, when writing *Wij slaven van Suriname* ('We Slaves of Suriname') in the 1930s 'to arouse Surinamese self-respect'.[2]

Bitter resentment has often been voiced in the colonies in response to the self-satisfied metropolitan version of history once taught there. The reaction of twentieth-century nationalists was predictable: a new, staunchly anti-colonial version of the colonial past had to be developed and circulated. Insofar as this came to pass, there was little room for subtleties. This lack of nuance did not matter to the Netherlands, which since the 1960s liked to think of itself as progressive and solidary. There had never been much interest in the West Indian past and, besides, it was barely considered part of Dutch history. This attitude now began to make way for humility and a – somewhat eager – willingness to admit guilt for everything bad that had ever been done in 'the West'. Yet this politically correct mode of bending over backwards essentially also testifies to contempt.

The development of a counter-history, a truly local account of this past, did not run smoothly. One of the problems encountered by the nationalists was how to deal with the divisions among their own population. Understandably, nationalist discourse prefers to obfuscate these divisions rather than elucidate them. Anyone who tells potentially divisive stories about the past, perhaps raising painful questions about the present, may bank on a certain degree of scepticism. All this is logical. The Netherlands has her own taboos regarding her colonial past, as well as many other issues – as have other nations. Nevertheless, while the character of Dutch society and its past are constantly being questioned and criticized today – whether or not in connection with its colonial past – this appears to be a far more delicate affair in Suriname and the Antilles. And thus one encounters the strange paradox that while, until recently at least, any entreaty to define and protect domestic national identity was met with awkward embarrassment in the Netherlands, it was matched by overly sympathetic Dutch reactions to similar attempts in Suriname, the Dutch Antilles or Aruba. In the process of nation building, these small, 'young' countries are apparently entitled to take whatever liberties they see fit in the interpretation of their history, and criticism is politely subdued for fear of being denounced as neo-colonialist.

Like any metropolitan historian working on his nation's erstwhile colonies, a Dutch researcher writing on the Dutch Caribbean is soon confronted with peculiar choices which, in this context, have a different sensitivity than if he or she were researching some distant phase or place in the history of Holland, France or, for that matter, Cuba. Although themes such as slavery, ethnicity and 'race' are not at all as strongly polarized in the Dutch Caribbean as they are elsewhere, especially in the United States, there is still an unmistakable tendency for polarization. Caution is therefore advisable. But how much? What is there for an historian of the Dutch Caribbean to do? There is a lot that needs to be brought to light, which otherwise, unjustly, is as good as ignored by Dutch historiography. Too much is still shrouded in silence and without this 'silenced history' of slavery, of colonial exploitation and neglect, neither the past of the Dutch Caribbean, nor of the Netherlands can be properly understood and written.[3] But where is the point of equilibrium between empathy and distance?

It often seems tempting to give precedence to empathy over distance. Anyone imagining the bloodcurdling scenes that must have taken place almost everyday on Suriname's plantations, would be more inclined to denounce slavery than to place it within a comparative context which might moderate the commonly held belief that slavery in Suriname was exceptionally sadistic. And whoever does so risks being suspected of veneering over something that should only be spoken off in terms of abhorrence.[4] Yet a researcher who does not maintain a distance from his or her subject will find it difficult to reach new perspectives and in this sense the pursuit of a certain distance should go without saying.

Thus, whoever writes on slavery without addressing slave resistance does not write history but creates myths; but the same is true of anyone who writes on slavery while excluding privileged, accommodating and even collaborating Afro-Caribbeans from the account. Whoever writes the post-war history of Curaçao without discussing the May 1969 revolt obscures the rigid stratification of socio-racial classes which had previously prevailed; whereas not daring to critically question the political and social achievements of Afro-Caribbean emancipation since May 1969 serves only to sustain new myths. Whoever describes Surinamese nationalism as proof of an aroused, triumphant self-awareness in relation to the Netherlands, without taking into consideration the deep ethnic divides, the massive resentment against the nationalist endeavour and the woeful inequities of independence will, perhaps despite the best of intentions, contribute to the ever-faltering start of the republic. This is not the way. Whoever applauds the achievement of Aruba's separate status should also be willing to question the awkward debate about who is a 'true' Aruban. Whoever struggles to envisage the entire island of St Martin as a single nation should be willing to address the fact that its population is still divided along many different lines and apparently has no qualms about being so. And so on, and so forth.

A firm and 'unique' national identity is no less diligently sought in the Dutch Caribbean and its diaspora than elsewhere in the region. The mixed accomplishments of decolonization are usually spoken of with the greatest of caution. And as far as history is given a role in the formulation of this new identity, it is all too frequently done so in defensive terms, in an atmosphere appositely described as 'collective victimology' by the prolific Dutch writer of Surinamese background, Anil Ramdas.[5] Although not particularly useful, this defensive attitude is understandable. Even where Antilleans and

Surinamese no longer feel like hammering on the anvil of colonial guilt, the guilt still exists. Even if it is the task of the historian to deduce and refute, and ultimately to offer the opportunity of a more balanced judgement; even if it is therefore also his or her task to establish that the Dutch slave trade was of secondary importance – this same historian should also raise the question in the Netherlands as to why at the turn of the millennium there was still not a single monument to slavery in the Netherlands.[6]

This reveals the Netherlands' ambivalent attitude towards her own colonial past. Expressing abhorrence about the wrongs perpetrated *over there* is easy, because this history is still not regarded as part of the national history. The Dutch seventeenth-century Golden Age is the epoch of Rembrandt, the Amsterdam canals, of Grotius, Spinoza, of the Dutch East India Company and perhaps Piet Hein's silver fleet – but not the beginning of the West Indian slave trade. Since 1945, the Dutch have been enthusiastic criticizers of the Germans, and many wearily observed the controversies surrounding a new holocaust memorial in Berlin which frequently made the Dutch press in the 1990s. But as long as there was no Dutch monument to commemorate the slave trade, wouldn't the Dutch have been well advised to keep a low profile on this part of the *Vergangenheitsbewältigung*, the German coming to terms with the Nazi past? Slavery was not a holocaust, and the equation between the two phenomena is sometimes advanced for reprehensible motives. But a living past really can go back four hundred years, and not just fifty.

I have mentioned the Dutch slave trade, but not the Netherlands' role in Indonesia and the traumatic transfer of sovereignty between 1945 and 1949. On the face of it, this Asian story presents just as many reasons for discussing colonial guilt. But although the heated debates in the Dutch press might suggest otherwise, this question has long since lost its urgency, especially since Indonesians regard the Dutch and a Dutch admission of guilt to be far less relevant than Antilleans or Surinamese do. This is yet another distinction between East and West. A complex of guilt and ensuing obligations can come to dominate a relationship in cases where the past has not been confronted and when there is a vast and inescapable imbalance of power and wealth. This pattern pertains to the relationship that binds the Netherlands and the Dutch Caribbean, but for obvious reasons much less to the relationship between the Netherlands and Indonesia.

The paradoxical 'Dutchification'

To reiterate, what links the Dutch Caribbean and the Netherlands is primarily the past. Throughout this history they came to share more and more: the Dutch language, the Surinamese more than the Antilleans; a shared nationality, still valid today for Antilleans; the transatlantic nature of the Antillean and Surinamese communities. These factors make these parts of the Caribbean 'Dutch' and fundamentally different from the surrounding countries with their 'French', 'British' or 'Spanish' characteristics. But at the same time it should be established that neither Suriname, nor Aruba, nor any other of the five Netherlands Antilles really resemble the Netherlands, anymore than they do each other – Guadeloupe and Martinique resemble France and each other significantly more.

The differences within the 'Dutch Caribbean' are largely attributable to the different purposes each part served within the West Indian territories of the colonial empire; purposes which were primarily determined by their environment, natural resources and location. But this heterogeneity also points to the scant interest the Netherlands had in making the Caribbean colonies truly Dutch. This story has already been told in the previous chapters. A significant section of what was already a small white population in the 'West' was not even of Dutch origin. The few Dutch families who did stay lost their sense of affinity with patria over the generations. They, along with other Europeans and a small Dutch civil service apparatus stood atop a population that seemed to inhabit another world beyond the realms of work and authority; the divisions began with the languages that were spoken by the colonial subjects, though these were eventually adopted by more and more whites.

Only after the abolition of slavery, and especially in the twentieth century, did Dutch policy become more geared towards assimilation. And here the paths of Surinamese and Antillean history diverge. In Suriname the Creole elite supported the infusion of Dutch culture into Suriname. The education system, in which Dutch was the official language, was to play a decisive role in this. The attempt at assimilation passed laboriously, partly because of an influx of tens of thousands Asian contract workers. Suriname's insertion into Dutch culture made significant progress when, in the period following the Second World War, elites from the new immigrant groups decided to follow Dutch models for individual and national advancement. Thence arose the paradox of a growing willingness to assimilate, which ultimately did not suit the Netherlands. The moment the process of decolonization became more imminent was precisely when the colony began increasingly to identify with the Netherlands.

Although Suriname became independent in 1975, it was more a consequence of the missionary zeal of a small number of strongly Dutch-oriented Creole intellectuals and Dutch pressure, than of a broad-based movement in Suriname itself. The level of resistance to

independence reflected the success of a late, but unexpectedly successful, assimilation policy. Rather than settling down in the Latin
American world to which, geographically speaking, Suriname belongs,
most of her nationals – whether they stayed or emigrated – chose to
continue ties with the Netherlands.

On the Antilles the Netherlands demonstrated itself to be a rather
absent-minded colonizer. Until the twentieth century the most important intervention made by the Netherlands, after colonization, was the
abolition of slavery – in ethical respects a positive intervention, in
economic terms ultimately a rather futile one. A cultural offensive by
the government was launched late in the day, in the twentieth century. On the Windward Islands English continued to be the dominant
language, while on the Leeward Islands it was Papiamentu. So it was
in the eighteenth century, and so it remains today. With the current
language problems that exist within the Kingdom, the Netherlands is
reaping the rewards of centuries of negligent colonialism.

In view of this, there is an irony to the course of decolonization.
Suriname, with its age-old and almost exclusive orientation towards the
Netherlands was finally persuaded to accept independence. Antillean
and Aruban politicians resisted pressure to follow suit. With imposed
independence hanging like the sword of Damocles above their heads,
they began to stress the 'centuries of solidarity' that had existed between
the Antilles and the Netherlands – certainly not the strongest in the
string of generally convincing arguments they have put on the table over
the last few decades. However, their arguments illustrate how much an
imaginary history can be turned to serve political ends, particularly in
the context of the Dutch Caribbean in which almost nothing happened
in the way the colonizer had envisaged.

Dutch identity and the Caribbean

It is hard enough to speak of cultural homogeneity within the 'Dutch'
Caribbean – partly due to the major language differences – without
including the Netherlands in this cultural domain. This limited level of
resemblance points to an incapacity on the part of the Dutch, but also to
the lack of interest the Netherlands had, until well into the twentieth
century, of drawing 'the West' into her own cultural sphere.

Dutch society had very little interest in the Caribbean, more or less
from the seventeenth century until the mid-twentieth century. Europe
was important, as were the East Indies and, later, the United States. But
not the West, and certainly not after hopes of a West Indian Eldorado
had definitively evaporated by the mid-eighteenth century. In the inter-

im, business, including the slave trade, was carried on with iron cynicism. The delay before the Dutch finally abolished slavery was yet another indication of this. In vain we scrutinize this history for a trace of the 'embarrassment of riches' considered so characteristic of the Dutch.[7]

Much changed following the Second World War. Indonesia was 'lost' and through the vicissitudes of decolonization, and especially the exodus, Suriname and the Antilles soon began to attract metropolitan attention. For the first time the Dutch Caribbean became an issue, albeit to the displeasure of the mother country. The increase in Dutch involvement was matched by its growing ambivalence. Where in previous centuries the Dutch had regarded their own culture as being too superior for the West, there now emerged a certain embarrassment, a guilty realization that this minor European culture could not be imposed on the Caribbean. It was therefore helpful that colonial ties were now waning. Complete overseas autonomy was being demanded and anxiously respected, also in education policy and language politics. Dutch instruments of cultural policy, such as Sticusa, were dismantled.[8] Some contentedly believed that the Netherlands had finally learned its place. However, this about turn might just as well be understood as a new expression of disinterest, even condescension; the final refusal to build up something in 'the West'.

It has since become clear that the Dutch Antilles and Aruba will long remain within the Kingdom, while independence has not really detached Suriname from the Netherlands. This conclusion provokes new questions, including the significance of 'the West' to Dutch identity, and vice versa. The first question is easier to answer than the second. The fact that, unlike half a century years ago, the Dutch are now aware of the existence of the former colonies in the Caribbean, is primarily a consequence of the exodus. On a somewhat more intellectual level, the issue of decolonization has perhaps left a few traces on the thinking of Dutch identity and foreign policy, even if the struggle for Indonesian independence is considered more important. Nonetheless, even the 1990s debates about Dutch identity generally ignored the Dutch Caribbean, or at best referred to this unique product of colonialism indirectly.

An influential collection of essays published in the mid-1990s, *Het nut van Nederland* (The Point of the Netherlands) is an apposite illustration. In the introductory article, Paul Scheffer argues that the quest for a Dutch identity has recently received a significant impulse, to the point of becoming crucially important, due to two radical developments: European unification and large-scale immigration, as a consequence of which the Netherlands is developing into a multicultural society. Not all the authors in the book agree with the consequences Scheffer attaches to this.

However, his explanation – the dual cause behind the flourishing identity debate – produces virtually no rejoinders. The Dutch Caribbean plays an implicit part in this context, namely, as the producer of migrants. In all other respects it is ignored by the authors. The problems of decolonization, linguistic relationships and transatlantic relations are all left out of the picture. The fact that the Kingdom of the Netherlands consists of two Caribbean partners alongside the Netherlands is not even mentioned, while a piece on Belgian Flanders is included. This is as painful from an Antillean and Aruban perspective as it is telling about Dutch attitudes – and it is certainly not exceptional.[9]

The Dutch identity that is subsequently construed contains a number of familiar constants: a love of mediocrity, a predilection for consensus, a tendency towards tolerance and openness, a striving for equality, a democratic tradition, a welfare state and a tradition of legal justice are spoken of positively and respectfully by all. On the other hand they also refer to an absence of *savoir vivre*, a feigned indifference to national culture, a lack of cultural awareness, and a quasi-humility, which even in the nineteenth century was already loathed as 'an all too conspicuous, tiresome phenomenon in the Netherlands today, in which general character is worn as false modesty'.[10] Self-satisfaction is touched upon by many of the authors. It is remarkable that colourlessness, dullness, or dowdiness are apparently not considered typical characteristics, even though many foreign observers have picked up on these in the past, and actually the 'multicultural society' is often applauded as being a curative antidote to a supposed Dutch greyness.[11]

And if we project this 'Dutch identity', with all its vagueness and contradictions, onto Dutch Caribbean society? Little is clarified. We should not, of course, expect too much from simply placing a rather 'essentialist' characterization of Dutch identity like a mould over the heterogeneous package of Dutch Caribbean societies. As much as Dutch identity, Dutch Caribbean identities are 'in the making', full of contradictions, both individually and collectively. The Dutch mould, itself also mutable, only fits here and there. The Dutch model of *verzuiling* or 'pillarization', had its day in Suriname in the period of *verbroederingspolititiek*, the fraternizational politics that linked the major ethnic pillars; but this model works less by the day. In a general sense, an identification with the Western world and its values characterizes much of the Dutch Caribbean outlook, as it does in other Caribbean societies. Yet even comparatively speaking, there appears to be little else of use in the box of supposedly metropolitan features. The Dutch Caribbean cannot be accused of a predilection for mediocrity; the traditions of democracy and legal justice, which the Dutch deprived their colonies of for so long, have received some serious blows in the former colonies in the postcolonial era; the struggle for social equality has been mainly rhetorical; and neither is false modesty a conspicuous Dutch Caribbean feature.

Imagining an identity

So what then makes a Dutch Caribbean identity? Whatever it is, there is no formula. In the end we arrive at the identity of every individual island and the diverse ethnic identities of Suriname – anything but a single, defined identity. Attempts have been made to formulate an overarching, national identity, but these have been more prescriptive than descriptive. The poem 'Wan bon', by the Surinamese nationalist poet Dobru, written in the 1960s and incessantly quoted ever since, provides a striking example:

Wan bon	One tree
someni wiwiri	so many leaves
wan bon.	one tree.
[...]	[...]
Wan Sranan	One Suriname
someni wiwiri	so many hair sorts
someni skin	so many skins
someni tongo	so many languages
Wan pipel.	One people.[12]

Moving phrases, but most of it would remain rhetoric. In the 1980s the military regime of Desi Bouterse was the first to seriously take the project of nation building in hand. In Paramaribo and elsewhere in the country, slogans and large posters appeared clearly inspired by the Cuban example. A united Surinamese people, heroic in a social-realist style, rallied behind the banners of production, unity and struggle. A concept was introduced of centuries of struggle against colonialism and imperialism, culminating in the 'triumph of the revolution'. This blueprint underlay the brightly coloured, historical panels that were placed in the grounds in front of the presidential palace. Continuity was depicted as running from the heroic Amerindians, the Maroons, the slaves and contract workers via Anton de Kom to the military. A dominant enemy, the Netherlands, lent coherence to the whole. In the mid-eighties, however, the Maroons took up arms against the military; just as in the past they were discounted as uncivilized and backward. Shortly thereafter the military was forced to withdraw, making way for the fragile construction of the New Front in which old ethnic parties were once again content to adhere loosely to the rhetoric of *wan bon*, while practising strictly ethnic policies. The resulting, unfocused, nationalism continued to be marked predominantly by Creole symbolism.

As dependent on Dutch assistance as the New Front was, it only permitted itself to pay cautious lip service to an anti-colonial, nation-building rhetoric. Since then, Suriname has been ruled alternately by the New Front and parties with roots in the period of military rule. All in all, the project of nation building has progressed little.

The irony is that independent Suriname, in its search for a national identity, takes its references from the Netherlands far more than the Netherlands Antilles or Aruba do. In some respects, people in Suriname have little choice. The greatest challenge – ethnic plurality – is given a wide berth: highlighting it is risky and nowadays barely permissible.[13] Unlike the Afro-Surinamese population, the Hindustanis take their 'country of origin' as part of their frame of reference. Modern media, especially the Bollywood film industry, have strengthened this tendency, and the Indian Embassy in Paramaribo stimulates this interest. However, this ethnic identification cannot, by definition, have any significance for other population groups and thwarts the project of 'colour-blind', ethnically neutral nation building.

For the Netherlands Antilles the greatest problem is diversity and the limited cohesion between the islands. It is clearly deemed more acceptable to speak openly about this issue on the islands than it is to fully address the issue of ethnic division in Suriname. Thus in 1996 the official Antillean Commission for Nation Building published a report openly addressing the need to build a stronger sense of national identity among the five islands. The report exuded an atmosphere of new beginnings, right down to the title: *One people, One Effort, One Nation*. It speaks of efforts that need to be made, of an agenda aimed at getting islanders more involved with each other, of developing symbols such as a national Hall of Fame, of a more focused organization of events around the flag, of the national anthem, and so on. It speaks of striving towards a 'human image': an Antillean who is aware, critical, creative and respectful; who cooperates and has a sense of responsibility; who loves his or her country; who has a sense of self-esteem; and who strives to preserve 'nature, humanity and an own identity'.[14]

These are noble, but not specifically Antillean *desiderata*. Surmounting the divisions between the islands is implicitly central to all the efforts of the Commission, but how this relates to the above remains uncertain. Moreover, since the publication of this optimistic report, the intended policy for a political restructuring of the Netherlands Antilles-of-five has been shattered once more on the intractability of reality. It requires much imagination and optimism today to believe that the *One people, One Effort, One Nation* will ever have any significance beyond the insular.

Another remarkable blind spot in the Commission's report – as in much of the Antillean discourse on national identity – is the issue of constitutional status and the Antillean diaspora in the metropolis. In spite of its evident importance to postcolonial status, with all that implies, and in spite of evident 'return' of the Dutch at the time of publication, the entire report *One people, One Effort, One Nation* dedicates only a few, very general paragraphs to the Netherlands. Neither the intensification of ties with the Kingdom, nor the fact that the diaspora numerically comprises the 'second island' of the Antilles – and potentially in the future the first – seems to have presented the commission with sufficient reason to seriously reflect on this aspect.[15]

Aruba, with its separate status within the Kingdom, is by far the better off; not only materially, but also in terms of nation building. Supported by most of the local population, its political leadership has fought and won a campaign for its independent status within the Kingdom against both the Netherlands and Curaçao; it therefore has a clear nationalist heritage. Having achieved separate status, it went on to experience a sustained economic boom, which in itself is something to be proud of. The country of Aruba proudly presents its unique *mestizo* character and is regarded as a success on all accounts. Whoever questions this presumed success, whether in relation to the level of integration between 'native' Arubans and the post-oil immigrants, or to the democratic and judicial standards observed by local government and business, touches a very tender nerve. Even so there is every reason to affirm that Aruba cherishes an idea of solid national identity not readily found elsewhere in the Dutch Caribbean.

Nowhere in the Dutch Caribbean is there an open and animated debate about national identities – less so it seems than anywhere else in the region. This does not mean that there are not many vague notions of identity in circulation. At an intellectual level there is also a certain anxious protection of 'our own' identity. Criticism of symbols of identity such as local languages, versions of history or cultural expressions, is not received lightly, whether it comes from compatriots or outsiders. *Het Nut van Nederland* suggests that in the Netherlands, national identity is 'unlimitedly taken for granted' and points to the relaxed attitude of a debate in which many stress precisely the undefined nature of the national character. Several contributors to this book believe it is possible for the Dutch to be this nonchalant about their own history and national symbols because these have become so deeply absorbed over many centuries as to no longer require explanation. 'What perhaps best typifies the Netherlands is a self-conceit which believes it needs no words', writes Paul Scheffer, although he does add, 'perhaps these words are needed now'. The eminent historian E.H. Kossmann is one of those sceptics who consider the notion of national identity to be 'too complicated, too multifaceted and too variable' for an inclusive judgement to be possible.

'Better to studiously walk around it, view it from all angles, but do not enter into it; treat it like a huge jellyfish on the beach.'[16]

This relaxed attitude has been typical of the Dutch identity debate for decades, insofar as there was a debate at all. Conversely, inasmuch as identity is debated in the Dutch Caribbean, it is far from relaxed. Uncertainty, contradiction and criticism are not appreciated, even less so scepticism and humour; the mere idea of comparing Caribbean identity with something as repugnant as a jellyfish! In this vacuum of uncertainty, the core elements of identity are not there for the picking. The colonial past may be part of this identity, as may be the languages, or the Netherlands; folklore may even be part of this identity, though it never spread very far, nor was it ever held in much regard socially, and is today increasingly repressed. All this makes awkward questions all the more disturbing.

Ultimately this chapter says little about the way of life and thinking of 'the' Surinamese, Antillean and Aruban populations. Rather, it stresses the enormous diversity, and any talk of a single, shared culture must be secondary to a discussion of these radical differences. But in another sense too, the identity discussed here is far removed from the daily reality of most Arubans, Antilleans or Surinamese. In order to better understand that lived identity, one has to personally experience life there, read novels, listen to music and so on. And throw in the couple of ethnographies that are not yet too out of date.

For present purposes, I am not concerned with presenting an alternative ethnography, and neither am I equipped to do so.[17] I do not want to paint vignettes of the life of a Bonairean teacher, a Hindustani taxi driver, a Curaçaoan politician, a Chinese shopkeeper, an Aruban receptionist, an Afro-Surinamese civil servant, let alone of a Dominican cleaning lady on St Martin. Neither their lifestyles, nor the ways in which they interact are discussed here. I am mainly concerned here with questioning the way in which nationalist discourse prefers to present local identity. This reveals a strong inclination to completely abstract those concrete lives and to search for an ideal image of what people once were or once wanted to be. It is apparently hard to suppress the tendency to iron out the creases of the past and to distil from the present only what is convenient. The nation builders seem to have something else on their minds than reading novels, ethnographies or historical studies. The view that diversity and contradiction are not only problematic, but also a pleasant challenge, seems to be unpopular if not offensive.[18]

Highlighting the continuing appeal of Winti to emphasize that the nominally strictly Christian Afro-Surinamese population still adhered to its religious heritage forged in slavery was once a necessary correction.

However, now the relevant question is not only how Winti relates to Christianity, but how this religion is changing and perhaps acquiring new meanings through the secularization of societies on both sides of the Atlantic. To take another example, how many hundreds-of-thousands of MacDonald's burgers have to be eaten in Willemstad before this snack becomes defined as more typical of the eating habits of Curaçaoan school children than *funchi*?[19] What does *simadan* – enthusiastically held up by folklorists as their own harvest festival – still have to say about the contemporary culture of the Leeward islands where there is practically no agriculture left? Are Surinamese poems like *Wan bon*, with their representation of an ethnic coming together, any less rhetorical today than they were 1975?

Much of what is supposed to pass as unique national heritage seems to be construed in a context of denial, of a negation of development over time, a refusal to acknowledge internal conflicts and oppositions both in the past and the present. The normative national or island identity thus formulated seems even further removed from reality than much of what is said about Dutch identity.

A Caribbean identity?

The whole of the Caribbean shares a history of colonialism and bonded labour culminating in structurally similar patterns of creolization throughout the region. However, the cultures and colonial policies of the European countries involved differed considerably from one another. This includes the great variety of sources from which each repopulated its own colonies. The outcomes of these parallel processes of demographic and cultural creolization consequently differ greatly. The collective identity of the Caribbean, a region that likes to be regarded as a single cultural area, is therefore paradoxical: what is shared, besides a past, is a large degree of heterogeneity inherited from history. History and heterogeneity automatically force questions of island versus collective Caribbean identity to the fore.[20]

The identity of each of the Caribbean countries is almost by definition sought in the unique, in what people 'have' and 'are', away from the colonizer of the past. The larger countries became independent early on, shedding their identification with the European motherland first and most effectively. That this also entailed an armed struggle greatly enhanced the process of nation building. Whereas elsewhere historical myths had to be more or less invented, here they were distilled 'from the real past'. Historical struggle and heroism therefore became a crucial part of national identity, just as the Eighty Years' War against the Spanish once was a crucial element in Dutch nation building. All indispensable myths. Thus, in Caribbean context, Cuban, Haitian and perhaps Dominican identities have all been easier to formulate and experience as patently individual national characters. This remained the case even when, in the twentieth century, these nations were the first to come under the aegis of the new superpower, the United States.

Then there is the unique case of Puerto Rico: an 'unincorporated territory', yet for most practical purposes part of the United States. The island has struggled to define its identity vis-à-vis an as yet predominantly Anglo-Saxon American culture and partly because of this has preferred to engage with the cultural sphere of its former colonizer, Spain. In a certain respect, Puerto Rico's nation building, with all its ambivalence and taboos, comes closest to the Dutch Caribbean experience. Here too there is an issue of language and failed bilingualism, an exodus, an extreme dependence on a 'motherland' which is as overwhelming and irritating as it is envied and admired – and, moreover, in this case, also close by.

Until a few decades ago, the rest of the region – the former British, Dutch and, with the exception of Haiti, French Caribbean – and certainly its elites, still primarily looked to the mother country for their identities. A shared predicament of national identity emerged: how much distance do we want to take from 'our' European culture? Insofar as Suriname and the Netherlands Antilles differed from their British and French peers in the 1950s, they did so primarily in the sense that their culture less clearly reflected and emulated that of the mother country, beginning – it may be repeated – with language.

Developments since then have only served to strengthen the anomalous, ambivalent position of the Dutch Caribbean. The French Caribbean, which has been incorporated into France as a group of three overseas provinces, have only become more French. Of course, this was met with eloquent dissent, articulated in *négritude, créolité* and *antillanité*. However, there can be no doubt that almost the entire population has, almost without interruption, held France up as the model for its language, frame of reference and place in the world.

For the British Caribbean, to a certain extent, the opposite is true. Independence for the vast majority of colonies led to a dual shift in the debate around identity. On the one hand the focus on a unique character was stronger. This development was sustained by an understanding that although the West Indian Federation had collapsed, they still belonged to a collection of British Caribbean countries, and that together they were reasonably large and carried a certain amount of weight in the region. On the other hand it emerged that the United States, and even Canada, in many respects began to replace Britain as it began to consciously to turn away from its Caribbean empire. Thus the initially bifurcated character of the Anglophone Caribbean exodus increasingly tilted towards the U.S. The reaction to this shift in orientation was ambivalent. Besides resentment and rancour about the colonial past, an increasing need to preserve something of Britain seems to have developed, even if only as a counterweight to an intrusive American influence. Consequently, much of what Britain left behind – not only the language, including U.K. spelling, but also political, legal and educational institutions and traditions, saying nothing of the phenomenon of cricket – were preserved with conviction. It is therefore possible for a stronger sense of unity to exist within this part of the Caribbean because it is unmistakably a sub-region: at least a dozen countries, all English-speaking, despite their limited physical and population sizes together forming something resembling a political block and a cultural sphere, a collection in itself, 'separate' in the Americas perhaps, but linked to each other and, through their language, part of the dominant Anglo-American world.

In this context the development of the Dutch Caribbean falls out of line in several respects. Orientation towards the Netherlands has increased, but so too has the level of ambivalence. The essential dimension of the fiasco of Suriname's independence is that it barely reduced her isolation from her immediate surroundings, an isolation which underlines how little interest the outside world has in the country, and vice versa. Suriname today continues to look to the Netherlands rather than the Caribbean, despite nearly thirty years of independence; interest in India is primarily cultural and limited to the Hindustanis; the orientation towards Africa is scant and purely rhetorical; while for most Surinamese of Javanese origins, Indonesia is nothing but a vague notion. That the Dutch language has only gained ground since 1975 speaks volumes. The choice is as pragmatic as it is frustrating and it is precisely this frustration that feeds the ever-present ambivalence towards Dutch culture; a duality that is remarkable even when compared with other Caribbean countries.

This last point is also more true today than ever before for the Netherlands Antilles and Aruba. Traditionally the islands, unlike Suriname, were strongly oriented towards the local region and the U.S., but over the last few decades a fundamental shift has occurred towards the Netherlands, at least in the realms of politics and migration. Pragmatism rather than affection for the motherland has dictated this shift. The comprehension of this, strengthened by the feeling that the level of affection for its Caribbean territories has never run deep on the North Sea coast, is adding to frustration and ambivalence. It is in this context that Papiamentu takes on such an enormous symbolic meaning and becomes central to the formulation of an identity. And it is almost inevitable that a critical questioning of the practical uses of that language should provoke such bitter reactions, and that barely any attempts have been made to infuse the ties of the Kingdom with a more profound cultural significance. Not only do the islands give this issue a wide berth, so too does the erstwhile colonizer.

Suriname's involvement with the Netherlands has remained constant, while the other islands' has increased. History, language and the diaspora prop up a relationship which generates more ambivalence than enthusiasm. And there is more: a large collection of fantasies about a paradise overseas and so much more should now be mapped on the basis of serious research, unhampered by an excessive concern about what may or may not be said in a postcolonial context. What one would map is, in a certain respect, typically Caribbean, in the sense that here too culture is becoming creolized, cross-fertilizing, and that the context of this culture building is strongly asymmetrical in relation to the outside world. Within the limitations of this outside world, in its extremely small scale with its extreme heterogeneity, the Dutch Caribbean is without doubt unique, even from a Caribbean point of view.

The Netherlands was long a negligent colonizer; later it became a partner bound by an ambiguous sense of shame and annoyance. It got the Caribbean empire it deserved: areas which are not Dutch but which now, with a view to their limited viability and in the absence of any attractive alternatives, seem to have little choice but to cling on tightly to the Netherlands. Examining this awkward predicament is the first task facing anyone attempting to find words for the unique identity of what in these pages has been lumped together under the fictitious banner of a single 'Dutch' Caribbean.

Postscript

Loosely covering nearly four centuries of history, *Paradise Overseas* strives to map the contemporary Dutch Caribbean and its continuing links to the Netherlands. The original, more elaborate version was published half a decade ago. It may seem preposterous to provide a postscript so soon, as if the last five years have made a crucial difference to the previous centuries. Indeed, this brief retrospective glance mainly reflects on minor change alongside predominant continuity.

After several decades of depletion caused by the exodus to the Netherlands, the population of Suriname is increasing again. The crucial new factor is that much of this growth derives from both the legal and illegal immigration of Brazilians, who within a decade may come to make up some ten per cent of all inhabitants. While successive Surinamese governments have made a point of striving to insert the country more firmly into the Caribbean, particularly by joining CARI-COM, this new migration may prefigure a rather different geopolitical destiny.

In 2003, Suriname changed the name of its national currency from the *gulden* inherited from colonial times to the Surinamese dollar. The convenience of this is that the Surinamese no longer have to pay tens of thousands guilders for a soft drink or a bread roll, as the new dollar has been set at a much higher intrinsic value. Psychologically, it may be a comfort to the Surinamese that they are no longer constantly confronted with the fact that their *gulden* has come down to a mere fraction of its original value. Likewise, the choice for 'dollar' rather than '*gulden*' symbolizes their government's preference for breaking loose from its colonial heritage. Unfortunately, progress made in the real world of economics remains another story. The traditional, overwhelming dependence on the bauxite industry, some large-scale agriculture, Dutch development aid, and remittances of the Surinamese community in the Netherlands has not been broken. The elaborate state apparatus remains a troublesome burden to the treasury, a challenge hard to face for electoral reasons. The two significant growth sectors in the economy are gold mining and drug trafficking. Both exercise a strong corruptive pressure on the state, while the huge gains reaped in these sectors benefit only a few Surinamese.

Suriname has remained a parliamentary democracy, and there is no reason to think this will change again in the near future. Whether this democracy functions is another question. The last decade has seen an alternation of terms of office between the traditional coalition based on ethnic parties and a new one with a firm foothold in the period of military rule. The traditional ethnic parties seem to be on the defensive, which is a remarkable development in view of the country's otherwise strong ethnic divisions. Some may read this as an encouraging step in the process of nation building. Others may stress that the credibility of many of the new parties, with their roots in the military period and the soaring crime and corruption which came in its wake, leaves much to be desired and actually invites the observation that Suriname's incorporation into its geographic habitat follows precisely the wrong trajectory.

The latter observation is coming increasingly to prevail in The Hague. With the change of generations in Dutch politics, the engagement with Suriname is waning. So is the disillusion about the results of development aid. This is only partly offset by the lobby of the Surinamese Dutch. Less Dutch political involvement might not worry Surinamese politicians, but it does economically. The 'golden handshake' of 1975 is nearly exhausted.

Judging by the past, one would expect the negotiation of a possible renewal of aid relations to be close to the top of the bilateral agenda, but it is not. The Hague demonstrates little interest in proceeding down the chosen path. Thus, after a delay of several decades, the transfer of sovereignty might indeed end in the severing of the postcolonial ties. The fact that many Surinamese on both sides of the Atlantic deplore this idea seems to be decreasingly relevant to Dutch policy-making.

The Dutch engagement with the Netherlands Antilles and Aruba is not much more amiable, it just happens to be constitutionally cemented. A recent survey suggests that over half of the Dutch population would rather see Curaçao, and probably the other islands as well, becoming independent. This attitude was also prevalent some thirty years ago.[21] Of course, the constitutional realities dictate that Dutch politicians must continue down another track, along which the Dutch will continue to reaffirm their presence at the expense of Antillean and Aruban autonomy, and thus deepen rather than sever their presence in the Caribbean. Sadly, this policy originates less in a positive commitment than in an increasing weariness of whatever reminds the Dutch of these remnants of empire.

What, then, are these reminders? We may start with Aruba, which presently elicits only few such reminders. Since its start as a separate country within the Kingdom, Aruba has been an economic success. As long as this economic miracle does not shatter and migration to the Netherlands remains negligible, the island may happily reap the benefits of postcolonial protection without experiencing many limitations of its domestic autonomy. The balance, however, is precarious: by definition, its small economy with its dependence on tourism and service industries is extremely vulnerable to external threats beyond its control, including international terrorism and crime.

Excluding calamities, there are two structural factors which can and probably will draw the Dutch further into Aruban politics. The first is the ongoing changes in the island's population. Growth has brought with it a rather heavy and permanent level of immigration from mainly Spanish-speaking neighbouring countries. The implications of this, for instance for the educational system, are increasingly being felt in Aruba. In the long run these will pose new challenges to the question of Aruban identity. In the short run, they are bound to elicit critical Dutch interest, because of issues of citizenship and educational and financial liabilities.

The second factor, which might end up drawing Aruba further under the Dutch umbrella, is not as much connected with the island itself, but rather with the precarious condition of the Netherlands Antilles at large. A dual crisis has characterized the five-island nation for much of the past decade. First, there is the endemic economic crisis with its repercussions both on the islands, particularly Curaçao, and through emigration also in the Netherlands. Second, there is an unwillingness – with St Martin at the forefront, followed by Curaçao – to continue with the five-island entity of the Antilles. The Hague has consistently declared its refusal to give in to these centrifugal wishes, yet it seems most likely that in the end Dutch politicians will have to reconsider. The evident trade-off would on the one hand entail the substitution of the fictitious 'country' of the Netherlands Antilles with a system of direct relations between each of the islands and the metropolis. On the other hand, the Dutch would hereby finally attain the firmer grip on island government they have been striving for over many years. There are many complications in this scenario, yet it is hard to seriously believe in any other outcome. Should this scenario come true, Aruba would most likely be put under strong pressure to conform. In spite of the many political complications, an alternative is difficult to come by.

This is all politics. The question which permeates much of this book is, of course, how a postcolonial relationship, and changes therein, impinge upon local identities. Suffice it here to reiterate a few conclusions. First, with over one-third of the Caribbean populations living in the metropolis, 'local identity' has become an ever more elusive concept. Remarkably, this is an issue hardly addressed on the Western side of the Dutch Caribbean. Second, there is now an interesting sequel to the historical paradox that Suriname, by far the most 'Dutch' of all Caribbean territories, was the only one to break its postcolonial ties. By not choosing that path, the islands inadvertently embarked on a route that has drawn them further into the Dutch world than ever before, as the experience of the past decade indicates. Thus, the first paradox is followed up by a second one. Hesitantly, at times with a dragging of feet, and perhaps with dubious outcomes, the Surinamese are indeed moving into other geopolitical spheres; for the younger generations, at least, the Netherlands is gradually becoming a nation at a distance. For the Antilleans and even the Arubans the opposite pertains, yet there is little indication that this sobering fact has been seriously incorporated into the rhetoric of national identity, which more than ever now focuses on narrow, *insular* markers only.

As during colonialism, metropolitan power prevails in the postcolonial relationship. Dutch supremacy was never complete nor fully effective, but there is no denying that the Netherlands dictated the parameters of colonization. In the dismantling of the remnants of empire the Dutch somehow lost control – hence the extensive Caribbean community in the Netherlands, hence the failure of the policy to make the Antilles a six-island sovereign state. Even so, the relation between the former colonizer and its colonies remains highly asymmetrical in this postcolonial era. The very slow process of disengagement between Suriname and the Netherlands is not sought, let alone dictated by Paramaribo, but by The Hague. The price the Antilles and Aruba continue to pay for voting against sovereignty is to conform more than ever with Dutch standards. That price might be reasonable and the compensation attractive, on most accounts, yet it is evident that the metropolis continues to set the parameters.

We may now conclude with some reflections on Dutch identity in relation to its Caribbean heritage. First, there has been a remarkable, almost overnight rediscovery within the Netherlands of Dutch Caribbean history, and particularly its downsides. In the 1997 first edition of *Het paradijs overzee* I cynically remarked upon the absence of any official monument in the Netherlands commemorating the Dutch Atlantic slave trade and slavery. Only two years later, the Dutch government responded positively to petitions from Caribbean organizations in the Netherlands who urged for such a national monument to be erected. Moreover, the prestigious Prince Claus Foundation for culture and development worldwide published a book to commemorate slavery. The national monument, made by the Surinamese sculptor Erwin de Vries, was inaugurated in Amsterdam in the presence of the Queen of the Netherlands and the Dutch Prime Minister in 2002, on 1 July, Emancipation Day. A state-sponsored national institute for education and research on slavery and its legacies was established exactly one year later.[22]

The whole process was clearly contextualized by all the players involved as signalling not only a new Dutch awareness of the downsides of its own national history, but equally as a commitment to the inclusion of the descendants of these enslaved Africans now living in the Netherlands. Political interest and press coverage were generally positive, even if as time progressed some scepticism developed regarding black identity politics and internal dissent among the groups involved. Press coverage certainly helped. Recent surveys among the Dutch population indicate that these forgotten chapters have been retrieved from oblivion. In one such survey, respondents mentioned colonialism and particularly the Atlantic slave trade and slavery as being among the worst episodes in Dutch history.[23]

Once on the agenda, there was certainly no effort to silence the hesitant debate. Some controversy was voiced about obvious issues such as comparative angles to the justifications and harshness of Dutch slavery, and particularly about slavery's contemporary legacies. Probably the most volatile issues of the debates were the claim of a privileged 'African' understanding of this past, as well as propositions regarding psychological legacies left by slavery, particularly white racism and cultural trauma among the descendants of slaves. None of these debates were new to anyone familiar with the Caribbean or 'plantation America' in general – but certainly the 'Black Atlantic' had never been as clearly present in the Netherlands before.[24]

This is not to say that the Netherlands has now somehow fully incorporated its Caribbean antecedents into its understanding of its own identity. Much less so, that Dutch society is in the process of happily incorporating the new cultures of the many recent migrants into 'local' identity. More so than five years ago, Dutch public debate today is very much focused on the drawbacks of multiculturalism, often boiling down to straightforward xenophobia. With around one million Muslims now living in the Netherlands, much of the debate is about the position of Islam and its adherents in Dutch society. Increasingly distinctions are being made between the country's Muslim population on the one hand, and the various postcolonial immigrants and their offspring on the other. The advantage of belonging to the latter category is clear, as the emergence of reasonably successful identity politics among all postcolonial migrant communities attest.

Will a better understanding of Dutch history in the Caribbean and of the Caribbean antecedents to Dutch identity translate into a continuing positive commitment to the former colonies? There is much reason for doubt. The once strong commitment to Suriname is little by little losing ground, mainly because The Hague sees many problems and few advantages. The move towards establishing a firmer grip on the Antilles and Aruba is inspired more by a weary longing to prevent the islands from generating problems for the Netherlands than on genuine commitment. All in all, not much has altered over the last three decades, and there is no particular reason to assume it will change. The question remains as to how the Caribbean community in the Netherlands, having literally brought colonial history home to the metropolis, will position itself in the future, and what will be the direction, intensity and outcome of their commitment to the nations of their ancestors.

Notes

1 This chapter was originally written in 1997 as the closing chapter of *Het paradijs overzee*. The text offered here follows the original with minor revisions and additions, except for the final section, 'Postscript'.
2 De Kom 1981:49. See also Chapter 6.
3 The concept of 'silencing history' is of course borrowed from Trouillot 1995.
4 It should not be surprising in this respect that my perhaps rather naive attempts to contextualize common clichés about the extreme harshness of Surinamese slavery (Oostindie 1993b, reprinted in Dutch in *Het paradijs overzee*) were occasionally

180   *Paradise Overseas*

denounced as shamelessly reactionary, albeit it only once in print (Shell 1992, Hoetink & Oostindie 1993).

5 Ramdas 1996:202, 1993:33.
6 This has changed since; see the 'Postscript'.
7 Schama 1988. See also chapter 2.
8 Sticusa: the Amsterdam-based Foundation for Cultural Cooperation within the Kingdom (1948–1988). See Oostindie & Klinkers 2003, Chapter 10.
9 Koch & Scheffer 1996, Scheffer 1996. In response to a request by the Dutch government to explore the possible tensions between 'national identity' and internalization, the prestigious Raad voor Maatschappelijke Ontwikkeling (1999) published a report on Dutch identity in which Dutch colonial history and its legacies are not even mentioned in passing.
10 The liberal patriot Johannes van Vloten, 1873, quoted by Kossman (1996:57).
11 For example, Joustra 1993.
12 Quoted in Van Kempen 1995:336–7.
13 Cf. the premise of the exhibition *Sranan; Culture in Suriname* (Binnendijk & Faber 1992), and the commentary on it by Price & Price (1996:98–9).
14 Commissie Natievorming 1996:58–9. Without beating about the bush, the commission stated: 'All subjects (including the exact sciences) which are taught in schools must serve the aims described here above.' (p. 58).
15 In 1997, the government of the Netherlands Antilles decided a national anthem was needed 'for the purpose of strengthening solidarity between the islands of the Netherlands Antilles and national identity'. A competition was organized to this end. Antilleans living both on the islands and elsewhere – thus mainly in the Netherlands – were invited to submit their proposals for music and words of a national hymn. The language could be Papiamentu and/or English, not Dutch (*Antilliaanse Nieuwsbrief* 38(7/8)1997).
16 Scheffer 1996:29. Kossmann 1996:68.
17 In recent publications Allen, Heijes & Marcha (2003), Antonius (1996) and Marcha & Verweel (2000, 2003) provide useful materials for an ethnography of contemporary Curaçao. In these publications, there is a strong emphasis on legacies of slavery identified in terms such as 'culture of shame', 'inferiority complex' and the like.
18 See Broek 1994, Oostindie 1997a.
19 *Funchi* is a staple of cornmeal paste.
20 Hall 1995. The idea of a cultural area underpins Knight's authoritative handbook *The Caribbean* (1990), which, incidentally, in spite of its many merits, forms no exception to the rule that in the 'comparative' study of the region, the Dutch Caribbean is at best marginally addressed. For the connections between ethnicity and nation building, see also Oostindie 1996a and Chapter 5 in this book..
21 A majority of 54% responded that Curaçao should become independent, 10% opted for the status of a province, 21% for the status quo; 15% apparently had no opinion (ANP, 12–8–2003). By way of comparison: in the mid-1970s there were even clearer Dutch majorities (62–78%) in favour of independence of both Suriname and the Antilles (Oostindie & Klinkers 2001, II:73).
22 Oostindie 1999. See Oostindie 2001 for a thoroughly revised English version, including several contributions on the history and politics of the Dutch commemoration.
23 The survey was held in 1999 (*Historisch Nieuwsblad*, July 2000). According to a very recent survey, by 2003 a sample of respondents even overestimated the share of the Dutch in the Atlantic slave trade (*Historisch Nieuwsblad*, May 2003).
24 Gilroy 1993.

Bibliography

Abbring, H.J.
1834   *Weemoedstoonen uit de geschiedenis van mijn leven, of Mijn reis naar Curaçao, en vlugtige beschouwingen van dat eiland gedurende mijn tienjarig verblijf op hetzelve.* Groningen: Van Boekeren.
Aldrich, Robert & John Connell
1992   *France's overseas frontier; Départements et Territoires d'Outre-Mer.* Cambridge: Cambridge University Press.
1998   *The last colonies.* Cambridge: Cambridge University Press.
Allen, Rose Mary
1992   'Katholicisme en volkscultuur, een dialectische relatie; Een aanzet tot de studie van het "beschavingswerk" van de Curaçaose rooms-katholieke kerk in de periode 1824–1915', in: B. Boudewijnse, H. Middelbrink & C. van de Woestijne (eds.), *Kerkwandel en lekenhandel; De rooms-katholieke kerk op Curaçao*, pp. 15–30. Amsterdam: Het Spinhuis.
Allen, Rose Mary, Coen Heijes & Valdemar Marcha (eds.)
2003   *Emancipatie & acceptatie; Curaçao en Curaçaoenaars. Beeldvorming en identiteit honderdveertig jaar na de slavernij.* Amsterdam: SWP.
Alleyne, Mervyn C.
2002   *The construction and representation of race and ethnicity in the Caribbean and the world.* Kingston, Jamaica: The University of the West Indies Press.
Alofs, Luc
1996   *Slaven zonder plantage; Slavernij en emancipatie op Aruba, 1750–1963.* Aruba: Charuba.
Alofs, Luc & Leontine Merkies
1990   *Ken ta Arubiano? Sociale integratie en natievorming op Aruba.* Leiden: Caraïbische Afdeling KITLV.
Anderson, Benedict R.O'G
1983   *Imagined communities; Reflections on the origin and spread of nationalism.* London: Verso.
1992   *Long-distance nationalism; World capitalism and the rise of identity politics.* Amsterdam: CASA.
Anonymous
1870   'Suriname en zijne vooruitzichten', *De Economist* 2:769–71.
Antonius, Roland C.M.
1996   *Calls from the social desert; On the political socialization of adolescent youth in Curaçao.* [Dissertation, University of Amsterdam.]

Bakker, Eveline, Leo Dalhuisen, Maurits Hassankhan & Frans Steegh
1993   *Geschiedenis van Suriname; Van stam tot staat.* Zutphen: Walburg Pers.

Bartelink, E.J.
1916   *Hoe de tijden veranderen; Herinneringen van een ouden planter.*
            Paramaribo: Van Ommeren.
Baud, Michiel, Kees Koonings, Gert Oostindie, Arij Ouweneel & Patricio Silva
1996   *Etnicidad como estrategia en America Latina y el Caribe.* Quito: Ediciones
            Abya-Yala.
Belmonte, B.E.C.
1855   *Neêrlands West-Indië in zijne belangen en Dr. W.R. van Hoëvell in zijne
            'Slaven en vrijen'; Slavernij – emancipatie – kolonisatie.* Leiden: Van den
            Heuvell.
Bender, Thomas (ed.)
1992   *The antislavery debate; Capitalism and abolitionism as a problem in his-
            torical interpretation.* Berkeley: University of California Press.
Benítez-Rojo, Antonio
1989   *La isla que se repite; El Caribe y la perspectiva posmoderna.* Hanover: Del
            Norte.
Benoit, P.J.
1980   *Reis door Suriname; Beschrijving van de Nederlandse bezittingen in
            Guyana [...].* Zutphen: Walburg Pers. [Originally 1839.]
Bernabé, Jean, Patrick Chamoiseau & Raphaël Confiant
1989   *Eloge de la créolité.* Paris: Gallimard.
Best, Lloyd
1967   'Independent thought and Caribbean freedom', *New World Quarterly*
            3–4:13–34.
Binnendijk, Chandra & Paul Faber (eds.)
1992   *Sranan; Cultuur in Suriname.* Amsterdam: KIT; Rotterdam: Museum voor
            Volkenkunde.
Blakely, Allison
1993   *Blacks in the Dutch world; The evolution of racial imagery in a modern
            society.* Bloomington: Indiana University Press.
Blom, Anthony
1787   *Verhandeling van den landbouw in de Colonie Suriname.* Amsterdam: Smit.
Blom, Anthony [& Floris Visscher Heshuysen]
1786   *Verhandeling over den landbouw, in de Colonie Suriname, volgens eene
            negentien-jaarige ondervinding zamengesteld, door Anthony Blom, en met
            de noodige ophelderingen en bewysredenen voorzien, door Floris Visscher
            Heshuysen [...].* Haarlem: Van der Aa.
Bolland, O. Nigel
1992   'Creolization and Creole societies; A cultural nationalist view of Caribbean
            social history', in: Alistair Hennessy (ed.), *Intellectuals in the twentieth-
            century Caribbean I. Spectre of the new class; The Commonwealth
            Caribbean*, pp. 50–79. London: Macmillan.
Boogaart, Ernst van den
1982   'Colour prejudice and the yardstick of civility; The initial Dutch con-
            frontation with black Africans 1590–1635', in: Robert Ross (ed.), *Racism
            and colonialism; Essays in ideology and social structure*, pp. 33–54. Den
            Haag: Nijhoff.
Boogaart, Ernst van den, Pieter C. Emmer, Peter Klein & Kees Zandvliet
1992   *La expansión holandesa en el Atlántico.* Madrid: Mapfre.
Boomgaard, Peter & Gert Oostindie
1989   'Changing sugar technology and the labour nexus; The Caribbean,
            1750–1900', *Nieuwe West-Indische Gids/New West Indian Guide* 63:3–22.

Bosch, G.B.
1829–36 *Reizen in West-Indië.* Utrecht: Van der Monde. 2 delen.
1843 *Reize in West-Indië en door een gedeelte van Zuid- en Noord-Amerika; Derde deel: Reize naar Suriname in brieven.* Utrecht: Bosch.
Boxer, C.R.
1957 *The Dutch in Brazil, 1624–1654.* Oxford: Clarendon Press.
1965 *The Dutch seaborne empire 1600–1800.* London: Hutchinson.
Breugel, G.P.C. van
1834 *Aansporing ter bevordering van het godsdienstig onderwijs der slaven en kleurlingen op plantaadjen, bijzonder gerigt aan eigenaren van plantaadjen in de kolonie Suriname, en aan andere weldenkende Christenen.* Haarlem: Van Loghem.
Broek, Aart G.
1994 *Onenigheid is een genoegen; Omtrent identiteit beneden de wind.* Curaçao: Amigoe.
Bruijne, Ad de
2001 'A city and a nation; Demographic trends and socioeconomic development in urbanising Suriname', in: Rosemarijn Hoefte & Peter Meel (eds.), *20th century Suriname; Continuities and discontinuities in a new world society*, pp. 23–47. Kingston: Ian Randle Publishers; Leiden: KITLV Press.
Bruijne, G.A. de & A. Schalkwijk
1994 'Kondreman en P'tata; Nederland als referentiekader voor Surinamers?' in: A.J. Brahim et al. (eds.), *Suriname in het jaar 2000*, pp. 225–41. Baarn: Bosch & Keuning.
Buddingh', Hans
1995 *Geschiedenis van Suriname.* Utrecht: Spectrum.
Buisman, Jan Willem
1992 *Tussen vroomheid en verlichting; Een cultuurhistorisch en -sociologisch onderzoek naar enkele aspecten van de verlichting in Nederland (1755–1810).* Zwolle: Waanders.
Burton, Richard
1993 'Ki Moun Nou Ye? The idea of difference in contemporary French West Indian thought', *New West Indian Guide* 67:5–32.

Carlin, Eithne & Jacques Arends
2002 *Atlas of the languages of Suriname.* Leiden: KITLV Press.
Chamberlain, Mary
1997 *Narratives of exile and return.* London: Macmillan.
Choenni, Chan E.S. & Kanta Sh. Adhin (eds.)
2003 *Hindostanen; Van Brits-Indische emigranten via Suriname tot burgers van Nederland.* Den Haag: Sampreshan.
Chumaceiro, Az., A.M.
1879 *Is Curaçao te koop?* Den Haag: Belinfante.
Clarke, Colin A. (ed.)
1991 *Society and politics in the Caribbean.* London: Macmillan.
Clifford, James
1988 *The predicament of culture; Twentieth-century ethnography, literature, and art.* Cambridge: Harvard University Press.
Cohen, Robert
1991 *Jews in another environment; Surinam in the second half of the eighteenth century.* Leiden: Brill.

184   *Paradise Overseas*

Cohen, William B.
1980   *The French encounter with Africans; White response to blacks 1530–1880.* Bloomington: Indiana University Press.

Commissie Natievorming
1996   *One people, one effort, one nation; Aanzet tot een beleidsplan voor de structurering van het proces van natievorming in de Nederlandse Antillen.* [Curaçao]: s.n.

Costa Gomez, Moises Frumencio da
1935   *Het wetgevende orgaan van Curaçao; Samenstelling en bevoegdheid, bezien in het kader van de Nederlandsche koloniale politiek.* Amsterdam: Paris.

Croes, Rudolf M.
1987   *Welvaart zonder ontwikkeling; De invloed van de oliemaatschappijen op de Arubaanse economie 1928–1948.* Leiden: Caraïbische Afdeling, KITLV.

Curtin, Philip D.
1964   *The image of Africa; British ideas and action, 1780–1850.* Madison: University of Wisconsin Press.

Dahlhaus, G.J.M.
1924   *Monsigneur Martinus Joannes Niewindt, eerste apostolisch vicaris van Curaçao; Een levensschets, 27 Aug. 1824–12 Jan. 1860.* Baasrode: Bracke-Van Geert.

Dalhuisen, Leo, Ronald Donk, Rosemarijn Hoefte & Frans Steegh (eds.)
1997   *Geschiedenis van de Antillen; Aruba, Bonaire, Curaçao, Saba, Sint Eustatius, Sint Maarten.* Zutphen: Walburg Pers.

Dash, J. Michael
2000   'Review of Marie-Hélène Laforest, Diasporic Encounters: Remapping the Caribbean (2000)', *New West Indian Guide* 75:148–50.

Davis, David Brion
1966   *The problem of slavery in western culture.* Ithaca: Cornell University Press.
1975   *Slavery in western culture; The problem of slavery in the age of revolution 1770–1823.* Ithaca: Cornell University Press.
1984   *Slavery and human progress.* New York: Oxford University Press.

Debrot, Cola
1985   *Verzameld werk I; Over Antilliaanse cultuur.* Amsterdam: Meulenhoff.

Dekker, J.H.
1982   *Curaçao zonder/met Shell; Een bijdrage tot bestudering van demografische, economische en sociale processen in de periode 1900–1929.* Zutphen: Walburg Pers.

Derveld, F.E.R.
1981   *Politieke mobilisatie en integratie van de Javanen in Suriname; Tamanredjo en de Surinaamse nationale politiek.* [Dissertation University of Leiden.]

Dew, Edward
1978   *The difficult flowering of Surinam; Ethnicity and politics in a plural society.* Den Haag: Nijhoff.
1994   *The trouble in Suriname, 1975–1993.* New York: Praeger.

Dijk, Kees van
2003   'The magnetism of songs', *Bijdragen tot de Taal-, Land- en Volkenkunde* 159:31–64.

Dissel, S. van
1857   *Curaçao; Herinneringen en schetsen.* Leiden: Sijthoff.
Doel, H.W. den
2000   *Afscheid van Indië; De val van het Nederlandse imperium in Azië.* Amsterdam: Prometheus.
Domínguez, Jorge I., Robert A. Pastor & R. DeLisle Worrell (eds.)
1993   *Democracy in the Caribbean; Political, economic, and social perspectives.* Baltimore: Johns Hopkins University Press.
Doorn, J.A.A. van
1994   *De laatste eeuw van Indië; Ontwikkeling en ondergang van een koloniaal project.* Amsterdam: Bert Bakker.
Drescher, Seymour
1987   *Capitalism and antislavery; British mobilization in comparative perspective.* New York: Oxford University Press.
1990   'The ending of the slave trade and the evolution of European scientific racism', *Social Science History* 14:415–50.
1991   'British way, French way; Opinion building and revolution in the second French slave emancipation,' *American Historical Review* 96:709–35.
1995   'The long goodbye; Dutch capitalism and antislavery in comparative perspective', in: Gert Oostindie (ed.), *Fifty years later; Antislavery, capitalism and modernity in the Dutch orbit*, pp. 25–66. Leiden: KITLV Press. [Pittsburgh: University of Pittsburgh Press 1996.]
Duff, Ernest A.
1990   'Cultural imperialism in the Caribbean; The challenge of the 1990s', *Caribbean Affairs* 3-1:38–48.
Dijck, Pitou van
2001a   'Continuity and change in a small open economy; External dependency and policy inconsistencies', in: Rosemarijn Hoefte & Peter Meel (eds.), *20th century Suriname; Continuities and discontinuities in a new world society*, pp. 48–70. Kingston: Ian Randle Publishers; Leiden: KITLV Press.
Dijck, Pitou van (ed.)
2001a   *Suriname; The economy; Prospects for sustainable development.* Kingston: Ian Randle Publishers; Amsterdam: Roozenberg.

Eensgezindheid
1804   *Verzameling van uitgezochte verhandelingen, betreffende den landbouw in de kolonie Suriname; Opgesteld door het Landbouwkundig Genootschap De Eensgezindheid, gevestigd in de devisie Matappika, binnen dezelve kolonie.* Amsterdam: Gartman & Uylenbroek.
Elkins, Stanley Maurice
1971   *Slavery; A problem in American institutional and intellectual life.* Chicago: University of Chicago Press. [Originally 1959.]
Emden, Egbert van, H.G. Roux & J. Frouin
1848   *Onderzoek ten gevolge der circulaire van den heer Otto Tank [...].* Paramaribo: Muller Az.
Emmer, Pieter C.
1974   *Engeland, Nederland, Afrika en de slavenhandel in de negentiende eeuw.* Leiden: Brill.
1980   'Anti-slavery and the Dutch; Abolition without reform', in: Christine Bolt & Seymour Drescher (eds.), *Anti-slavery, religion, and reform; Essays in memory of Roger Anstey*, pp. 80–98. Folkestone: Dawson: Archon.

1993   'Between slavery and freedom: The period of apprenticeship in Suriname (Dutch Guiana), 1863–1873', *Slavery & Abolition* 14–1:87–113.

1996   'Capitalism mistaken? The economic decline of Surinam and the plantation loans, 1773–1850; A rehabilitation', *Itinerario* 20–1:11–8.

1998   *The Dutch in the Atlantic economy, 1580–1880.* Aldershot: Ashgate Variorum.

2000   *De Nederlandse slavenhandel 1500–1850.* Amsterdam: De Arbeiderspers.

Emmer, Pieter C. & Wim Klooster

1999   'The Dutch Atlantic, 1600–1800; Expansion without empire', *Itinerario* 23–2:48–69.

Fasseur, Cees

1995   *De weg naar het paradijs en andere Indische geschiedenissen.* Amsterdam: Bert Bakker

Fermin, Philippe

1770   *Nieuwe algemeene beschryving van de Colonie van Suriname.* Harlingen: Van der Plaats.

1778   *Tableau historique et actuel de la Colonie de Surinam, et des causes de sa décadence.* Maastricht: Dufour & Roux.

Fernandes Mendes, H.K.

1989   *Onafhankelijkheid en parlementair stelsel in Suriname; Hoofdlijnen van een nieuw en democratisch staatsbestel.* Zwolle: Tjeenk Willink. [Dissertation University of Leiden.]

Fouse, Gary C.

2002   *The story of Papiamentu; A study in slavery and language.* Lanham: University Press of America.

Frank, David B.

1993   'Political, religious, and economic factors affecting language choice in St. Lucia'. *International Journal of the Sociology of Language* 102:39–56.

Frijhoff, Willem Th.M.

1992   'The Dutch enlightenment and the creation of popular culture', in: Margaret C. Jacob & Wijnandt W. Mijnhardt (eds.), *The Dutch Republic in the eighteenth century; Decline, enlightenment, and revolution*, pp. 292–307. Ithaca: Cornell University Press.

Furnivall, J.S.

1945   'Some problems of tropical economy', in: Rita Hinden (ed.), *Fabian colonial essays*. London: Allen & Unwin.

Gallandat, D.H.

1769   *Noodige onderrichtingen voor de slavenhandelaaren.* Middelburg: Gillissen.

Gilroy, Paul

1993   *The black atlantic; Modernity and double consciousness.* London: Verso.

Gobardhan-Rambocus, Lila

2001   *Onderwijs als sleutel tot maatschappelijke vooruitgang; Een taal- en onderwijsgeschiedenis van Suriname, 1651–1975.* Zutphen: Walburg Pers.

Goslinga, Cornelis Ch.

1956   *Emancipatie en emancipator; De geschiedenis van de slavernij op de Benedenwindse eilanden en het werk der bevrijding.* Assen: Van Gorcum.

1971   *The Dutch in the Caribbean and on the Wild Coast 1580–1680.* Assen: Van Gorcum.

1985   *The Dutch in the Caribbean and in the Guianas 1680–1791.* Assen: Van Gorcum.

1990   *The Dutch in the Caribbean and in Surinam 1791/5–1942.* Assen: Van Gorcum.

Gowricharn, Ruben S.

1993   'Integratie als normatief proces', in: Ruben S. Gowricharn (ed.), *Binnen de grenzen; Immigratie, etniciteit en integratie in Nedeland*, pp. 173–84. Utrecht: De Tijdstroom.

Grasveld, Fons & Klaas Breunissen

1990   *Ik ben een Javaan uit Suriname.* Hilversum: Stichting Ideële Filmprodukties.

Green, William A.

1976   *British slave emancipation; The sugar colonies and the great experiment 1830–1865.* Oxford: Clarendon.

Haakmat, André

1996   *Herinneringen aan de toekomst van Suriname; Ervaringen en beschouwingen.* Amsterdam: Arbeiderspers.

Hall, Stuart

1995   'Negotiating Caribbean identities', *New Left Review* 209:3–15.

Hannerz, Ulf

1992   *Cultural complexity.* New York: Columbia University Press.

Hartsinck, Jan Jacob

1770   *Beschryving van Guiana, of de Wilde Kust, in Zuid-America [...].* Amsterdam: Tielenburg.

Heeckeren van Waliën, G.P.C. van

1826   *Aanteekeningen, betrekkelijk de kolonie Suriname.* Arnhem: Thieme.

Heijer, Henk den

1994   *Geschiedenis van de WIC.* Zutphen: Walburg Pers.

Helman, Albert

1976   *Zuid-zuid-west.* Amsterdam: Querido. [Originally 1926.]

1983   *De foltering van Eldorado: Een ecologische geschiedenis van de vijf Guyana's.* Den Haag: Nijgh en Van Ditmar.

Helsdingen, W.H. van

1957   *Het Statuut voor het Koninkrijk der Nederlanden.* Den Haag: Staatsdrukkerij- en Uitgeverijbedrijf.

Hering, J.H.

1779   *Beschrijving van het eiland Curaçao, en de daar onder hoorende eilanden Bon-Aire, Oroba en Klein Curaçao [...].* Amsterdam: Van Selm.

H[erlein], J.D.

1718   *Beschryvinge van de volk-plantinge Zuriname [...].* Leeuwarden: Injema.

Hermans, W. Fr.

1969   *De laatste resten tropisch Nederland.* Amsterdam: De Bezige Bij.

Hira, Sandew

1983   *Van Priary tot en met De Kom; De geschiedenis van het verzet in Suriname 1630–1940.* Rotterdam: Futile.

Hira, Sandew (ed.)

2003   *Het dagboek van Munshi Rahman Khan.* Den Haag: Amrit; Paramaribo: NSHI.

[Hirsch Ballin, E.M.H.]

1990   *Schets van een Gemenebestconstitutie voor het Koninkrijk der Nederlanden.* Den Haag: KabNA.

Hobsbawm, Eric J.
1990   *Nations and nationalism since 1870; Programme, myth, reality.*
          Cambridge: Cambridge University Press.
Hoefte, Rosemarijn
1990   *De betovering verbroken; De migratie van Javanen naar Suriname en het
          rapport-Van Vleuten (1909).* Dordrecht: Foris.
1998   *In place of slavery; A social history of British Indian and Javanese labor-
          ers in Suriname.* Gainesville: University Press of Florida.
Hoefte, Rosemarijn & Peter Meel (eds.)
2001   *20th century Suriname; Continuities and discontinuities in a new world
          society.* Kingston: Ian Randle Publishers; Leiden: KITLV Press.
Hoefte, Rosemarijn & Gert Oostindie
1991   'The Netherlands and the Dutch Caribbean; Dilemmas of decolonisation',
          in: Paul Sutton (ed.), *Europe and the Caribbean,* pp. 71–98. London:
          Macmillan.
Hoefte, Rosemarijn & Gert Oostindie (eds.)
1996   *Echo van Eldorado.* Leiden: KITLV Uitgeverij.
Hoetink, H.
1958   *Het patroon van de oude Curaçaose samenleving; Een sociologische
          studie.* Assen: Van Gorcum.
1967   *Caribbean race relations; A study of two variants.* London: Oxford
          University Press.
1969   'Race relations in Curaçao and Suriname', in: L. Foner & Eugene D. Genovese
          (eds.), *Slavery in the New World; A reader in comparative history,* pp. 179–87.
          Englewood Cliffs: Prentice-Hall.
1972   'Suriname and Curaçao', in: David W. Cohen & Jack P. Greene (eds.),
          *Neither slave nor free; The freedman of African descent in the slave soci-
          eties of the New World,* pp. 59–83. Baltimore: Johns Hopkins University
          Press.
1973   *Slavery and race relations in the Americas; Comparative notes on their
          nature and nexus.* New York: Harper.
1985   '"Race" and color in the Caribbean', in: Sidney W. Mintz & Sally Price
          (eds.), *Caribbean contours,* pp. 55–84. Baltimore: Johns Hopkins
          University Press.
1995   'Zwaarmoedige gedachten bij een afscheid', in: Henny E. Coomans,
          Maritza Coomans-Eustatia & Peter Prins (eds.), *Caraïbische cadens; Liber
          amicorum opgedragen aan de Gevolmachtigde Minister van de
          Nederlandse Antillen Edsel A.V. [Papy] Jesurun,* pp. 70–3. Bloemendaal:
          Stichting Libri Antilliani.
Hoetink, Harry & Gert Oostindie
1993   'Robert Shell's "Rangton van Bali"; A note on the Dutch historiography of
          slavery', *Kronos; Journal of Cape History* 20:107–9.
Hoëvell, Wolter R. van
1854   *Slaven en vrijen onder de Nederlandsche wet.* Zaltbommel: Noman. Twee
          delen.
Holt, Thomas C.
1992   *The problem of freedom; Race, labor, and politics in Jamaica and Britain
          1832–1938.* Baltimore: Johns Hopkins University Press.
Hoogbergen, Wim S.M.
1990   *The Boni Maroon wars in Suriname.* Leiden: Brill.
1992   *'De bosnegers zijn gekomen!' Slavernij en rebellie in Suriname.*
          Amsterdam: Prometheus.

Hostmann, F.W.
1850   *Over de beschaving van negers in Amerika, door kolonisatie van Europeanen [...].* Amsterdam: Sulpke.
Huender, Suzanne
1993   *Un spil di presente/Un porta pa futuro; Geschiedbeleving en nationale identiteit op Curaçao.* [M.A. thesis Universities of Leiden and Nijmegen.]
Huntington, Samuel P.
1993a   'The clash of civilizations?', *Foreign Affairs* 72(3):22–49.
1993b   'If not civilizations, what?', *Foreign Affairs* 72(5):186–94.
Hulst, Hans van
1997   *Morgen bloeit het diabaas; De Antilliaanse volksklasse in de Nederlandse samenleving.* Amsterdam: Het Spinhuis.

Israël, Jonathan I.
1995   *The Dutch republic; Its rise, greatness, and fall 1477–1806.* Oxford: Clarendon.

Jacobs, Jaap
1999   *Een zegenrijk gewest; Nieuw-Nederland in de zeventiende eeuw.* Amsterdam: Prometheus-Bert Bakker.
Jacob, Margaret C.
1992   'Radicalism in the Dutch enlightenment', in: Margaret C. Jacob & Wijnandt W. Mijnhardt (eds.), *The Dutch republic in the eighteenth century; Decline, enlightenment, and revolution,* pp. 224–40. Ithaca: Cornell University Press.
Jacob, Margaret C. & Wijnandt W. Mijnhardt (eds.)
1992   *The Dutch republic in the eighteenth century; Decline, enlightenment, and revolution.* Ithaca: Cornell University Press.
Jansen van Galen, John
1995   *Kapotte plantage; Suriname een Hollandse erfenis.* Amsterdam: Balans.
2000   *Hetenachtsdroom; Suriname, erfenis van de slavernij.* Antwerpen/Utrecht: Contact.
Jongh, Th. P.M. de
1966   *De krimpende horizon van de Hollandse kooplieden; Hollands welvaren in het Caribische zeegebied.* Assen: Van Gorcum.
Jordan, Winthrop D.
1968   *White over black; American attitudes toward the negro 1550–1812.* Chapel Hill: University of North Carolina Press.
Joustra, Arend (ed.)
1993   *Vreemde ogen; Buitenlanders over de Nederlandse identiteit.* Amsterdam: Bert Bakker.
[Juda, M.]
1869   *Derde open brief aan allen die belang stellen in de toekomst van Suriname.* Amsterdam: Van der Made.

Kagie, Rudie
1989   *De eerste neger; Herinneringen aan de komst van een nieuwe bevolkings- groep.* Bussum: Wereldvenster.
Kals, Joannes Guiljelmus
1756   *Neerlands hooft- en wortel-sonde, het verzuym van de bekeringe der heyde- nen, aangewesen en ten toon gespreid door drie leerredens gedaan en gemeen gemaakt door drie der voornaamste kerk-voogden in Engeland [...]; Uit 't Engelsch vertaalt, en met aanmerkingen verrykt [...].* Leeuwarden: Koumans.

190   *Paradise Overseas*

Kappler, August
1854   *Zes jaren in Suriname; Schetsen en tafereelen uit het maatschappelijke en militaire leven in deze kolonie.* Utrecht: Dannenfelser.
1881   *Holländisch-Guiana; Erlebnisse und Erfahrungen während eines 43 jährigen Aufenthalts in der Kolonie Surinam.* Stuttgart: Kohlhammer.

Kempen, Michiel van (ed.)
1995   *Spiegel van de Surinaamse poëzie; Van de oude liedkunst tot de jongste dichters.* Amsterdam: Meulenhoff.

Klerk, C.J.M. de
1953   *De immigratie der Hindostanen in Suriname.* Amsterdam: Urbi et Orbi.

Klooster, Wim
1994   'Subordinate but proud: Curaçao's free blacks and Mulattoes in the Eighteenth Century', *New West Indian Guide* 68:283–300.
1997   *The Dutch in the Americas, 1600–1800; A narrative history with the catalogue of an exhibition of rare prints, maps, and illustrated books from the John Carter Brown Library.* Providence, R.I.: The John Carter Brown Library.
1998   *Illicit riches; Dutch trade in the Caribbean, 1648–1795.* Leiden: KITLV Press.

Knight, Franklin W.
1990   *The Caribbean; The genesis of a fragmented nationalism. 2nd edition.* New York: Oxford University Press.

Knippenberg, Hans
1992   *De religieuze kaart van Nederland; Omvang en geografische spreiding van de godsdienstige gezindten vanaf de Reformatie tot heden.* Assen: Van Gorcum.

Koch, Koen & Paul Scheffer (eds.)
1996   *Het nut van Nederland; Opstellen over soevereiniteit en identiteit.* Amsterdam: Bert Bakker.

Koelewijn, Cees & Peter Rivière
1987   *Oral literature of the Trio Indians of Suriname.* Dordrecht: Foris.

Kolfin, Elmer
1997   *Van de slavenzweep en de muze; Twee eeuwen verbeelding van slavernij in Suriname.* Leiden: KITLV Press.

Koloniaal Verslag
1863   *Koloniaal verslag; Bijlage van het verslag der handelingen van de Tweede Kamer der Staten-Generaal.* Den Haag: Algemeene Landsdrukkerij.

Kom, Anton de
1981   *Wij slaven van Suriname.* Bussum: Wereldvenster/Amsterdam: Contact. [Originally 1934.]

Kossmann, E.H.
1992   'The Dutch republic in the eighteenth century', in: Margaret C. Jacob & Wijnandt W. Mijnhardt (eds.), *The Dutch republic in the eighteenth century; Decline, enlightenment, and revolution*, pp. 19–31. Ithaca: Cornell University Press.
1996   'Verdwijnt de Nederlandse identiteit? Beschouwingen over natie en cultuur', in: Koen Koch & Paul Scheffer (eds.), *Het nut van Nederland; Opstellen over soevereiniteit en identiteit*, pp. 56–68. Amsterdam: Bert Bakker.

Kuitenbrouwer, Maarten
1978   'De Nederlandse afschaffing van de slavernij in vergelijkend perspectief',
            Bijdragen en Mededelingen betreffende de Geschiedenis der Nederlanden
            93:69–101.
Kunitz, J.D.
1805   *Surinam und seine Bewohner oder Nachrichten über die geographischen,*
            physischen, statistischen, moralischen und politischen Verhaltnisse dieses
            Landes während einer zwanzigjährigen Aufenthalts daselbst, gesammelt.
            Erfurt: Beyer & Maring.

Lammens, Adriaan François
1823   *Redevoering ten betooge: dat de sterfte of het afnemen van het getal der*
            negerslaven, in de kolonie Suriname, niet zoo zeer aan mishandelingen,
            maar hoofdzakelijk aan andere oorzaken moet toegeschreven worden [...].
            Amsterdam: Stenvers Leeneman van der Kroe.
1982   *Bijdragen tot de kennis van de Kolonie Suriname [...] tijdvak 1816 tot*
            1822. [G.A. de Bruijne (ed.).] Amsterdam: Vrije Universiteit; Leiden:
            KITLV. [Originally 1822, 1846.]
Lampe, Armando Rudolfo
1988   *Yo te nombro libertad; Iglesia y Estado en la sociedad esclavista de Curazao*
            (1816–1863). Nijmegen: s.n. [Dissertation Vrije Universiteit of Amsterdam.]
Lamur, Humphrey E.
1985   *De kerstening van de slaven van de Surinaamse plantage Vossenburg*
            1847–1878. Amsterdam: Centre for Caribbean Studies, University of
            Amsterdam.
Lans, W.H.
1829   *Proeve over de oorzaken van verval en de middelen tot herstel der*
            Surinaamsche plantaadjen. Den Haag: Van Cleef.
1842   *Bijdrage tot de kennis der Kolonie Suriname.* Den Haag: Nederlandsche
            Maatschappij van Schoone Kunsten.
1847   *Emancipatie door centralisatie; Schets van een ontwerp tot behoud van*
            Suriname. Den Haag: Noordendorp.
Lenders, Maria
1996   *Strijders voor het lam; Leven en werk van Herrnhutterbroeders en -zusters*
            in Suriname 1735–1900. Leiden: KITLV Uitgeverij.
Lennep Coster, G. van
1836   *Herinneringen mijner reizen naar onderscheidene werelddeelen.*
            Amsterdam: Schleijer.
1842   *Aanteekeningen, gehouden gedurende mijn veblijf in de West-Indiën, in de*
            jaren 1837–1840. Amsterdam: Schleijer.
Lewis, Gordon K.
1983   *Main currents in Caribbean thought; The historical evolution of Caribbean*
            society in its ideological aspects 1492–1900. Baltimore: Johns Hopkins
            University Press.
Lier, Rudolf A.J. van
1971   *Frontier society; A social analysis of the history of Surinam.* Den Haag:
            Nijhoff.
Linde, J.M. van der
1987   *Jan Willem Kals; Leraar der Hervormden, advocaat van indiaan en neger.*
            Kampen: Kok.

Maingot, Anthony P.
1994   *The United States and the Caribbean*. London: Macmillan.
Malouet, V.P.
1802   *Collection de mémoires et correspondances officielles sur l'administration des Colonies, et notamment sur la Guiana française et hollandaise*. Parijs: Baudouin.
Manley, Michael
1987   *Up the down escalator*. London: Deutsch.
Marcha, Valdemar F. & Paul Verweel
2000   *De waarheid van Curaçao*. Amsterdam: SWP.
2003   *De cultuur van de angst; Paradoxale ketenen van angst en zwijgen op Curaçao*. Amsterdam: SWP.
Meel, Peter
1990a   'Money talks, morals vex: The Netherlands and the decolonization of Suriname 1975–1990', *European Journal of Latin American and Caribbean Studies* 48:75–98.
1990b   'A reluctant embrace: Suriname's idle quest for independence', in: Gary Brana-Shute (ed.), *Resistance and rebellion in Suriname; Old and new*, pp. 259–89. Williamsburg: College of William and Mary.
1993   'The March of Militarization in Suriname', in: Anthony Payne & Paul Sutton (ed.), *Modern Caribbean Politics*, pp. 125–46. Baltimore: Johns Hopkins University Press.
1998   'Towards a typology of Suriname nationalism', *New West Indian Guide* 72:257–81.
Meiden, Gerard Willem van der
1986   *Betwist bestuur; Een eeuw strijd om de macht in Suriname 1651–1753*. Amsterdam: De Bataafsche Leeuw.
Mintz, Sidney W.
1989   *Caribbean transformations*. New York: Columbia University Press. [Originally 1974.]
Mintz, Sidney W. & Richard Price
1992   *The birth of African-American culture; An anthropological perspective*. Boston: Beacon Press. [Originally 1976.]
Moes, C.M.
1845   'Redevoering over de ware menschlievendheid, als den volkomensten band van alle maatschappelijke vereeniging', *Surinaamsche Almanak*, pp. 129–53.

Naipaul, V.S.
1981   *The middle passage; Impressions of five societies – British, French and Dutch – in the West Indies and South America*. New York: Vintage. [Originally 1962.]
Nassy , David de Is. C. et al.
1788   *Essai historique sur la Colonie de Surinam [...] par les régents et réprésentants de ladite Nation Juive Portugaise*. Paramaribo: s.n.
Nederveen Pieterse, Jan
1990   *Wit over zwart: Beelden van Afrika en zwarten in de Westerse populaire cultuur*. Amsterdam: Koninklijk Instituut voor de Tropen.
Nettleford, Rex
1988   'Creolisation in the Caribbean arts', in: Michiel Baud & Marianne C. Ketting (eds.), *'Cultuur in beweging'; Creolisering en Afro-Caraïbische cultuur*, pp. 53–74. Rotterdam: Erasmus Universiteit Rotterdam.

1990   'Threats to national and cultural identity', in: Anthony T. Bryan, Edward
            Greene & Timothy M. Shaw (eds.), *Peace, development and security in the*
            Caribbean; Perspectives to the year 2000, pp. 241–54. London: Macmillan.

Oldendorp, C.G.A.
1987   *History of the mission of the Evangelical Brethren on the Caribbean*
            islands of St. Thomas, St. Croix, and St. John [Johann Jakob Bossard, ed.].
            Ann Arbor: Karoma. [Originally 1777.]
Olwig, Karen Fog
1993   *Global culture, island identity; Continuity and change in the Afro-*
            Caribbean community of Nevis. Reading: Harwood Academic Publishers.
Oomens, Maria
1986   'Veelwijverij en andere losbandige praktijken; Bevolkingspolitiek tegen-
            over Surinaamse plantageslavinnen in de 19e eeuw', *Jaarboek voor*
            vrouwengeschiedenis 7:152–71.

Oostindie, Gert J.
1986   'Kondreman in Bakrakondre; Surinamers in Nederland 1667–1955', in:
            Gert Oostindie & Emy Maduro, *In het land van de overheerser II;*
            Antillianen en Surinamers in Nederland, 1634/1667–1954, pp. 1–131.
            Dordrecht: Foris.
1988   'Caribbean migration to the Netherlands; A journey to disappointment?' in:
            Malcolm Cross & Han Entzinger (eds.), *Lost Illusions; Caribbean minori-*
            ties in Britain and the Netherlands, pp. 54–72. London: Routledge.
1989   *Roosenburg en Mon Bijou; Twee Surinaamse plantages, 1720–1870.*
            Dordrecht: Foris.
1990   'Preludes to the exodus; Surinamers in the Netherlands 1667–1960s', in:
            Gary Brana-Shute (ed.), *Resistance and rebellion in Suriname; Old and*
            new, pp. 231–58. Williamsburg: College of William and Mary.
1992   'The Dutch Caribbean in the 1990s; Decolonization, recolonization?',
            Caribbean Affairs 5–1:103–19.
1993a   'The economics of Suriname slavery', *Economic and Social History in the*
            Netherlands 5:1–24.
1993b   'Voltaire, Stedman, and Suriname slavery', *Slavery & Abolition* 14–2:1–34.
1994   *Caraïbische dilemma's in een 'stagnerend' dekolonisatieproces*. Leiden:
            KITLV Uitgeverij.
1995b   'Migrations et identités des populations Caribéennes aux Pays-Bas', in:
            Fred Reno (ed.), *Identité et politique de la Caraïbe et de l'Europe multi-*
            culturelles, pp. 59–80. Parijs: Economica.
1997   *Het paradijs overzee; De 'Nederlandse' Caraïben en Nederland.*
            Amsterdam: Bert Bakker [3rd ed. Leiden: KITLV Uitgeverij, 2000.]
1998   'The delusive continuities of the Dutch Caribbean diaspora', in: Mary
            Chamberlain (ed.), *Caribbean migration; Globalised identities*, pp.
            127–47. London: Routledge.
2003   'Squaring the circle; Commemorating the VOC after 400 years', *Bijdragen*
            tot de Taal-, Land- en Volkenkunde 159:135–61.
Oostindie, Gert (ed.)
1995a   *Fifty years later; Antislavery, capitalism and modernity in the Dutch orbit.*
            Leiden: KITLV Uitgeverij. [Pittsburgh. University of Pittsburgh Press
            1996.]
1996   *Ethnicity in the Caribbean; Essays in honor of Harry Hoetink*. London:
            Macmillan.

194   *Paradise Overseas*

1999a   *Dromen en littekens; Dertig jaar na de Curaçaose revolte, 30 mei 1969.* Amsterdam: Amsterdam University Press.
1999b   *Het verleden onder ogen; Herdenking van de slavernij.* Amsterdam: Arena/Den Haag: Prins Claus Fonds voor Cultuur en Ontwikkeling.
2001   *Facing up to the past; Perspectives on the commemoration of slavery from Africa, the Americas and Europe.* Kingston: Ian Randle/The Hague: Prince Claus Fund.

Oostindie, Gert & Inge Klinkers
2001   *Knellende Koninkrijksbanden; Het Nederlandse dekolonisatiebeleid in de Caraïben, 1940–2000.* Amsterdam: Amsterdam University Press. 3 vols.
2003   *Decolonising the Caribbean; Dutch policies in a comparative perspective.* Amsterdam: Amsterdam University Press.

Oostindie, Gert & Emy Maduro
1986   *In het land van de overheerser II; Antillianen en Surinamers in Nederland, 1634/1667–1954.* Dordrecht: Foris.

Oostindie, Gert & Alex van Stipriaan
1995   'Slavery and slave cultures in a hydraulic society; Suriname', in: Stephan Palmié (ed.), *Slavery and slave cultures in the Americas*, pp. 78–99. Knoxville: University of Tennessee Press.

Oostindie, Gert & Peter Verton
1998a   'Ki sorto di reino?/What kind of kingdom? Antillean and Aruban views and expectations of the Kingdom of the Netherlands', *New West Indian Guide* 72:43–75.
1998b   *Ki sorto di reino?/What kind of kingdom? Visies en verwachtingen van Antillianen en Arubanen omtrent het Koninkrijk.* Den Haag: SDU Uitgevers.

Oppenneer, Herman
1995   *Kid Dynamite; De legende leeft.* Amsterdam: Mets.

Paasman, A.N.
1984   *Reinhart; Nederlandse literatuur en slavernij ten tijde van de verlichting.* Leiden: Nijhoff.

[Paddenburg, G.G. van]
1819   *Beschrijving van het eiland Curaçao en onderhoorige eilanden; Uit onderscheidene stukken, bijdragen en opmerkingen opgemaakt, door een bewoner van dat eiland.* Haarlem: Bohn.

Patterson, Orlando
1982   *Slavery and social death; A comparative study.* Cambridge: Harvard University Press.

Pattullo, Polly
1996   *Last resorts; The cost of tourism in the Caribbean.* London: Cassell/Latin America Bureau; Kingston: Ian Randle.

Paula, A.F.
1993   *'Vrije' slaven; Een sociaal-historische studie over de dualistische slavenemancipatie op Nederlands Sint Maarten 1816–1863.* Zutphen: Walburg Pers.

Payne, Anthony & Paul Sutton (eds.)
1993   *Modern Caribbean politics.* Baltimore: Johns Hopkins University Press.
2001   *Charting Caribbean development.* London: Macmillan.

Pistorius, Thomas
1763   *Korte en zakelyke beschryvinge van de Colonie van Zuriname [...].* Amsterdam: Crajenschot.

Poeze, Harry et al.
1986   *In het land van de overheerser I; Indonesiërs in Nederland 1900–1950.*
        Dordrecht: Foris.
Postma, Johannes Menne
1990   *The Dutch in the Atlantic slave trade 1600–1815.* Cambridge: Cambridge
        University Press.
Price, Richard
1983   *First-time; The historical vision of an Afro-American people.* Baltimore:
        Johns Hopkins University Press
1990   *Alabi's world.* Baltimore: Johns Hopkins University Press.
2001   'The miracle of creolization; A retrospective', *New West Indian Guide*
        75:35–64.
Price, Richard (ed.)
1976   *The Guiana Maroons; A historical and bibliographical introduction.*
        Baltimore: Johns Hopkins University Press.
Price, Richard & Sally Price
1996   'Museums, ethnicity and nation-building; Reflections from the French
        Caribbean', in: Gert Oostindie (ed.), *Ethnicity in the Caribbean; Essays in
        honor of Harry Hoetink,* pp. 81–105. London: Macmillan.
1999   *Maroon arts; Cultural vitality in the African diaspora.* Boston: New
        Beacon Press.
Putte, Florimon van
1999   *Dede pikiña ku su bisiña. Papiamentu – Nederlands en de onverwerkt
        verleden tijd.* Zutphen: Walburg Pers.

Raad voor Maatschappelijke Ontwikkeling
1999   *Nationale identiteit in Nederland. Internationalisering en nationale iden-
        titeit.* Den Haag: Staatsdrukkerij.
Ramdas, Anil
1992   *De papagaai, de stier en de klimmende bougainvillea.* Amsterdam: De
        Bezige Bij.
1994   *Ethiek als vitaal belang.* Amsterdam: De Bezige Bij.
1996   *De beroepsherinneraar en andere verhalen.* Amsterdam: De Bezige Bij.
Ramos, Aarón Gamaliel & Angel Israel Rivera (eds.)
2001   *Island at the crossroads; Politics in the non-independent Caribbean.*
        Kingston: Ian Randle; Boulder: Lynne Rienner.
Raynal, G.F.
1774   *Histoire philosophique et politique des établissements et du commerce des
        Européens dans les deux Indes.* Amsterdam: s.n.
Renkema, W.E.
1970   'Anno 1869; Curaçao los van Nederland? Dat nooit!!!', *Kristòf* 3:1–8.
1981   *Het Curaçaose plantagebedrijf in de negentiende eeuw.* Zutphen: Walburg
        Pers.
Renselaar, H.C. van
1963   'De houding van de Creoolse bevolkingsgroep in Suriname ten opzichte
        van andere bevolkingsgroepen (in het bijzonder ten opzichte
        van Hindostanen)', *Bijdragen tot de Taal-, Land- en Volkenkunde*
        119:93–105.
Richardson, Bonham C.
1989   'Caribbean migrations 1838–1985', in: Franklin W. Knight & Colin A.
        Palmer (eds.), *The modern Caribbean,* pp. 203–28. Chapel Hill: University
        of North Carolina Press.

Riemer, Johann Andreas
1801   *Missions-Reise nach Suriname und Berbice; Zu einer am Surinamflusse im dritten Grad der Linie wohnende Freynegernation, nebst einige Bemerkungen über die Missionsanstalten der Brüderunität zu Paramaribo.* Zittau/Leipzig: Schöpfische Buchhandlung.
Römer, René A.
1974   'Het 'wij' van de Curaçaoënaar', *Kristòf* 1–2:49–62.
1979   *Een volk op weg/Un pueblo na kaminda; Een sociologisch historische studie van de Curaçaose samenleving.* Zutphen: Walburg Pers.
Römer-Kenepa, Nolda
1992   'Onderwijs als veiligheidsklep; De rooms-katholieke kerk en het volksonderwijs op de Nederlandse Antillen 1824–1863', in: B. Boudewijnse, H. Middelbrink & C. van de Woestijne (eds.), *Kerkwandel en lekenhandel; De rooms-katholieke kerk op Curaçao,* pp. 33–52. Amsterdam: Het Spinhuis.
Rummens, Joanna W.A.
1991   'Identity and perception; The politicalization of identity in St. Martin', in: Harry P. Díaz, Joanna W.A. Rummens & Patrick D.M. Taylor (eds.), *Forging identities and patterns of development in Latin American and the Caribbean,* pp. 265–78. Toronto: Canadian Scholars' Press.

Said, Edward W.
1993   *Culture and imperialism.* London: Vintage.
Sansone, Livio
1992   *Schitteren in de schaduw; Overlevingsstrategieën, subcultuur en etniciteit van Creoolse jongeren uit de lagere klasse in Amsterdam 1981–1990.* Amsterdam: Het Spinhuis.
Schalkwijk, Aart & Ad de Bruijne
1997   *Van Mon Plaisir tot Ephraïmszegen; Welstand, etniciteit en woonpatronen in Paramaribo.* Amsterdam: Instituut voor Sociale Geografie, Universiteit van Amsterdam; Paramaribo: Leo Victor.
Schama, Simon
1988   *The embarrassment of riches; An interpretation of Dutch culture in the Golden Age.* New York: Fontana.
Scheffer, Paul
1996   'Land zonder spiegel; Over de politieke cultuur in Nederland', in: Koen Koch & Paul Scheffer (eds.), *Het nut van Nederland; Opstellen over soevereiniteit en identiteit,* pp. 10–39. Amsterdam: Bert Bakker.
Schiltkamp, J.A. & J.Th. de Smidt (eds.)
1973   *West Indisch plakaatboek; Suriname; Plakaten, ordonnantiën en andere wetten, uitgevaardigd in Suriname 1667–1816.* Amsterdam: Emmering.
Scholtens, Ben
1994   *Bosnegers en overheid in Suriname; De ontwikkeling van de politieke verhouding 1651–1992.* Paramaribo: Afdeling Cultuurstudies/Minov.
Schutte, G.J.
1974   *De Nederlandse patriotten en de koloniën; Een onderzoek naar hun denkbeelden en optreden 1770–1800.* Groningen: Tjeenk Willink.
Sedney, Jules
1997   *De toekomst van ons verleden; Democratie, etniciteit en politieke machtsvorming in Suriname.* Paramaribo: Vaco.
Sekou, Lasana M.
1996   *National symbols of St. Martin; A primer.* Sint-Maarten: House of Nehesi Publishers.

Shell, Robert
1992   'Rangton van Bali (1673–1720); Roots and resurrection', *Kronos; Journal of Cape History* 19:163–75.
Siwpersad, J.P.
1979   *De Nederlandse regering en de afschaffing van de Surinaamse slavernij 1833–1863.* Groningen: Bouma; Castricum: Hagen.
Social science encyclopedia
1985   *The social science encyclopedia.* Adam Kuper & Jessica Kuper (eds.). London: Routledge & Kegan Paul.
Soest, J.J. van
1977   *Olie als water; De Curaçaose economie in de eerste helft van de twintigste eeuw.* Zutphen: Walburg Pers.
Speckmann, J.D.
1963   'De houding van de Hindostaanse bevolkingsgroep in Suriname ten opzichte van de Creolen', *Bijdragen tot de Taal-, Land- en Volkenkunde* 119:76–92.
1965   *Marriage and kinship among the Indians in Surinam.* Assen: Van Gorcum.
Staatscommissie
1855   *Eerste rapport der staatscommissie, benoemd bij Koninklijk besluit van 29 november 1853, no. 66, tot het voorstellen van maatregelen ten aanzien van de slaven in de Nederlandsche koloniën; Suriname.* Den Haag: Van Cleef.
1856   *Tweede rapport der staatscommissie, benoemd bij Koninklijk besluit van 29 november 1853, no. 66, tot het voorstellen van maatregelen ten aanzien van de slaven in de Nederlandsche koloniën; de Nederlandsche West-Indische eilanden en bezittingen ten kuste van Guinea.* Den Haag: Van Cleef.
Stedman, John Gabriel
1796   *Narrative, of a five years' expedition against the revolted negroes of Surinam, in Guiana, on the Wild Coast of South America; From the year 1772 to 1777 [...].* London: Johnson & Edwards.
1799–1800 *Reize naar Surinamen, en door de binnenste gedeelten van Guiana.* Amsterdam: Allart.
St-Hilaire, Aonghas
2001   'Ethnicity, assimilation and nation in plural Suriname', *Ethnic and Racial Studies* 24:998–1019.
2003   'Globalization, urbanization, and language in Caribbean development; The assimilation of St. Lucia', *New West Indian Guide* 77:65–84.
Stipriaan, Alex van
1989   'The Suriname rat race; Labour and technology on sugar plantations 1750–1900', *Nieuwe West-Indische Gids/New West Indian Guide* 63:94–117.
1993   *Surinaams contrast; Roofbouw en overleven in een Caraïbische plantagekolonie 1750–1863.* Leiden: KITLV Press.
1995   'Suriname and the abolition of slavery', in: Gert Oostindie (ed.), *Fifty years later; Antislavery, capitalism and modernity in the Dutch orbit*, pp. 117–41. Leiden: KITLV Press. [Pittsburgh: University of Pittsburgh Press 1996.]
1995   'Debunking debts; Image and reality of a colonial crisis; Suriname at the end of the 18th century', *Itinerario* 19–1:69–84.
2000   *Creolisering; vragen van een basketbalplein, antwoorden van een watergodin.* Rotterdam: Erasmus Universiteit Rotterdam.

Stols, Eddy
1971   *De Spaanse Brabanders of de handelsbetrekkingen der Zuidelijke Nederlanden met de Iberische Wereld, 1598–1648.* Brussel: Palais der Academiën.
Stuart, Stephanie
1993   'Dominican Patwa; Mother tongue or cultural relic?', *International Journal of the Sociology of Language* 102:57–72.
Suriname
1872   *Suriname en de opheffing van het pauperisme in Nederland; Uitgegeven door een Vereeniging van Surinamers.* Leiden: Somerwil.

Tank, Otto
1848   'Circulaire; Aan de heeren eigenaars en administrateurs van plantaadjes in de kolonie Suriname', *Berigten uit de Heiden-Wereld* 6:93–6, 14:95.
Teenstra, M.D.
1835   *De landbouw in de kolonie Suriname voorafgegaan door eene geschied- en natuurkundige beschouwing dier kolonie.* Groningen: Eekhoorn.
1842   *De negerslaven in de kolonie Suriname en de uitbreiding van het christendom onder de heidensche bevolking.* Dordrecht: Lagerweij.
1852   *Beknopte beschrijving van de Nederlandsche overzeesche bezittingen voor beschaafde lezers uit alle standen, uit de beste bronnen en eigen ervaring in Oost- en West-Indië geput.* Groningen: Oomkens.
Thoden van Velzen, H.U.E. & W. van Wetering
1988   *The Great Father and the danger; Religious cults, material forces, and collective fantasies in the world of the Surinamese Maroons.* Dordrecht: Foris.
Trommelen, Jeroen
2000   *Dwars door Suriname; Drie Guyana's in een tegendraads portret.* Amsterdam: Arena.
Trouillot, Michel-Rolph
1995   *Silencing the past; Power and the production of history.* Boston: Beacon Press.
1998   'Culture on the edges; Creolization in the plantation context', *Plantation Society in the Americas* 5:8–28.
Tulchin, Joseph S. & Ralph H. Espach (eds.)
2000   *Security in the Caribbean; The challenge of regional cooperation.* Boulder, CO: Lynn Rienner.
Turner, Mary
1982   *Slaves and missionaries; The disintegration of Jamaican slave society 1787–1834.* Urbana: University of Illinois Press.

Usselinx, Willem
1608   *Naerder bedenckingen, over de zee-vaerdt, coophandel en de neeringhe, als mede de versekeringhe van den staet deser vereenichde landen in de teghenwoordighe vrede-handelinghe met den Coninck van Spangnien [...].* S.l.: s.n.

Veer, G.S. de
1861   'Aanteekeningen over de emancipatie der slaven in de Ned[erlandsche] West-Indische koloniën', *Themis; Regtskundig Tijdschrift* 2:169–228.
Verberk, Geneviève, Peer Scheepers & Maurits Hassankhan
1997   'Etnocentrisme in Suriname', *OSO; Tijdschrift voor Surinaamse Taalkunde, Letterkunde, Cultuur en Geschiedenis* 16–2:133–45.

Vereniging
1990   *Vereniging Ons Suriname 18 januari 1919–18 januari 1989* [...].
            [Amsterdam: Ons Suriname].
Verton, Peter C.
1977   *Politieke dynamiek en dekolonisatie; De Nederlandse Antillen tussen
            autonomie en onafhankelijkheid.* Alphen a/d Rijn: Samson.
1996   'Aruba; eiland apart, kleine samenleving, autonoom land', in: [J. de Ruiter
            et al.,] *Met alle respect; Rapport van de commissie van onderzoek in het
            kader van de samenwerking tussen Aruba en Nederland op het gebied van
            criminaliteitsbestrijding,* pp. 73–86. Den Haag: SDU Uitgevers.
Vianen, Bea
1973   *Het paradijs van Oranje.* Amsterdam: Querido.

Waal Malefijt, Annemarie de
1963   *The Javanese of Surinam; Segment of a plural society.* Assen: Van Gorcum.
Walcott, Derek
1990   *Omeros.* London: Faber & Faber.
Walle, J. van de
1974   *Beneden de wind; Herinneringen aan Curaçao.* Amsterdam: Querido.
1975   *Een oog boven Paramaribo; Herinneringen.* Amsterdam: Querido.
Walvin, James
1973   *Black and white; The negro and English society 1555–1945.* London:
            Penguin.
Warren, George
1667   *An impartial description of Surinam upon the continent of Guiana in
            America [...].* London: Godbird, Brooke.
West India Commission
1993   *Time for action; Report of the West India Commission.* Kingston: The
            Press – University of the West Indies.
Williams, Eric E.
1970   *From Columbus to Castro; The history of the Caribbean 1492–1969.*
            London: Deutsch.
Winkels, W.E.N.
1856   *Slavernij en emancipatie; Eene beschouwing van den toestand der
            slavernij in Suriname.* Utrecht: Andriessen.
Winter, Johanna Maria van
1953   'De openbare mening in Nederland over de afschaffing der slavernij',
            West-Indische Gids 34:61–90.
Wolbers, J.
1861   *Geschiedenis van Suriname.* Amsterdam: De Hoogh.

Yelvington, Kevin A.
2001   'The anthropology of Afro-Latin America and the Caribbean; Diasporic
            dimensions', *Annual Review of Anthropology* 30:227–60.

Zwager, H.H.
1980   *Nederland en de verlichting.* Haarlem: Fibula-Van Dishoeck.

Index